Medical Billing, Coding, and Reimbursement

How to Run Your Own Home Medical Billing Service

Second edition, 2008

Loretta Sinclair

MEDICAL BILLING, CODING, AND REIMBURSEMENT

HOW TO RUN YOUR OWN HOME MEDICAL BILLING SERVICE

Second edition, 2008

LORETTA SINCLAIR

A DIVISION OF WINEPRESS PUBLISHING GROUP

Annotation Press (a division of WinePress Publishing, PO Box 428, Enumclaw, WA 98022) functions only as book publisher. As such, the ultimate design, content, editorial accuracy, and views expressed or implied in this work are those of the author.

ISBN 13: 978-1-59977-006-2
ISBN 10: 1-59977-006-7
Library of Congress Catalog Card Number: 2006927648

DEDICATION

Thank you God for all of the gifts and talents that You have trusted me with;

Thanks to my parents for not killing me while I was growing up;

Thank you Chris and Kelly,
my support and my inspiration;

And last but absolutely not least,

Thanks to Roger,
for making me whole again.

DISCLAIMER

This manual is meant to be a companion guide to the ICD-9, CPT, and HCPCS manuals that are reference materials for medical billing. Depending on the volume of CPT and ICD-9 manuals you are using, the codes may vary slightly from the answers in the appendix section of this book. Some codes may be deleted from older manuals or changed to new codes. Please follow the instructions of your specific reference manual and extend the answers out to their most current and correct conclusions, understanding that these codes are updated on a yearly basis. If using an older manual, please adjust your answers. Please refer to the Deleted Codes section in the beginning of the manual if you have questions about your specific edition.

CPT, ICD-9, and HCPCS manuals are expensive if purchased brand new. All three are updated yearly by the AMA ™ and other publishers. Older manuals are good training tools. When an office purchases a new set of reference manuals, they will often either keep the older ones for possible use later on or donate them for education and training purposes. If you do not have a set of these reference manuals to use with the workbook section of this book, contact some local physicians' offices or hospitals and ask if they would be willing to donate some older manuals to you for teaching purposes. Most will be happy to comply.

All of the patient names, business information, addresses, social security numbers, insurance identification numbers, and any other identifying information contained within this manual are fictitious. They are intended solely for teaching purposes and any resemblance to any persons, either living or dead, is coincidental. This information has been contained within this billing manual for the express purpose of learning how to fill out insurance forms correctly and completely. It does not in any way constitute an actual insurance claim or services provided to any person, living or deceased.

This manual is also intended as advice for those learning the field of medical billing and those who intend to start their own medical billing service. Each business is individual, and what works for one business, or one area of the country, may not necessarily work in another. This book is not a guarantee of success in any field or business venture.

TABLE OF CONTENTS

INTRODUCTION, FAQS, OVERVIEW, AND CLAIMS PROCESS

INTRODUCTION

The medical billing field, whether office-based or home-based, is one of the largest growing and fastest changing fields in business today. New legislation and updated insurance company policies and regulations keep this fast-paced industry at the forefront of new technology, both in terms of patient care and the business end of collections and reconciliation. It is both an interesting and challenging field to be employed in. The satisfaction of being involved in something that can literally change or even save a patient's life is priceless. And from a financial standpoint, to be able to perform a simple bookkeeping task or explain a paperwork procedure that can possibly save someone thousands of dollars can be very rewarding.

As a home-based business, this can be extremely profitable, with the proper training and knowledge behind you. As with any field, if you get involved in something without a complete understanding of what you are doing and how you are doing it, this business venture can be disastrous both financially and professionally. Reputations and business references are on the line for you, as well as your financial security.

The information contained within this book is designed to be an in-depth guide to exactly what this business entails and what you will need to be prepared for when beginning a business of this sort. We will cover a brief overview of the billing process with all of the reference materials necessary to understand how claims are billed. From there, we will cover basic coding, the collection and revenue tracking process, and finally end up with running this type of business as a home-based entrepreneurial venture.

It is my hope that if you are not sure whether this field is right for you this book will help you make up your mind. If you do wish to proceed in this business venture, this book will offer you some sound advice and guidance along the way. And if you decide that you would rather be employed in another field, this book would have saved you money by showing you what to expect before you invested money that none of us really has to lose on a chance opportunity. Whatever your choice is, I wish you the best of luck in your business venture and sincerely hope that this book is of some value to you in your decision-making process.

FAQs

Frequently Asked Questions

1. Is this business right for me?

   This is a tough question to answer because each person is different. When you run a home-based bookkeeping service (medical or otherwise), you need to know that there will be large blocks of time when you will be working alone. Bookkeeping and accounting tend to be solitary types of work, and while you may have the interaction of others in the office, or some limited phone contact, the work is primarily a one-person job. When this business is run from the home rather than an office-based setting, you lose part of that social contact. If you don't mind sitting alone in your home office and working for several hours at a time, this would be a good occupation for you.

   Another thing to remember is that this is essentially a bookkeeping business, so an aptitude for numbers and mathematical equations is essential. Accuracy is paramount when dealing with insurance entities and your patients' accounts. If you don't like to balance your checkbook, you may want to take a good close look at the day to day duties of a bookkeeper before investing a lot of money in this field.

2. How much does it cost to start?

   The start-up costs can be minimal. There is little that is absolutely required in the way of equipment. A computer and your software package will be your most expensive purchases at first. If you already have a computer that is compatible with your software package, you can use that and upgrade to a newer computer later. A few reference manuals and office supplies are all that will be essential initially. Furniture, new phones, etc., can all be added later after you have a steady cash flow coming in from your business.

   While financial aid may be available from local entities for you, the process will be a long and arduous one. You should plan on footing most of the start-up costs yourself, and then work through the paperwork process to be reimbursed when you can. If you wait on the approval process of the bank, good business opportunities could be lost in the down time. The loan process is a significant amount of paperwork to go through, and many entities will not finance start-up businesses. Statistics show that most new businesses will fail in the first five years. These statistics don't account for the people who just decide that being self-employed isn't for them, nor does it account for those businesses that are so successful they are purchased by other companies. Financial institutions will insist on previous bank statements, tax records, client contracts, outstanding A/R, applications, and more than likely collateral for the loan. This will take a significant amount of time. If you have a business opportunity and can initially fund this undertaking yourself, I would suggest you do that.

3. What do I need to know?

    You will need to know the basics of the industry; that is, what is a claim form? What are the specific codes that are used by the insurance companies? And, how to use your specific computer programs. The industry has standards that remain the same from insurance company to insurance company. Once these standards are understood and maintained, billing to all insurance companies will be routine.

4. Where can I learn?

    Most community colleges and adult education centers have classes in how to learn medical insurance billing. In addition, many technical schools will have programs as well, although these will be more expensive. You can also volunteer at a local doctor's office or hospital in exchange for training and education. Most medical offices are happy to exchange knowledge for hours. Each side gets something out of the deal.

5. How do you get clients?

    Clients can be solicited in a number of ways. There are specific advertising methods that are more effective than others, but advertising will be your main key. Also, word of mouth will land you more clients than anything else. Referrals from happy clients are as valuable as gold in this industry, so take care of that very first client you get.

6. Do I need a partner?

    Some people feel more comfortable working with another person, especially if that person has more experience in this field than they do. While working with another person might be nice, or even convenient, it is not by any means necessary. This can be a very successful one-person business if you put everything into it.

7. If I get into trouble, who will be there to help me?

    Certainly there are always people around to assist you if you need it. If it is a computer question or problem, you can call either the software company or your computer warranty company. If you are past the warranty period, there are plenty of computer stores that will work on your computer for a nominal fee. If it is an industry question you struggle with, contact the insurance company involved or your local government insurance authority. If it is a business question, you can contact your Better Business Bureau, Small Business Development Association, or even another billing service in your area. Most people are happy to help, as long as you don't take too much of their own business time.

8. Where do I find the right computer and software package?

    A little investigation will be required here first. You will need to determine what kind of billing you would like to do and what insurance companies are most commonly dealt with in those particular fields. From there, phone calls need to be placed for prices and compatibility. As with any other major purchase, you must be a smart shopper and look around at what would be the best deal for your unique situation.

9. What is the best way, logistically, to move work around from office to office?

    That depends on where your clients are located in reference to your place of business. Are they within driving distance, or are they a greater distance away? Do you have other obligations (like small children) that will interfere with a regular delivery schedule? Can you reasonably pick up and deliver work, should you hire a courier, or would a mail account like FedEx or UPS be better? Determine what works best for you and your situation first, before you land that big client, so you will be ready to answer all their questions when they ask them.

10. Can I really run this from my home?

   Yes, it can be done. You will need to have some space that is uniquely yours. Ideally, your own room is the best situation, but you can make do a part of a room (i.e. corner of a living room or dining room). You will need to ensure that your documents and work will not be disturbed by anyone in the household. Also, confidentiality has to be maintained for the patients. Your computer needs to be protected from hackers and other intruders. If you can work within these parameters, you can run this business from anywhere.

11. How much money can I realistically expect to make?

   As in any job or business venture, that depends on how many hours you put into it and the types of clients that you land. You can make anywhere from a modest part time income to over six figures a year for an average full time job. Just remember, like anything else, this is above all a job. It is not a get-rich-quick scheme. You will need to work hard everyday, just like any other profession. There is always a financial risk when you begin your own business, but the rewards are also great if you are willing to go after them.

12. Will this industry be around five years from now?

   This industry is constantly changing and developing. It will be around for some years to come as a steady source of work and income, but constant attention to the changing business environment is necessary to keep up on all of the new industry trends. Continuing education is an absolute must with both the insurance and computer advances.

   The home medical billing service is a great small business to get into. You will have more control of your job, clients, hours, and money than at a traditional job. You will have the freedom to work into your schedule the things that are important to your life and the chance to make your own valuable career choices. With a few learned basic concepts and minimal purchases, you could be well on your way to entrepreneurship and all of the benefits that come with that status. This field is wide open right now, with enough work to keep an army of people busy for years to come. The specific information contained within this book will hopefully guide you through the vast masses of choices out there on the subject and give you some good solid information on which you can base your business decisions.

OVERVIEW

This book will give an in-depth overview with working exercises for the following topics.

THE CPT MANUAL

CPT stands for Current Procedural Terminology and is the reference manual used for coding of all out-patient procedures for the professional fee component of the physician's billing. A basic understanding and working knowledge of this book is essential for success in this field.

THE ICD-9CM MANUAL

ICD-9CM stands for International Classification of Diseases, 9th Edition, Clinical Modification, and is the reference manual used for coding of all diagnoses used in medical billing, either inpatient or outpatient. This book is used for both professional fee and facility fee claims. Understanding this manual is essential in proper filing of medical claims.

THE HCPCS MANUAL

The HCPCS manual is another book for which a brief familiarization is necessary. This manual is used less than the previously mentioned two, but knowledge and understanding are still required for this field. HCPCS stands for Healthcare Common Procedure Coding System, and is a continuation of the CPT coding system.

THE HCFA-1500 FORM

This form is the universal billing form for professional fees. Utilizing codes from all three manuals listed above, we will cover all aspects of filling out this form completely and accurately for submission to all insurance companies.

THE UB-04 FORM

This form is the universal billing form for facility and technical fees. Again, utilizing all three manuals listed above, we will cover complete instructions for completion and submission of this form. More complicated than the 1500 form, this document requires more coding and reference material to complete accurately. A complete understanding of all eighty-six fields for this claim form is essential for accurate filing and collections.

OVERVIEW OF THE BILLING PROCESS

An in-depth understanding of the entire claims process is an absolute must in order to have the most efficient collection process possible. We will cover what happens from the time that a patient makes an appointment through completion of all necessary forms.

OVERVIEW OF BILLING AND COLLECTIONS PROCESS

An overall understanding of the claim processing and collection procedure will be covered, from the time that a completed claim form is filed through payment being received within your office. By the time this chapter is finished, a complete understanding of the entire claims process should be realized with the ability to differentiate between all individual steps throughout the process.

SETTING UP AND RUNNING THIS BUSINESS AS A HOME-BASED ENTITY

All aspects of running this type of business as a home-based organization will be covered, including everything from initial set-up, to seeking clients, establishing a business presence within your neighborhood, to your own tax deductions and forms, and running your home around your business (and vice versa).

So, is this business really for you?

Let's find out.

CLAIMS PROCESS

The claims process can be a complicated one with many separate and distinct levels. It is simplified by breaking it down into individual steps that can be dealt with much easier on a smaller level.

PRE-REGISTRATION AND SCHEDULING

The Appointment

When a patient calls your office for a new appointment, certain information must be obtained up front to determine whether or not this patient will be covered by their insurance for your services. Primarily, find out if the patient has insurance coverage and through which carrier. If this is a carrier that you are contracted with, then you can proceed to the next step. If the patient has no insurance they should be informed that full payment is expected on the date of service, or payment arrangements need to be made with your office.

Eligibility

The individual's eligibility for the month of service must be established. Simply having an insurance card isn't good enough. While this is certainly a good beginning, further steps must be taken to ensure payment. Either take a photocopy of the patient's insurance card, or log the information from the card into the patient's chart, including insurance company name, address, and phone number, patient's ID and group numbers, and both patient and subscriber's full legal names. After this information is obtained, call the insurance company and verbally verify that the coverage hasn't been terminated for some reason (change of job is the most frequent) since the card has been issued. After firm eligibility has been established, an appointment for the patient can be scheduled.

Notification

Once an appointment has been scheduled, a written notification should be sent to the patient for their records. Under certain circumstances (if a lawsuit is involved for an auto accident or in the case of a worker's compensation injury), written notification must also go to the patient's attorney, insurance company, and employer. Check with your local insurance authorities for regulations on this to ensure that all legal parties are served with proper appointment notification well in advance of the patient being seen. This will also help to ensure prompt and proper payment of your claim.

Authorization

If prior authorization is required by the insurance company, the time to obtain this is before the patient is seen. Many insurance plans now fall under the heading of "capitation," or "managed care." This means that the patient is assigned a primary care physician within a certain network of physicians. That physician is responsible for all basic care for that patient. If the patient requires a service that the physician either cannot perform, or is not covered under the primary care physician's capitation contract, that physician may then refer that patient out to another provider for service. Before a referral can be made and the patient seen at another office, prior authorization must be obtained by the treating office from the insurance company. Make sure you understand your patient's insurance plan and its benefits and limitations before providing service.

Courtesy Reminder Notice

We all lead extremely busy lives these days and it is very easy to forget little things like doctor's appointments, especially if the appointment has been made way in advance. A courtesy reminder call twenty-four to forty-eight hours prior to the appointment is a good idea to make sure that the patient will be there, or give you enough notice to cancel and rebook the appointment if necessary. A reminder note in the mail will work as well, but it needs to be sent out in enough time for the patient to receive it twenty-four to forty-eight hours before the appointment day.

APPOINTMENT DAY

On the day of the appointment, there are a few things that need to be attended to prior to the patient being seen. First, a completed Patient Information Sheet must be obtained for all new patients. This will contain all personal, insurance, employer, and subscriber information. In the case of an established patient, this information needs to be re-verified and any changes updated and logged. If necessary, a quick phone call to re-verify eligibility may be done. This is a good idea if the patient is seen in a different month than the date the appointment was originally scheduled. Any co-pays and patient fees should be collected at this time as well. After all these initial details are attended to, the patient is ready to be seen.

Everything up to this point is routinely performed by the provider's office. It will be at this point that the billing service will then take over.

BILLING

Collection of Patient Information

The first step in the actual billing process is to enter all of the personal patient information into the computer. This includes patient address, date of birth, sex, marital status, employment status, and all pertinent insurance information. This can be obtained from the New Patient Information Sheet that the patient initially filled out on their first visit to the doctor's office. With this in the computer, you are ready to move on to the next step.

Collection and Coding of Charge Information

After the patient's personal and insurance information has been obtained, you are ready for the charge information. The physician or provider of service should provide you with what is commonly known as a "superbill." This is a sheet showing all of the charge information and diagnosis information for this particular visit. This superbill should have the date of service and a written listing of all procedures (with dollar amounts applied) for which the patient will be charged. It should also have a written diagnosis showing why the patient was seen. After this information is provided, the diagnoses and procedures should be coded using the CPT and ICD-9CM manuals. If necessary, help should be obtained from the treating healthcare professional to ensure proper coding. This information can then be entered into your billing program.

Claim Filing

After all billing and claim information is entered into the computer, a claim form, (or batch file for electronic claims) can be produced. The totals on these claims should be added up and compared to the dollar amounts totaled from the superbills for that date of service to make sure that all charges have been accurately entered into your billing system. After this is done, the claims can be filed (either electronically or mailed).

COLLECTIONS AND POSTING

Follow-up of Claims

1. When a claim has been filed and all appropriate information is contained within the claim form, assuming that eligibility is still viable, the claim should be paid within thirty to forty-five days. This is the average turnaround time for most insurance carriers. This can be a little faster with electronic claim submissions after the initial testing period for new providers is done. After thirty days, if your claims are not yet paid, then a follow-up phone call to the insurance company is required. Status on the unpaid claim should be requested at that time and the response logged either in the patient chart or in the computer system. If there is a problem with the claim, you should be notified at this time. Follow-up calls should be repeated at regular intervals until the claim is either paid or denied.
2. Once the claim is paid, the payment should then be reconciled against the provider contract to make sure that the payment is correct. The explanation of benefits (check stub) should be reviewed for any pertinent information relating to this claim. Additional patient liability should be noted and billed. If the patient has any secondary insurance coverage, that should be billed at this time with a copy of the original claim and the explanation of benefits showing what the primary insurance company has paid.
3. The payment should then be posted to the patient's account and a copy filed in your office for easy access for future reference. The original checks can then be deposited into the bank. Storage of records can either be the filing of the original paper document or a scanned image on the computer for easy reference. The preference is entirely up to you and your office.

DENIALS AND UNDERPAYMENTS

First, determine the reason for the denial or underpayment. If it is due to patient ineligibility on the date of service, then the patient or secondary insurance needs to be billed. If it is due to either an insurance error or clerical office staff error, an appeal needs to be written requesting the payment in full. If there is nothing that can be done to correct the denial, then the charge must be written off. Not all denials can be billed to the patients. If the error was on the part of your office, incorrect information that was billed, or not obtaining the proper authorizations, the patient cannot be billed for these errors. The only thing that you can bill the patient for is that which the patient bears some liability in. For instance, if the patient didn't tell you that a prior authorization was needed, or if they did not provide you with proper insurance information prior to being seen, then this amount can become patient liability. If the patient was actually seen for injuries relating to a work injury and they are asking you to bill their primary health insurance, when the denial comes back you can then bill the patient until they provide you with proper workers compensation information. If the patient's negligent actions cause you to be unable to collect on a bill, they can then become responsible for the bill. This can all be avoided with proper processing of all information before the patient is initially seen (see section A).

1. Occasionally you will run into what is known as a "pre-existing condition." This would apply if the patient has purchased an individual policy. A pre-existing condition is a medical condition that was documented before the policy took effect and is specifically excluded from covered benefits. For instance, you have a long history of back problems due to an injury that you sustained some years back. Due to your inability to work, you have no group health coverage and decide to purchase an individual policy that you pay for yourself. You will probably be required to have a medical examination, and release your medical records to the insurer before the policy will be issued. They will then issue a rider on the policy stating that any services in connection with the previous back injury are non-covered and therefore patient responsibility. Pre-existing

conditions are not applicable in a work environment. If you are accepted for employment with a company that covers its employees with healthcare, and you enroll in that coverage when first eligible, your coverage is full. Many offices will routinely perform a pre-employment physical to ensure that you are healthy enough for the workload they require and that you do not have any health problems that will be burdensome for their insurance carrier, causing premiums to be raised.

2.   Another thing you will run into routinely will be denied charges or disallowed amounts detailed out on the EOB. An example of this may be where the insurance company will pay for the office visit but then deny any other services that were performed that day stating that the other services should be included in the office visit. Or, they will deny the office visit as unnecessary but pay the ancillary services. When this happens, consult your contract language for the specific limitations on services performed. The CPT manual will detail out which services are generally included, or bundled, with others. If certain services are non-covered or should be included with other services, the details of these specifics should be laid out in your contract. Refer to that document for any questions, or if you have further questions after that, contact the insurance company directly. Denied charges should not be billed to the patient unless you have notified them previously that any non-covered services will be their responsibility and allow them to decide whether or not to have the services performed. If charges are still significant or overwhelming, the patient can apply for state, county, or federal aid at that point.

3.   There will also be incidents in which the patient will reach the lifetime maximum benefits payable under their contract. This is rare, but it does happen. When you have a patient who has undergone an extensive illness or injury (i.e. cancer), they will occasionally reach the maximum limitations of their policy. At this point, if the patient has any secondary insurance they should then take over as primary; or, if there is no other insurance, all charges will at that point then become the patient liability. While some patients will pick up an individual policy, it will generally come with a rider declining coverage for any pre-existing conditions. Make sure to read and understand what coverage the patient has so you can help them through difficult periods like these.

This, in a nutshell, is the billing and collection process. Specific procedures will be delved into in greater detail in the following chapters explaining all of the specifics for each step one at a time.

Most people will find a good medical terminology course extremely helpful in this field. There are many good self-study guides that can walk you through the basics of human anatomy and physiology as well. A strong basic understanding of the human body can be a big plus in trying to master the coding process. Also, certain insurance company denials will be related to billed procedures not being related to the diagnoses being reported. The more education you can obtain in this area, the more efficiently your job can be performed.

CODING

CPT

The CPT manual is a listing of all current procedures that have been assigned codes by the American Medical Association ™ for tracking purposes. Like the ICD-9 manual, these codes are divided up by categories and are listed either alphabetically or numerically for quick reference and ease of use in the book. CPT stands for Current Procedural Terminology. It contains all current procedure codes that are used for the professional component of a claims bill. This billing manual is updated and reprinted every year. It is highly recommended that you purchase a new one whenever they come available. It is the best way to keep up on new changes and codes to keep your billing accurate.

The CPT was established in 1966 by the American Medical Association ™ in order to ensure uniformity of billing among providers and also to allow a means of tracking to establish current trends in health care. The predecessor to the CPT was called the RVS (Relative Value Study). It contained much of the same information as the CPT but also contained an extra feature called the Relative Value. This was a numerical code that was assigned to each procedure code denoting a degree of difficulty for that particular procedure. This value was then used with a multiplier for each specialty section, giving a dollar value for any given procedure. When this system was challenged in court, it was determined that it constituted price fixing among the medical community and the book was rendered obsolete, although some health insurance carriers still refer to its contents occasionally (not the relative value system, but rather the coding section as a guide). The CPT then was published, without the Relative Value, and has been used ever since. The CPT, also known as Level I Professional Coding, covers outpatient professional charges. Its companion manual, the HCPCS guide, Level II for Expert coders, covers a more in-depth level of professional codes for procedures, professional services, supplies, and drugs in both the inpatient and outpatient settings. This will be covered in another chapter. Level III coding is for local regulations in your own geographical area. Since these are unique to your own specific city and state, we will not cover any of these codes here.

The CPT book is a guide to accurately report medical, surgical, and diagnostic services rendered to patients in the provider setting. It is comprised of five digit codes, along with two digit modifiers (see pages 261–262 in Appendix of this book) to further refine the procedure descriptions. There are also mandatory two-digit Place Of Service code that must be reported on your HCFA-1500 or UB-04 claim forms, which even further define the exact nature of the procedure being reported. These modifiers and place of service codes are also listed in the CPT manual. A list of these codes is contained in the Appendices Section of this book.

Like the ICD-9 coding manual, the CPT book contains symbols and annotations to help the coding process. These symbols and color-coded markings are explained in the beginning of the book. Review these markings each year, as they may change from volume to volume. Also in the front of the text is a section entitled Guidelines for Billing. This section explains all of the HCFA requirements for various coding procedures. It also lists criteria for unlisted procedures and special report procedures.

This book, like the ICD-9, is divided into two sections, one alphabetical and one tabular. The tabular section, the largest of the two, will contain the full descriptions of the service, publisher's annotations, and referrals to other codes or sections for accurate coding. The alphabetical section should only be used as a reference guide for the larger, more in-depth tabular section. For example: The alphabetical section contains an entry entitled Office and/or Other Outpatient Services. This then gives you a code range of 99271–99355. In order to determine the correct code, you must then turn to the Evaluation and Management Section of the book and review all of the codes in that range to determine which would be the best code for your particular patient (i.e. new patient, established patient, levels of service, place of service, etc.).

The Tabular Section of the CPT is broken down into the sections listed below.

99200-99499	Evaluation and Management
00100–01999	Anesthesia
99100-99140	Anesthesia
10000-69999	Surgery
10000–19499	Integumentary System
20000–29909	Musculoskeletal System
30000–32999	Respiratory System
33010–37700	Cardiovascular System
39000–39599	Hemic and Lymphatic Systems
39000–39599	Mediastinum and Diaphram
40490–49999	Digestive System
50010–53899	Urinary System
54000–55980	Male Genital System
55970–55980	Intersex Surgery
56000–58999	Female Genital System
59000–59899	Maternity Care and Delivery
60000–60699	Endocrine System
62000–64999	Nervous System
65091–68899	Eye and Ocular Adnexa
69000–69979	Auditory System
70000-79999	Radiology
80000-89999	Pathology and Laboratory
90700-99999	Medical Services (except anesthesiology)

So, for example, all radiological services would be in the 70000 range.

In addition, the CPT manual will also contain anatomical and procedural illustrations to help with the coding process. Refer to these often, especially for surgical and medical procedures.

One of the most helpful sections in the book is the section listing new, changed, and deleted codes. These should be gone through every year when the new CPT manual comes out. Review all codes in this section to see if any of the changes apply to your particular practice. It is generally located (depending on publisher) in the beginning of the book. Also, in the beginning is a section entitled Official Guidelines for Coding and Reporting. This section will give you complete instructions for how to use the book and its various sections to be in accordance with the official AMA^{TM} guidelines. Please review this section carefully and follow all instructions accordingly. It will save time and money later on.

The alphabetical section should never be used alone to code any procedure. It should only be used to refer you to the appropriate tabular section for further research. After determining which section to refer to, all codes in any given section should be reviewed for the code that meets all patient criteria. Coding from the alphabetical section alone can cause errors and under-reimbursement for not choosing the proper code.

The Evaluation and Management section of the CPT manual is one of the most challenging and one that will be used the most by the average biller. This section contains all of the codes for office visits, clinic visits, and hospital visits. Also referred to as the Medicine Section, this area has the most choices for any given visit, and will require an in-depth knowledge of why and where the patient is being seen. For example, office visits are split into categories by New Patient or Established Patient, and then further broken down by either a focused problem and examination, expanded problem and examination, detailed problem and examination, or comprehensive problem and examination. Hospital Observation codes, Emergency Room Visit codes, Consultation codes, and Inpatient Hospital Care codes are also broken down by these same criteria, beginning with new or established patient. Consultation codes are also determined by these criteria: initial consultation, follow-up consultation, and confirmatory consultation.

The first thing that needs to be done when coding for this section is to determine the following:

- Is this a new patient or an established patient?
- Where will the patient be seen (i.e. home, office, hospital, etc.)?
- What type of services will be performed (i.e. exam, consult, hospital care, ER services, etc.)?
- How much time was spent with the patient?
- How old is the patient (i.e. newborn care, prenatal care, etc.)

Once these basics are answered, you can proceed.

CPT EXERCISES

LET'S TRY SOME EXERCISES.

Review the Evaluation and Management Codes section of the CPT for these problems.

1. A new patient presents for an office visit. He is an adult male and requires a comprehensive history and exam, followed by medical decision making of a highly complex nature. What code would you use?

2. A new patient presents for an office visit. He is an adult male and requires a focused history taking and exam with medical decision making of a straightforward nature. What code would you use?

3. An established patient presents for an office visit. She is a middle-aged female and requires an expanded history taking and exam with medical decision making of a low complexity. What code would you use?

4. Your physician is called for a hospital visit. You have never seen this patient before. She is an older female patient. This visit will be for initial observation, with a detailed history and exam, with medical decision making of a low complexity. What code would you use?

5. Your physician is called back to the hospital for subsequent hospital care for this same patient. She now requires a more focused history and exam but still has medical decision making of a low complexity. What code would you use?

6. Can you have a subsequent hospital care visit for a new patient?

7. Your physician is called to the hospital for observation of an established patient. The history taking and exam is of a comprehensive nature and decision making is moderately complex. What code would you use?

8. Can you use an observation care code for a new patient?

9. You have a patient being discharged from the hospital and you are called for a discharge service evaluation. This evaluation will be less than thirty minutes in length and the patient is a middle-aged male. What code would you use?

10. You have a new patient that comes to your office for an consultation. This is an outpatient service at your office. It requires a detailed history and examination with medical decision making of a low complexity. What code would you use?

11. Your physician has an initial inpatient new-patient consult hospital visit with an elderly gentleman. It requires a focused history and exam, with straightforward decision making. What code would you use?

12. This same gentleman has a follow-up inpatient consultation. He is an established patient with a detailed history and exam, and decision making of a high complexity. What code would you use?

13. Can you have a follow-up inpatient consult on a new patient?

14. Your physician is called for a confirmatory consultation for a new patient. This will be a comprehensive history and exam, and require medical decision making of a moderate complexity. What code would you use?

15. Can you have a confirmatory consultation on an established patient?

16. A teenage boy is brought into the emergency room. This is a new patient for you. He requires a comprehensive history and exam and medical decision making of a high complexity. What code would you use?

(See answers in Section V)

These same criteria also hold true for the remaining sections of the Evaluation and Medicine section of the CPT (i.e. nursing home visits, home visits, domiciliary, board and care, custodial care, newborn care). You must gather as much information about the patient and the visit as you can prior to coding each service.

There are also lesser used codes for team conferences (99361–99362) and telephone calls (99371–99373). The preventive medicine and counseling codes should be reviewed for familiarity as well.

There are also modifiers that will enhance the basic codes. Some examples of these will be a modifier for two services in the same day or the same service using two different physicians. A table of CPT modifiers is located in the appendix section of this book. Please review these codes and familiarize yourself with them.

CPT – EXERCISE 1

Please look up the following codes in the CPT books (use the tabular section for this exercise). For Type of Visit, use Office Visit (OV), Hospital Visit (HV), Consultation (C), etc.
Patient Type (PT) refers to a new patient or established patient.

Code	Type	PT Type	Problem level
99201	_____	_____	_____
99211	_____	_____	_____
99218	_____	_____	_____
99221	_____	_____	_____
99232	_____	_____	_____
99238	_____	_____	_____
99244	_____	_____	_____
99254	_____	_____	_____
99252	_____	_____	_____

(See answers in Section V)

CPT-EXERCISE 2

Please look up the correct CPT codes for these procedures (use the alphabetical section of the book for this exercise):

Description	CPT Code
Miller Procedure	_____
Miscarriage, second trimester	_____
Excision, Metacarpal	_____
Paternity testing, blood type	_____
Face Lift	_____
In Vitro Fertilization	_____
Incision and Drainage, Skin with Fluid Collection	_____
Injection, Cyst, Kidney	_____
Intubation, Endotracheal tube	_____
Administration, Ipecac	_____
Excision, Intervertebral Disc Decompression	_____
Intermediate Care Facility Visits	_____

(See answers in Section V)

CPT – EXERCISE 3

Description	CPT Code
Sensitivity Study-Fungus	_____
Separation, Craniofacial, closed	_____
Excision, Stomach, total	_____
Gastric Bypass, Stomach	_____
Tetanus Immunization	_____
TB (Tuberculosis) Skin test	_____
Tachycardia, heart, recording	_____
Hysterosonography	_____
Heroin Screen	_____
Hernia Repair-Epigastric	_____
Drainage, Abscess, Liver	_____
Diverticulum, Meckel's, Excision	_____

(See answers in Section V)

CPT-EXERCISE 4

Please code the following:

Description	CPT Code

1. Office Visit-new patient-comprehensive   _____

2. Hosp Visit observation-new or established patient, initial   _____

3. Hosp visit-hosp care, initial, comprehensive of
    moderate complexity   _____

4. Hosp visit-subsequent visit-focused of low complexity   _____

5. Breast reconstruction with tissue expander
    subsequent expansion   _____

6. Laparoscopy, surgical transection of vagus nerves, truncal   _____

7. Diagnostic ultrasound, chest, echography chest
    B-scan with realtime image documentation   _____

8. Blood Tests (Chemistry/Path and Lab)
    Creatine   _____

    Copper   _____

    Chromium   _____

    Fluoride   _____

    Dihydrocodeinone   _____

9. Echocardiography, transthoracic for congenital
    heart anomalies, complete   _____

10. Cardiac Catheterization
    Right Heart Cath   _____

    Left Heart Cath   _____

11. Physical Therapy Evaluation   _____

12. Prescription and fitting of contact lenses   _____

13. Cochlear device implantation (Hearing aid)   _____

14. Thyroid Lobectomy   _____

15. Incision, Gastrotomy   _____

(See answers in Section V)

CPT – EXERCISE 5

Please code the following:

Description	CPT Code
1. Incision, soft tissue, superficial	_____
2. Incision, deep or complicated	_____
3. Repair, flexor tendon, primary, each tendon, each subsequent tendon	_____
4. Incision and Drainage, Knee joint, hematoma	_____
5. Fasciotomy, iliotibial open (tenotomy) knee joint or femur, thigh region	_____
6. Cholangiopancreatography	_____
7. Vasotomy, Incision vas deferens	_____
8. Vasectomy, excision vas deferens	_____
9. Cervical biopsy	_____
10. Excision endometrial sample (biopsy)	_____
11. Subdural tap, skull thru fontalenne or suture, infant	_____
12. X-ray teeth, diagnostic exam	_____
13. Venography, extremity, bilateral, radiological supervision and interpretation	_____
14. Diagnostic ultrasound, spinal canal echography	_____
15. Arthritis panel	_____
16. (Path and Lab) Blood test for Human Growth Hormone	_____

(See answers in Section V)

For additional exercises, please see the Medical Billing, Coding, and Reimbursement Supplemental Workbook.

ICD-9-CM

ICD-9-CM stands for International Classification of Diseases: 9th Revision, Clinical Modifications. In 1988 the Medicare Catastrophic Act was passed, which required all Medicare contracted medical offices to report to the federal government what diagnoses their patients were being seen for. This is for official tracking purposes so that appropriate funding could be designated for major health risks to the general population and trends in health care could be established. We've all seen the commercials that state something like "more Americans die from lung cancer every year than heart disease, stroke, and auto accidents combined." Official government tracking of the ICD-9 codes on insurance claim forms are how they determine these statistics. Since 1988, all commercial carriers, workers' compensation carriers, and both private and managed health care systems have adopted the use of this coding system. Uniformity of billing is essential for tracking purposes. The ICD-9, like the CPT manual, is updated every year, with a new edition published with all new codes, amended codes, and deletions noted. It is highly recommended to obtain a new version whenever one becomes available. It is necessary for accurate and complete billings. The addition/correction/deletion chapter is generally located (depending on publisher) in the beginning of the book. Also, at the beginning is a section entitled Official Guidelines for Coding and Reporting. This section will give you complete instructions for how to use the book and its various sections to be in accordance with official government guidelines. Please review this section carefully and follow all instructions accordingly. It will save time and money later on.

The ICD-9 is a reference manual for any biller to be able to find any code that has been established by the government. This book can seem complicated at a glance, but with a good foundation in how the book is set up, its use can be simplified considerably. A basic knowledge in both medical terminology and anatomy is required to ensure accurate coding and reimbursement for your claims. Initially set up to report only diagnoses of illnesses patients contracted, this book has since expanded to include conditions and injuries as well.

While the codes that exist in the ICD-9 book are official government codes, many private publishers have enhanced the basic government information with their own annotations to help make the coding process easier. For example, the basic three-digit code for *Diabetes* is 250. This code is carried out with a fourth and sometimes fifth digit past a decimal point, indicating whether or not there are complications accompanying the basic underlying disease. The code 250.3 indicates the patient has "diabetes with coma (with ketoacidosis)," but this is still not enough information as far as the government is concerned. They require a fifth digit to indicate whether or not this patient is a Type I or Type II diabetic and whether this patient is insulin dependent or not. The ICD manual itself will tell you whether a fourth or fifth digit is required for any given code.

Some private publishers have indicated annotations interspersed within the coding text to indicate when further coding or other attention is required in the coding process. While it is not necessary for you to know the complete medical complications for each and every patient involved, it is important for you to know whether or not a code can be carried out to the fifth digit or whether the basic three-digit code is enough. If further information is required, then you should refer the question to a physician or your medical provider for the final decision. These annotations will also refer you to other more commonly used codes or indicate deleted codes as well. These footnotes and annotations can be extremely useful in the coding process. Codes are there to further define, clarify, and list other possible choices for the coding process. Each publisher has their own set of symbols or color coding system for your help and convenience. Read the introduction chapter of these books to understand your specific publisher's notation system.

Other notations include new and deleted codes, codes that cannot be used as a primary diagnosis, non-specific codes, and when an additional digit is required. They also refer you to more commonly used codes. For example, if you were to look up the term "cancer," you would then see the words, *see also, Neoplasm*. It is important to remember that the laymen's terms and the medical terms are different. While the index section may contain such common terms as "heart attack, stroke, or broken leg," the tabular section will have these conditions listed under their official medical listings of "myocardial infarction," and "fracture tibia and/or fibula, left or right leg." The tabular section listings and index section listings will not be identical. This is why it is vital to check both sections when coding a patient's diagnosis, and to check with your health care professional if you have any questions at all.

All annotations and corresponding symbols are listed in the beginning of your particular ICD-9 book. Make sure to read the entire introduction section of your book to help you make the most informed coding choices.

The ICD-9 is divided into three sections, or volumes. Volume 1 is an alphabetical listing of diagnoses. Volume 2 is a tabular listing of diagnoses. And Volume 3 is an inpatient facility listing of procedure codes. Primarily, we will be dealing with the first two sections.

Volume 1–Alphabetical Listing

The alphabetical listing is generally in the beginning of the book. It is strictly an organized listing of the codes, with their corresponding tabular number indicated next to it. Under the main heading for each entry will be listed any sub-listings or complications for that entry, but this section contains very few, if any, annotations. Neither does it contain any descriptions of diagnoses or directions for coding of complications. The alphabetical listing should never be used to code alone. It should only be used as a companion to the tabular listing and as a reference to guide you to the correct tabular page in which to begin your coding research process. For example, to look up a patient with diabetes, you would go to the D section, find the heading of diabetes, which would refer you to the diagnosis category of 250. You would then flip back to the tabular section, go to section 250, and follow the directions for appropriate coding from there. While most are specific codes that will be carried out to either a fourth or a fifth digit, there are some non-specific codes that are three digit codes only. In the back of many books, there will be an appendix of non-specific three-digit codes that cannot be carried out. Spend some time becoming familiar with your book and the special features that it contains to help you with your coding procedures.

Volume 2–Tabular Listing

The tabular listing uses the same codes, only listed by their assigned number rather than alphabetical. This section, the largest in the book, will also contain all of the directions and footnotes to help you with all of your coding needs. Each section will begin with the main heading for that specific diagnosis, then have all of the sub-headings and complications listed underneath. If another code is more commonly used, this section will refer you to that other section for review before your final coding decision is made. Essential for this process is a good, clear description of the patient's condition from your health care professional. If there is any doubt whatsoever as to exactly what the patient's condition is, this needs to be referred back to them for clarification before you continue. Accurate coding is absolutely essential for the billing process. Many reimbursement rates are based on both the procedure and diagnosis codes that are listed. Incorrect coding could potentially lessen your maximum collection efforts. If intentional mis-coding in order to get a higher reimbursement rate is uncovered, felony fraud charges will result. Accuracy is essential.

Volume 3–Procedure Codes

This volume of the ICD-9 coding manual is for inpatient facility procedure codes. It is also separated into two sections, one alphabetical and one tabular. The tabular section is broken down further by the different systems of the body. This volume breaks down the codes exactly the same as the other two do, with annotations and referral notes to help the coding process along. Volume 3 also contains many helpful diagrams and illustrations to guide you. This section is not intended for use by private practice physicians.

Some independent publishers will even include, in their introductory sections, a self-test section for practice coding using their manuals.

Incorrect coding is one primary reason for denials of claims. This process can be frustrating and costly to correct. Claims need to be resubmitted and corrected, tying up your collections for a longer period of time until the problem can be sorted out, if it can be sorted out. Many times, when a diagnosis is changed in the middle of the claim process, a letter of explanation is required as to why this claim information has been changed. Once the claim is denied by the insurance carrier, it then goes into the appeal process—a long and sometimes costly process of medical review that can take months, or even longer, to complete. Every effort should be taken to make accurate coding choices at the beginning of the claim process to avoid this claim pitfall.

You should use multiple codes whenever possible. The more codes listed, the more accurate your claim will be. The first code listed on any claim will be referred to as the primary diagnosis, or chief complaint. This is the reason that the patient is being seen that day. For example, let's say you have a patient who is pregnant and has cut her finger. If her visit that day is due to her cut finger, then her primary diagnosis for that visit will be 883.0 (open wound, finger) and her secondary diagnosis will be V22.2 (pregnancy, single, uterine, without sickness). If her visit is for prenatal purposes, but her finger still needs attention, then the codes would be reversed. You need to list as many codes, in the order of their importance for that day's visit, as the claim will hold. This will give the claims examiner a complete picture of the patient's overall health situation and the reason for the office or clinic visit.

This same principle holds true for coding of procedures as well. The primary procedure is coded in the first spot, and any other minor procedures are coded below that. For example in the chiropractic field, the primary code might be for manipulation or spinal adjustment, and the lesser procedures would be perhaps ultrasound therapy or ice pack. X-rays would also be minor procedures as well, since they would be used as an ancillary service to the office visit for the initial problem.

When a condition is suspected, but not yet diagnosed, you will then code the symptoms rather than the suspected disease. For example, if a physician suspects a brain tumor and decides to do further testing to confirm the diagnosis, you will not immediately code the claim with a brain tumor. The resulting symptoms of the patient's condition may be headache (784.0), insomnia (780.52), and blurred vision (368.8). After the diagnosis is confirmed through further testing, a diagnosis of brain tumor (191.1) can then be coded.

The more advanced diagnoses such as cancer (also known as neoplasm) are a little more difficult to code. In your ICD-9 manual, under the heading of Neoplasm, there is a table. The main heading reads Neoplasm, and under that main heading is an alphabetical listing of the various body parts that can be struck by this disease. Across the top are headings of Primary, Secondary, CA in situ, Benign, Uncertain Behavior, and Unspecified. These categories depend on the current state of growth and advancement of the disease. It is vital that the correct category be chosen as your reimbursement rate, and the patient's benefits can depend on your coding choice. These categories will also change as the patient's condition improves, stabilizes, or degenerates. Review of these diagnoses with your health care provider on a regular basis is essential.

NEOPLASM, NEOPLASTIC

Location	Malignant Primary	Malignant Secondary	Malignant Ca in situ	Benign	Uncertain Behavior	Unspecified
Abdomen	195.2	198.89	234.8	229.8	238.8	239.8
– cavity	195.2	198.89	234.8	229.8	238.8	239.8
– organ	195.2	198.89	234.8	229.8	238.8	239.8
– viscera	195.2	198.89	234.8	229.8	238.8	239.8
– wall	173.5	198.2	232.5	216.5	238.2	239.2

Notice that the codes will change slightly depending on the category and place on the body. Cancers are usually referred to by their place of origin. So, for example, if a person has a malignant cancer that begins in the lungs and then spreads to the entire body, it will still be referred to as a primary diagnosis of Neoplasm, Malignant, Lung (162.9).

Another table contained within the ICD-9 manual is the Table of Drugs and Chemicals. Again, the main heading being Drugs/Chemicals, and beneath that is an alphabetical listing of the various drugs and chemicals that can be ingested. Across the top are the categories Poisoning, Accident, Therapeutic Use, Suicide Attempt, Assault, and Undetermined. Some insurance carriers do not cover anything dealing with suicide or attempted suicide. Accurate coding can determine whether this will be a covered service for your patient or not. Large patient balances could result in the case of insurance denials, so accurate coding to avoid this is essential. See the following example.

TABLE OF DRUGS AND CHEMICALS

Drug Name	Poisoning	Accident	Therapeutic Use	Suicide Attempt	Assault	Undetermined
Propanol	980.3	E860.4	---	E950.9	E962.1	E980.9
Acetaminophen	965.4	E850.4	E935.4	E950.0	E962.0	E980.0
Aconite (wild)	988.2	E865.4	-- -	E950.9	E962.1	E980.9
ACTH	962.4	E858.0	E932.4	E950.4	E962.0	E980.4

Other notations and abbreviations that are important to note are listed below.

NOS–Not otherwise specified.
NEC–Not elsewhere classified
SEE–redirects you to a more specific category or code
SEE ALSO–refers you to additional information
SEE CATEGORY–refers you to review the entire category before coding
OR–Operating Room procedure (code as inpatient)
NON–OR–outpatient or clinic procedure
USE ADDITIONAL CODE–incomplete coding for this diagnosis, needs further information
NEEDS ADDITIONAL DIGIT–coding needs to be carried out further, not specific enough

CODE FIRST UNDERLYING DISEASE–don't code complications of a disease without first coding the disease itself (only if already diagnosed. Do not code if a Rule Out diagnosis. In that case, code the symptoms, not any possible complications.)

There are also Admitting Diagnoses and Discharge Diagnoses for all hospitals and inpatient facilities. The admitting diagnosis is the reason that the patient has been brought to your facility. This can be a non-specific code such as Assault (E968.9), but then your discharge diagnosis must contain more detailed information such as Wound, Open, Head (873.8).

V codes and E codes are special sections that were added after the initial codes were created to include both injuries and conditions. V codes are knows as supplemental classifications, and E codes are related to external causes.

For example, looking into the back of the ICD-9 section in the V code section we will find the following:

V10   Personal history of malignant neoplasm
V11   Personal history of mental disorder

And looking further into the E code section of the manual, we will find the following:

E869   Accidental poisoning by other gasses and vapors
E870   Accidental cut, puncture, perforation, or hemorrhage during medical care

Make sure to review these sections carefully and become familiar with them completely.
Also included in the text are the Official Government Appendixes. These include:

Morphology of Neoplasms
Glossary of Mental Disorders
Classification of Drugs by AHFS (American Hospital Formulary Service) List
Classification of Industrial Accidents

List of Three-Digit Codes (codes that cannot be carried out any further and are acceptable for billing as they are)

Some private publishers will also include their own appendixes of

MDCs (Major Diagnostic Categories) and
DRGs (Diagnosis Related Groups)
Glossary of Markers and Annotations

MDCs and DRGs are government-created terms initially used for Medicare purposes, but that have since spread to widespread use within the insurance field. These terms refer to groups of diagnoses and services that have been lumped together and assigned a dollar value for reimbursement purposes. The reimbursement you will receive for a DRG patient will not be based on the procedure that was performed but rather a combination of the procedure and the diagnosis that patient may have. For example, two patients enter the hospital for the exact same procedure, but one has a diagnosis of cancer and the other of congestive heart failure. The claims would be paid at two separate rates based on the DRG values, regardless of the fact that they received identical procedures. The reasoning basis for this is that certain diagnosed patients require a higher level of care, regardless of the procedure performed. While the same service may have taken place, one patient may have been in treatment longer than the other and require much more extensive recovery and follow-up care than the other, all based upon that patient's diagnosis.

DRGs are very difficult calculations with a large number of variables to consider. There is software from several vendors available to help with this calculation, or your local Medicare intermediary should provide a DRG Prospective Payor System (PPS) download page for you. Search the Internet for the Medicare representative in your local area and follow the links to the DRG pricer download page. There will be a fully self-contained software calculation program that will download allowing you to price these inpatient procedures yourself. Since there are different Medicare intermediaries (payers) for different regions of the country, there isn't one Medicare source for this information. Often times reimbursement levels will be different depending on where your practice is as well. For example, a surgical procedure done in the heart of Los Angeles will probably have a higher reimbursement percentage than the same procedure done in a small doctor's office in rural Alabama. Geographic regions play a major role in determining compensation for a specific provider of service. Look to your local intermediary for your geographic-specific information.

Coding Process

The coding process from the physician's office should be a relatively simple one. Coding from a hospital-based setting may be more involved due to more steps being involved in obtaining the patient information. The process should look something like this:

The patient is seen within the doctor's office and treated for their various ailments. Upon completion of their visit for that day, a form should be generated with the patient's name and all personal information. That form should also have the services that were performed that day and a specific diagnosis. This information should either be already coded by the physician's office or be written out in detail. When this form is picked up by you for billing, it should be reviewed for accuracy and completeness. If there are any questions, or if there are any discrepancies, return the form to the provider's office for completion or correction. After complete information is received, you are ready to bill. If the form is not coded, use your CPT and ICD-9 manuals to look up the services and diagnoses, placing the codes onto the superbill for data entry into your computer system.

Hospitals and other facilities are more difficult to elicit information from. The superbill, or charge information sheet, may or may not contain diagnosis information. This may need to be pulled from chart notes, emergency room reports, or surgical reports. This process is known as abstracting. It can sometimes be a cumbersome and time consuming process. More detective work is necessary to be able to track down necessary information. A thorough working knowledge of the business processes of your facility will help you save valuable time and wasted energy in tracking down required billing information. Once this information is obtained, you are ready for the billing process.

ICD-9 EXERCISES

LET'S TRY SOME EXERCISES:

ICD-9 Exercise 1

Look up the following diagnoses using the tabular section in your ICD-9 manual.

717.43 _____

540.0 _____

E852 _____

V65.1 _____

722 _____

443.0 _____

251.2 _____

253.3 _____

090 _____

E880.1 _____

(See answers in Section V)

ICD-9 Exercise 2

Please look up the following codes from the tabular section of your ICD-9 manual.

E970 _____

V455.3 _____

780.7_____

196 _____

056.9_____

102.0_____

360.1_____

998.01_____

E828 _____

628.0_____

(See answers in Section V)

ICD-9 Exercise 3

Use the alphabetical section of your ICD-9 manual to look up the following codes.

Description	ICD-9 Code
Fear of Open Spaces	
with Panic Attacks	_____
Hysterical Parorexia	_____
Twisted Bowel (Colon)	_____
Elephantiasis, Eyelid	_____
Human Growth Hormone Deficiency	_____
Blood Clot Bladder	_____
Clumsiness	_____
Cold	_____
Osteoarthritis	_____
Traumatic Rotator Cuff Tear	_____
Jackson's Veil	_____
Open Ankle Wound	_____

(See answers in Section V)

ICD-9 Exercise 4

Description	ICD-9 Code
Whooping Cough	_____
Widening Aorta	_____
Onychitis	_____
Malignant Neoplasm, Connective Tissue NEC Abdomen, Primary	_____
Benign Neoplasm, Connective Tissue NEC Hand, Secondary	_____
Neoplasm, Brain NEC Uncertain Behavior	_____
Injury, Eyeball, Superficial	_____
Abdominal Wall Fissure	_____
Diseased Heart (Organic)	_____
Cirrhosis, Liver, Chronic	_____
Osler's Disease (polycythemia vera)	_____
Hanging	_____

(See answers in Section V)

ICD-9 Exercise 5

Please answer the following questions using your ICD-9 book as a guide:

1. Does the code 518 require a fourth digit?

2. A fifth digit?

3. What is the difference between 512.0 and 512.1?

4. What is the code 232.0 for?

5. What does the code 233.0 exclude?

6. What is the first tabular code in the book?

7. What is the last tabular code in the book? (excluding V codes and E codes)

8. Does V02 require a fifth digit?

9. Where are they?

10. Does V17 require a fifth digit?

11. What is the code V25 for?

12. What kind of stock does the code E805 refer to?

13. Are there any E codes with fifth digits?

14. What is Appendix A?

15. What is Appendix B?

16. What is Appendix C?

17. What is Appendix D?

18. What is Appendix E?

19. Where are the definitions and illustrations?

20. Where is the general glossary?

21. Where is the E code alphabetical list?

22. Where is the V code alphabetical list?

23. Where is the Table of Drugs and Chemicals?

24. Where is the summary of Additions/Deletions/Revisions from the tabular list?

25. What does NEC stand for?

26. What does NOS stand for?

27. Can you get around in this book now? (The correct answer here is *yes!*)

(See answers in Section V)

ICD-9 Exercise 6

Please code the following:

Description	ICD-9 Code
Manson's Disease (schistosomiasis)	_____
Semicoma	_____
Fracture Fibula, Closed	_____
Hippus	_____
Seizure	_____
Self-mutilation	_____
Glider Crash	_____
Dog Bite	_____
Tongue Tie	_____
False Labor	_____
Krukenberg's Spindle	_____
Neck Injury	_____
Heel Deformity (acquired)	_____
Mental Health Evaluation	_____
Allergy Examination	_____

(See answers in Section V)

ICD-9 Exercise 7

Please code the following:

Description	ICD-9 Code
Osteomalacia	_____
Chronic deformans hypertrophica	_____
Psoriasis	_____
Slowing heart	_____
Thumb Sucking (child problem)	_____
Cancer of stomach, primary	_____
Headache	_____
Hemorrhage, Intestine	_____
Herpes, genital	_____
Iron deficient anemia	_____
Jackson's membrane	_____
Ixodiasis	_____
Abdominal mass	_____
Herrick's anemia	_____
Foods intolerance NEC	_____
Manic depressive psychosis	_____

(See answers in Section V)

Now let's try some ICD-9 and CPT coding together.

ICD-9 and CPT Together – Exercise 1

1. You have a new patient who was admitted to the hospital on 7/3 and discharged on 7/8 for a total of six days. The initial hospital visit was comprehensive, with subsequent days being focused. The discharge on 7/8 took less than thirty minutes. Code this visit.

   Initial exam   _____

   Subsequent days _____   How many? _____

   Discharge exam   _____

   This patient was admitted for:

   Headache   _____

   and Diabetes   _____

2. You have an established patient who is seen in the office for a focused exam.

   What is the code?   _____

   This patient was seen for:

   Diarrhea due to bacteria NEC _____

   and gastric flu _____

3. You have a patient admitted to the hospital for observation. This is an established patient with a focused exam of low complexity. Patient was admitted on 7/3 and discharged on 7/5.

   Please code 7/3 (admit day)   _____

   7/4 (subsequent day)   _____

   and 7/5 (discharge day)   _____

This patient also had the following hospital testing:

   Hemoglobin Concentration (blood) _____

   Blood Cell Enzyme Activity   _____

   and Bleeding Time   _____

This patient was admitted for:

   Duchenne's Disease (muscular dystrophy) _____

   and Autonomic Imbalance   _____

4. You have a new patient who is seen as an outpatient in your office for a comprehensive visit.

    Please code the visit   _____

    This patient also had the following tests:

    X-ray of Right Ankle   _____

    X-ray of Right Lower Leg   _____

    This patient's diagnosis is:

    Broken Right Ankle Bone   _____

    Sprain Right Lower Leg   _____

5. You have a patient in the hospital. The doctor is called for a consult. Patient is admitted on 7/3 and discharged on 7/8 for a total of five days. The initial hospital consult is a detailed history of low complexity. The discharge consult took less than thirty minutes. Please code this hospital stay:

    7/3 (admit day)   _____

    Subsequent days   _____ How many? _____

    7/8 (discharge day) _____

    This patient's diagnosis is:

    Infectious bronchitis with obstruction to airway, chronic   _____
    and Endocrine Dysfunction   _____

6. You are called to exam a new patient in a skilled nursing facility (SNF). This will be a new patient comprehensive visit for evaluation and management. This visit is of high complexity decision making. Please code the

    Initial visit _____

    and any subsequent visits   _____

    This patient's diagnosis is:

    Emphysema with bronchitis, acute and chronic   _____

    and Congestive Heart Failure   _____

7. You are called to the emergency room to see a patient. This patient is not admitted. This visit is outpatient, treat and release. This is a new patient, comprehensive visit of high complexity. Please code:

    ER visit_____

This patient's diagnosis is:

Auto Accident, involving another motor vehicle   _____

Concussion with moderate loss of consciousness   _____

8. One of your patients delivers a child prematurely. The newborn infant is now your patient. This infant is admitted to the neonatal intensive care unit. Please code:

   Initial visit (date of birth)   _____

   Subsequent care days for a stable infant   _____

This patient's diagnosis is:

   premature birth NEC   _____

   underdeveloped lungs   _____

9. You have a patient that you see either in their own home or a board and care facility, which they sometimes enter for limited periods of time. This is a new patient.

   For a home visit with a detailed history, of moderate complexity, what is the initial visit code? _____

   For a Domiciliary, or Board and Care, Initial visit with an expanded history of moderate complexity, use which code? _____

This patient's diagnosis is:

   Undiagnosed disease   _____
   And Failure to Thrive   _____

(See answers in Section V)

ICD-9 and CPT Together – Exercise 2

Please code the following diagnostic testing and their corresponding diagnoses:

Procedure		Diagnosis	
Cesarean Section (delivery only)	_____	Pregnancy	_____
CAT Scan	_____	Headache	_____
Brain death (determination)	_____	Murder	_____
Chest X-ray	_____	Lung cancer, Malignant, primary	_____
Well Baby Care	_____	Newborn Infant, Single birth, born in hospital	_____
Throat Biopsy	_____	Throat cancer Malignant, secondary	
Sleep Study	_____	Sleep Apnea, Adult With Insomnia	_____
Sperm Washing	_____	Male Infertility	_____
Including Special Handling	_____		
Psychological Testing	_____	Schizophrenia	_____
Cardiac Massage	_____	Cardiac Arrest	_____

(See answers in Section V)

For additional exercises, please see the Medical Billing, Coding, and Reimbursement Supplemental Workbook.

HCPCS

The HCPCS (pronounced 'hick-picks") stands for Healthcare Common Procedure Coding System. It is the next level (Level II) coding system beyond the CPT. It is a uniform method of coding for all health care providers. Put together in 1983, prior to that there was no specific and uniform coding system for certain procedures, services, or supplies for reimbursement.

Level I coding, or the CPT (Current Procedural Terminology) manual, uses a five-digit number with a two-digit modifier. Many of these codes are generic in nature, (i.e. supplies 99070). Level II coding (HCPCS) was created to further define codes which the CPT is not specific enough about for reimbursement from insurance companies. These codes consist of a five-digit alpha-numeric code specific to certain sections within the book. Like the other two reference manuals we have used, the HCPCS is broken down into two major sections: an alphabetical index and a tabular section. The tabular section of the HCPCS book is broken down into the following chapters:

ICD-9 Code	Description
A0000–A0999	Transportation Services Including Ambulance
A4000–A8999	Medical and Surgical Supplies
A9000–A9999	Administrative, Miscellaneous, and Investigational
B4000–B9999	Enteral and Parenteral Therapy
C1000–C9999	Outpatient PPS
D0000–D9999	Dental Procedures
E0100–E9999	Durable Medical Equipment
G0000–G9999	Procedures/Professional Services (temporary)
H0001–H2037	Alcohol and Drug Abuse Treatment Services
J0000–J9999	Drugs Administered Other than Oral Method
J9000–J9999	Chemotherapy Drugs
K0000–K9999	Temporary Codes
L0000–L9999	Orthotic Procedures
L5000–L9999	Prosthetic Procedures
M0000–M0301	Medical Services
P0000–P9999	Pathology and Laboratory Services
Q0000–Q9999	Q Codes (temporary)
R0000–R5999	Diagnostic Radiology Services
S0000–S9999	Temporary National Codes (non–Medicare)
T1000–T9999	National T Codes est. for State Medicaid Agencies
V0000–V2999	Vision Services
V5000–V5999	Hearing Services

In addition to these sections, additional modifiers, called Physical Status Modifiers are also used to further pinpoint and fine tune the diagnostic condition of the patient. A complete list of these modifiers is contained in the Appendices Section of this book.

HCPCS EXERCISES

Let's try some exercises.

Please look up the following HCPCS codes (remember to cross reference them in the index section of the book):

1.   Dental bleaching, external, per tooth   _____

2.   Aztreonam   _____

3.   Brachytherapy, prostate   _____

4.   Body sock   _____

5.   Benbadryl   _____

6.   Gravlee jet washer   _____

7.   Nebulizer, aerosol mask   _____

8.   Mini-bus, non-ER transportation   _____

9.   Sodium Chloride Injection   _____

10. Hypertonic saline   _____

11. Irrigation Solution   _____

12. Dental Sealant   _____

13. Johnson's thumb immobilizer   _____

14. Albumarc   _____

15. Carbon filter   _____

16. Jenamicin   _____

17. IUD (Intra Uterine Device)   _____

18. Wig   _____

19.   Oral Zithromax   _____

20.   Wound cleanser   _____

21.   Shoe Wedges (range)   _____

22.   Zantac   _____

(See answers in Section V)

HCPCS EXERCISE 2

Let's try another exercise. Look up the descriptions for these codes in the HCPCS manual.

1. A0428   _____

2. C1122   _____

3. E02751   _____

4. G9016   _____

5. J1815   _____

6. L1500   _____

7. K0105   _____

8. S9435   _____

9. V5364   _____

10. V5299   _____

11. S0034   _____

12. Q3031   _____

13. P9060   _____

14. L8610   _____

15. K0098   _____

(See answers in Section V)

HCPCS REVIEW

Let's try some exercises. Using the glossary or your HCPCS manual, answer the following questions. In what section of the HCPCS manual would you find the following section headings?

1. Medical/Surgical Supplies

2. Dental Procedures

3. Table of Drugs

4. Vision Services

5. Prosthetic Procedures

6. Temporary National Codes

7. Temporary Codes

8. Drugs/Other than Oral

9. Durable Medical Equipment (DME)

10. Temporary Outpatient PPS

11. Modifiers

12. Pathology and Lab

(See answers in Section V)

The HCPCS manual also contains an extensive list of modifiers to further enhance these codes, identifying such items as which fingers and toes are to be treated and how many physicians are treating the patient at any given time. A list of these modifiers is located in the Appendix section of this book. Please review these codes (page 261) and familiarize yourself with them and their use.

For additional exercises, please see the Medical Billing, Coding, and Reimbursement Supplemental Workbook.

BILLING

AUDITING AND RECONCILING ACCOUNTS

How much money should be collected for each service performed? Is this amount the same for every patient you see? Are we collecting enough or too much from the patient? What is the patient responsible for? Are we maximizing our collection efforts?

These are questions that each provider's office must answer individually. The answers are not the same for every practice. In order to determine whether your office is collecting the maximum amount of reimbursement to which you are entitled, you will need to understand your insurance contracts and patient policies. Each one will need to be examined individually in order to ensure accuracy in billing and collections. Extra care should be taken before billing the patient for anything you are unsure about. If you don't know whether a service can be billed to the patient, then contact that patient's insurance carrier and ask the customer service representative.

In order to avoid charges of discrimination or price gouging, your charges for services must be the same for all patients. The amount that is collected from the insurance companies will vary based on the different types of contracts, but the charges must be equal. Also, the co-pays and patient portions must be collected from each patient equally. A professional courtesy discount can sometimes be applied under certain circumstances, but you should be very careful about writing off co-pays for certain individuals just because they are friends or neighbors. If you write off the co-pay of a neighbor who happens to be of the same ethnic group as you, but collect from another neighbor that you don't really know who happens to be of a different ethnicity, you have just opened up yourself for a discrimination lawsuit. Simple misunderstandings happen every day. If Medicare or any other governmental agency is involved in any way, your client could lose his license to bill for that entity. This is not something to mess around with. Simple gestures of goodwill can be turned around at the drop of a hat. Always protect yourself and your clients at all cost. You, as a billing service, could well be dragged into an ugly lawsuit simply by association. Always protect yourself.

In order to begin to understand the maximum collections for any given practice, you must first understand the contractual obligations and limitations for the various different kinds of insurance programs available to your patients. Here is a brief run down of what's most commonly available today.

CAPITATION

Capitation accounts, also known as managed care, is one of the fastest growing insurance types in the country. Sometimes it is also referred to as GMC (Geographic Managed Care). This plan offers the ability to keep healthcare costs to a minimum and therefore is very appealing to insurers. This plan is so popular that even state and federal government agencies are offering Managed Care options to their insured patients as an option for their healthcare choices. Medicare and Medicaid have capitation option as well, leading the way for other smaller privatized companies to follow.

The basis of capitation is simple. A provider is assigned a certain number of patients to care for based on your geographic region. So, for instance, if your practice is in the city of Sacramento and you estimated that you could care for one thousand patients enrolled with Health Plan of Sacramento, after signing contracts, you would be assigned one thousand patients to care for. These patients would then have to come to you as their primary care physician for all services. For any service you could not provide, you would then refer them out to a specialty office within the managed care system (another contracting provider). For each of these patients you would receive a monthly stipend. You would receive this same amount every month for every patient on your register, whether you ever see this patient or not.

Whenever the patient is seen, they will usually have what is called an office co-pay. This amount is assigned by the insurance company and is based on the patient's contract, either personal or group. The contract will state that a set amount (usually five or ten dollars) is due from that patient on each visit. This money needs to be collected directly from the patient, usually at the time of service, since the patient knows ahead of time that it is due. This, together with the monthly stipend, is your payment for these services. According to each capitation agreement, only certain services are covered under your contract. They usually include only routine services such as office visits and lab work. Any service not covered under the cap agreement would then revert to a fee-for-service plan. Refer to your contract for a list of covered and non-covered services. Your total amount then collected from each patient would be the total of their stipend paid to you, plus your co-pay if they were seen. For most capitation agreements, there is no billing required. However, some health plans will request that you send in a claim form for each patient seen, simply for tracking purposes. The insurance company will need to make financial estimates regarding the numbers of patients seen, most common diagnoses, and most common services provided. If you provide service above the basic services listed in your cap agreement, and you revert to a fee-for-service billing, a claim form would need to be generated so reimbursement can be made to you.

The idea behind capitation is that the insurance premiums and stipends paid for healthy patients that are rarely, if ever seen, then make up for the more costly patients who are seen more frequently. This idea works well in most cases; however, a few very ill or injured patients on one roster could then cause your provider to lose money for the year. Careful record keeping needs to be kept in order to determine whether or not this is the case. Since your stipend amount will be paid to you in one large monthly check each month, you have two choices as far as posting these payments goes. You can divide the check by the number of patients you have enrolled in that plan and post the stipend to each individual patient account each month. Or, you can simply post the large bulk check to a miscellaneous account instead. It is entirely up to the preference of your specific office. The first option will require considerably more work, but shows a more accurate reflection of which patients you are making money from and which ones you are losing from. The other is easier and less costly as far as processing hours. Record keeping on individual patients will be more difficult but not impossible.

FEE FOR SERVICE

Fee for Service contracts have been the most common through the last few decades. They consist of a bill being generated for each and every service being performed and being filed with the various insurance companies for reimbursement. A check would then be cut to your office for each patient seen. Will the reimbursement for all Fee for Service patients be the same? The answer is no. If you have one patient who is insured with Insurance A that pays claims at 80 percent based on their contract rate with you, and another patient who has Insurance B that pays at 65 percent, the reimbursement rates will differ. In addition to that, patient liability amounts will vary as well. Even though two patients have the same insurance carrier, one may have a five hundred dollar per year deductible, while another may have one thousand dollars. This amount is assigned and tracked by the insurance carrier, so any questions regarding patient liability should be directed to them.

This is where you need to learn how to read the Explanation of Benefits very carefully. An Explanation of Benefits, or EOB, is the check stub that is attached to each check that comes to your office for insurance benefits. It explains who the payment is for and has a breakdown of how they arrived at their payment. For example:

Let's say you sent a bill to the insurance carrier for one hundred dollars for an office visit. This insurance carrier pays at 80 percent. They would then show an allowable amount of eighty dollars, and the remaining twenty dollars would have to be written off based on your negotiated contract. Then, the insurance company applies thirty dollars to the patient's yearly deductible, leaving you a payment of fifty dollars. The patient then needs to be billed for the thirty dollars. Your total payments from all sources (insurance company and patient combined) should equal what your contract rate is (80 percent in this case). Remember, you can never bill a patient for a disallowed contracted amount. If you have any questions regarding this, contact the insurance carrier directly.

HMO

HMO stands for Health Maintenance Organization. A Health Maintenance Organization is a healthcare provider with its own infrastructure and support staff. Generally, this will be an organization where the physicians and other providers are employees rather than contracting physicians. The HMO will generally own its own building and other facilities (i.e. labs, radiology centers, etc.) and will not refer patients out from their own facility unless there is no other way to provide service for them. Also referred to as private hospitals, patients without their specific insurance are not allowed to be seen in these facilities unless a life-threatening emergency occurs.

If contacted by an HMO to provide service to a patient, a written authorization needs to be obtained from the HMO to ensure payment. Generally, they will approach you with a fee schedule and ask if their standard contract rates are acceptable. After a signed document is obtained, patients can be referred to you for services. Even with a contract in place, services will not be paid without prior written authorization for each and every patient seen. When seen within the context of the HMO, the patient will be billed only for their individual co-pay amount at the time of the appointment, and the rest would be paid under a capitation agreement between the employer and the HMO.

PPO

PPO stands for Preferred Provider Organization. This is a group of contracting providers, each with their own offices set up, all affiliated with one insurance provider. This insurance provider is responsible for seeing that specialties of all types are covered under the contract so that patients could then stay with the PPO network for their care. The patient would have their choice of approved physicians and providers from a list provided by the insurance company. If they stay within the PPO network, the patient would have only their co-pay and deductible (if applicable) to pay. The patient can choose to be seen by any doctor, but if they choose a doctor outside the network (not on the approved list) that patient then becomes financially responsible for the entire visit, regardless of co-pay or deductible amounts. Before making any appointments for PPO patients, make sure you are an approved provider for their particular insurance company. A phone call to the customer service number on the patient's insurance card will tell you this if you don't know for sure.

With both an HMO and a PPO situation, the patient will be assigned what is called a Primary Care Physician (PCP). This is your main healthcare provider and will be the initial contact point for all services. If the PCP cannot provide services and needs to refer you to another specialty, they will make those arrangements and let you know where you will need to be seen for your healthcare issue. If services are not approved and referred through the PCP, they will be denied.

CONTRACTED PAYERS

Contracted payers would be any Fee for Service contract that you have. PPO practices would be an example of a contracted provider. These will be standard contracts for most insurance carriers in your area in which you have agreed, in writing and in advance, to accept a certain reimbursement amount for services. These are generally written as a percentage of charges, although many companies are now converting to a flat rate amount for specific services. For example, an office visit would be payable at the rate of fifty dollars, regardless of what your charge might be. Any patient liability would then be applied to the allowable amount of fifty dollars and a check cut to you for the final amount. The reimbursement amounts for various different services will be detailed out in your contract. Make sure you understand all of the contract language and clauses. If you have trouble reading it, call the insurance company for help.

In certain states and under federal regulations, there are laws that govern timely payment of claims. Interest and penalties can be applied if payments are received over a certain time period. Check with your local and federal insurance authority to know what the time limitations and maximum allowable interest and penalty amounts for your area are.

COBRA BENEFITS

COBRA benefits (Consolidated Omnibus Budget Reconciliation Act) is a federal law that enables an employee to continue with their group coverage for a limited period when certain circumstances would warrant the termination of that insurance. Examples of such circumstances would be job layoff, termination, voluntary job termination, divorce, reduction in hours (either temporary or permanent), or long-term disability. What this means to the patient is that they have the right to continue to have medical coverage at their own expense through a previous or part-time employer, until new insurance arrangements can be made through perhaps a new employment situation. This will generally get people past the probationary period at a new job in which insurance benefits are not usually covered. This is especially important when a sick child is affected. It helps to maintain consistency of treatment and some form of normalcy for the patient during a transition period.

As far as billing is concerned, all available information needs to be obtained for your files: date of separation from your job, date COBRA benefits took effect, number of dependents, etc. While this information will not be necessary for the billing form, COBRA claims for benefits are looked at more closely and questioned more often than traditional Employer Group Health Plan (EGHP) claims. Having this information handy in your files will save you the trouble of trying to get in touch with the patient or subscriber later on when the claim is denied.

CO-PAY

Co-pay is a flat amount that is assigned as patient liability for each visit or service provided. These are generally connected with HMO or PPO claims. It will be a set amount, like five or ten dollars per visit. This amount will be greater for more involved services (i.e. emergency room visits). This amount will not change for the life of the contract and is payable to the office at the time that services are rendered.

DEDUCTIBLE

This is the amount assigned by the insurance company that is patient liability. Generally it will be a flat amount per year. For example, if a patient's deductible amount is five hundred dollars per year, then the first five hundred dollars in allowed charges will be patient liability, and after that the insurance would begin to pay. So, using our previous example, if you had an office visit for which the charge was one hundred dollars and your contract rate was 80 percent, then the allowed amount would be eighty dollars, with twenty dollars being written off to your contract allowance. The entire eighty dollars would then be applied to the patient's deductible, and so on, until their five hundred dollars was met. The insurance can only apply to the deductible the contract amount that they would be responsible to pay.

You cannot bypass the insurance company in any case and accept monies directly from the patient without filing a claim with the insurance company first. The insurance company needs to track and apply this deductible amount to their claims within their system. If you collected five hundred dollars directly from the patient without billing the insurance carrier, they would have no way of knowing that the patient had already paid you and would apply another five hundred dollars to the patient's liability. All transactions must go through the claims process for accurate processing of these amounts. The only exception to this would be if for some reason the patient specifically did not want a service billed to the insurance company. Then, private arrangements can be made, making sure that the patient understands they will still be responsible for an additional deductible amount over and above the amount you are collecting from them. It would be a very good idea to get an agreement like this in writing to protect yourself from problems later on down the road.

COINSURANCE

Coinsurance is the amount of each claim that belongs to the patient, aside from the deductible. For example, a patient's contract might read: "Patient is liable for a deductible of the first five hundred dollars in expenses for each calendar year, after which insurance will pay 75 percent of contracted rate, with patient liable for 25 percent of contract rate, to a maximum of twenty-five hundred dollars per calendar year."

In this example, you must still find out what the contracted rate is first. This will be a separate figure from the 75/25 percent split mentioned above. Using our original example of the one hundred dollar office visit, the contracted rate is eighty dollars (80%). Then we apply the figures above. The insurance will pay 75 percent of the contracted rate (eighty dollars) making the insurance payment sixty dollars. The remaining 25 percent (twenty dollars) is then the patient's coinsurance amount due, bringing the total collected from both parties up to the allowable rate of eighty dollars (80 percent of the original one hundred dollar charge). This process will be followed until the patient's maximum out of pocket amount for the year has been met, at which time the insurance company will then begin reimbursement at 100 percent of the contracted rate, until the next calendar year begins again. Each transaction will be listed on the Explanation of Benefits (EOB). If either you or your patient disagrees with the insurance company figures, you must contact the customer service office directly for their insurance.

AUTO INSURANCE (MEDICAL PAYMENTS)

When a patient gets into an auto accident, the auto insurance is automatically the primary carrier for that injury. Medical payments, also known as med-pay, are subject to the limitations of the policy and generally have a cap on the amount of benefits that can be paid out. The problem is that they pay claims on a first-come-first-paid basis, so if the patient has extensive injuries and is seen at the emergency room, or worse yet trauma center, there is a very good chance that by the time your bill gets in there, benefits will be exhausted. When this happens, coverage will then revert to the patient's private health insurance, but the claim must first be filed (on paper) with a letter from the auto carrier showing the denial of coverage. When there is a third party involved—let's say the patient was hit by another party and their auto insurance is primary due to fault—the process will be the same. Both auto insurance companies need to be billed and should coordinate with one another as to who is actually at fault and therefore prime. You will receive a denial letter from one and either a payment or a benefits exhausted letter from the other. Any unpaid portion will then be billed to your health insurance carrier. If the auto insurance carrier pays the claim in full, you may keep the entire payment, since you are probably not contracted with this carrier. If, however, the auto insurance carrier pays you only a portion of the bill since this is all that is left in the insured's med-pay account, and you have a balance that will be billed to the health insurance carrier, you will only be able to collect up to the maximum allowable amount that the health insurance carrier would have paid. So, for example, if your bill is $150, the auto insurance paid you fifty dollars and your contract with the health insurance carrier allows you to only be reimbursed at seventy-five dollars, then you can only collect the remaining twenty five dollars from the health carrier (the difference between what the auto insurance paid and what the health insurance company is contractually liable for). This will usually be written into your health insurance carrier's contract with the physician under the Coordination of Benefits clause. It is an effective cost-saving measure for the consumers. Again, if you need help with the contract language and limitations of the policy, contact the insurance carrier directly for clarification.

NO INSURANCE

If a patient has no insurance, then 100% of the bill is their responsibility. You cannot, however, charge them any more than you would charge any other entity. If your charge for an office visit is $100.00 for insured patients, then it must also be $100.00 for uninsured patients as well. Many offices will offer a discount to patients for payment in full on the date of service. This is acceptable so long as the discount applies to everyone equally.

MEDICAID

When you register with your state agency to become a Medicaid provider, you are at that time given a provider manual and a fee schedule. This entity is to be treated just as you would a Fee for Service contracted payer. Reimbursement levels will be very low in comparison to other insurance companies. Many payers will not sign Medicaid contracts due to the high volume patient loads and low reimbursement rates. Many individual state Medicaid programs are moving toward the Capitated Managed Care (GMC) type accounts with providers being reimbursed a set amount each month for every patient enrolled with their office. This is an effective way for cost containment within the state budgeting and finance system for healthcare. Patients would then be responsible for their individual co-pays at the time of service. Some Medicaid patients also have a deductible with the state as well. Also known as the Share of Cost Program, the state determines how much a patient is able to pay for their medical services, and after that amount has been applied and met by the patient, Medicaid will then step in and pay the remaining amount of the bill. Share of Cost amounts are generally applied on a monthly basis rather than a yearly basis.

LOCAL AND COUNTY PROGRAMS

Every county and local authority will have limited medical funding available for its residents. These are very limited programs and will generally run under a capitation or GMC (Geographic Managed Care) type of program or homeless indigent program. What this means is that there will rarely be a fee-for-service type of billing associated with it. If you are a contracted provider, you will receive a monthly allotment to see these patients, usually with no billing attached; or if you are non-contracted you will not see them, as there will be no prior approval for your office. Most facilities that contract for these types of coverage are larger hospitals and facilities who can afford a business loss. These types of contracts rarely make the providers any money and are more of a community service program for the homeless, elderly, victims of violent crimes, or the severely abused.

In larger urban areas you will also see contracts with local police authorities to perform evidentiary examinations. These will consist primarily of sexual assaults and other violent acts where DNA or other trace evidence must be removed from the victim and sent for extended testing. These contracts will exist directly between the police (requesting) authority and the provider. The patient will never be involved in the financial aspect of these services at all.

MEDICARE

Medicare is the federal government-based insurance for retired persons, established to ensure that no working American is caught without insurance coverage after their employment period ends. There are two options for the patient to choose. They are the traditional Fee-For-Service plan, in which the patient can choose any doctor or hospital and a new capitated plan in which the patient is assigned to a medical network for their care. Capitated plans are more cost effective and save both the patient and the government money. Providers are then either paid by individual service as the patient is seen or they receive their capitation payment monthly. In addition to both of these service payment options, Medicare also has a reimbursement program called the Diagnostic Related Group, or DRG. This is generally reserved for inpatient hospital services or surgical procedures. What this means is that certain diagnoses are related together in reimbursement groups, together with related services, making a DRG group. When you submit a claim with your appropriate ICD-9 and CPT codes, those codes are then run through the Medicare system, and if your diagnoses and procedure codes are part of these groupings, you will receive a DRG determined reimbursement from their calculations. Patient deductibles and coinsurance amounts will still apply. Specifics on DRG reimbursement amounts and related information are listed on the Internet.

Medicare benefits coverage is divided into two sections. They are commonly referred to Part A and Part B. One is automatic for any taxpayer, and the other is voluntary. Part A benefits are for inpatient hospital coverage only and are automatic. If you are a taxpayer and have paid into Social Security, you will have Medicare Part A coverage. Believe it or not, there are a significant number of people who are not covered under this. These are people who have never worked for one reason or another—perhaps there is family money they have lived off of, or they may have been taken by the kindness of others, or are families who have been long-term welfare recipients. For whatever reason, there are persons for whom Medicare is not a given thing. They have the option of buying into the Medicare program at their own expense and after they are of eligible age. A spouse of a working person is eligible for Medicare benefits under the spouse's Social Security number. So, in the case of a woman whose job was to stay home and take care of children, she is eligible for both Social Security and Medicare under her husband's coverage. Part B Medicare benefits are for outpatient services, and enrollment in this is voluntary. There is a charge for this service, deducted from your Social Security benefits monthly. The charge is minimal as compared to the benefit for this service. Most Medicare enrollees choose both Part A and Part B coverage. It is unusual to find someone with only Part A coverage, although it does happen.

Medicare Part D is the new drug coverage enacted in recent years to help uninsured Medicare patients with the cost of their prescription medications. It can be opted either as fee-for-service, or HMO entitlement just like their Part A and Part B coverage. This insurance coverage should be billed out by pharmacy providers, like any other drug coverage for other insurance companies.

Medicare is generally always the primary carrier once the patient becomes eligible. In unusual and specific circumstances, an insurance carrier could be primary over Medicare, such as if the elderly patient or their spouse is still employed full-time after the age of Medicare eligibility. Also in the case of End Stage Renal Disease patients, the insurance is automatically primary for the first thirty-six months of dialysis and care, then coverage reverts to Medicare as primary after that. Contact your local Medicare intermediary for questions regarding these issues.

The important thing to note is that Medicare is the leader in legislative and policy healthcare trends. Whatever Medicare does, policy-wise, generally all other insurance carriers will follow in a short period of time. If there is one major carrier to watch for changes and industry trends, it is Medicare. You should keep up on what all carriers are doing, but pay special attention to the Medicare intermediaries and governmental policymakers.

WORKERS' COMPENSATION

Workers' compensation is a system set up to cover workers injured on the job. Payment can follow any of the methods described above, from contracting payers, Fee for Service, to DRG reimbursement. The only difference is that the patient should never be liable for any services once approved by the insurance company. A written authorization should always be obtained from the insurance carrier prior to any service being performed, aside from emergency services.

There are two sides to the workers' compensation system: Evaluation and Treatment. Once a claim is accepted by the insurance company and treatment is approved, it will be treated just like any other claim. Claim forms must be filed, and reimbursement will follow either your contracted rate or your state's own accepted official workers' compensation fee schedule.

The evaluation side is more difficult. Not every claim that is filed for workers' compensation is accepted. There are many factors that need to be determined. For example, if your patient is in construction and he falls off a roof while at work, liability is pretty clear. But, in the case of a secretary who has been typing for fifteen years and develops carpal tunnel syndrome, it is not so clear. Let's say she worked for five different employers over that time period. There could be what is called cumulative trauma, which means that not one single employer is solely responsible for her claim, but rather the liability needs to be apportioned to all five equally. This is where the claims process can get tricky. Just because a claim is denied by an insurer doesn't mean that the patient hasn't been injured or that they aren't in need of care. It may simply mean that there are more insurance companies involved than just one and the appropriate liability factor needs to be determined legally. Sometimes these cases need to be brought before a judge to determine apportionment or even causation. Back injuries are a common diagnosis that is denied initially, until it can be proven that the employee truly did injure themselves at work, and not riding bulls in the local rodeo over the weekend. In either case, the patients should not be billed for these services. If you choose to see an injured worker before their claim has been accepted, you run the risk of the insurance denying your claim as non-covered or not approved. At this point there is little you can do to get it paid. If your claim is part of the evaluation process, you can file a lien against any possible future compensation out of the legal case and then wait for a court date. If it is treatment you are providing, without authorization your claims will be rightly denied and must be written off by you.

When is the patient liable for workers' compensation claims? Generally speaking, never. If you choose to see a patient whose claim has not been accepted by the insurance company, then you are not guaranteed payment in any way and run the risk of not getting paid at all. An agreement must be made up front as to who will be responsible for the bill in the event that the claim is denied. If you agree to take on the client on a lien basis (collecting only when the case is settled and there is a cash settlement involved), then if that case is lost, you are denied compensation. The only other way you can collect from the patient is if ordered to by the court. This is generally only done in the case of clear fraud. I have seen it happen. This is where private detectives with sub-rosa tapes follow the patient around without their knowledge to catch them in the act of something they claim they cannot do, such as lifting heavy boxes or the like. It does happen, and you need to be aware of it. Aside from these limited circumstances, the patient is not liable for his workers' compensation bills.

NON-COVERED SERVICES/ DENIED SERVICES

If a service is listed in your contract as non-covered and your office provides this service to a patient anyway, it must be written off, unless the patient is notified ahead of time (and preferably in writing) that it is non-covered and they will be solely responsible for payment. If a service is provided and then subsequently denied by the insurance company, this also must be written off. You cannot bill the patient for anything that they were not notified ahead of time they would be responsible for. Refer to your insurance manual or customer service representative for specifics about your individual contract.

If a patient comes in and is told that a specific service is not covered, and he chooses to have this service anyway, then he can be billed for that service. If a patient chooses to leave his insurance network and go to another provider, then responsibility for that charge is also his; likewise, if he obtains services without properly informing you of his insurance or allowing you to obtain the proper prior authorization, then he is also responsible for payment of that claim.

COORDINATION OF BENEFITS

Coordination of Benefits is a term used to indicate when two insurance companies are in contact with each other. This eliminates fraud in the industry and helps to keep healthcare costs down. When you become insured by a company, your eligibility goes into their database. If you are also covered, say by a spouse or other insurance company, you are then listed as eligible with them as well. These companies then contact one another and contact you to verify the purposes of your visit and who would then legally be the primary carrier. This way you cannot make claims to multiple companies for the same services and pocket the monies after the original bill is paid. If two companies coordinate benefits, they will, based upon the nationally accepted rules of primacy (listed below), determine who is the primary payer and who is secondary. If auto insurance is involved, the private insurance company will work directly with the auto insurance carrier to determine what benefits have been paid and to whom. Some information may be required from your office to speed this process along. If an insurance company requests information from you, it generally means that your benefits will be tied up until an answer is received. It is in your best interest to return this information as soon as possible so that your claims can be paid in a timely manner.

RULES OF PRIMACY

If a patient is covered by more than one insurance company, who is the primary carrier? In the case of an employer group health plan, the employee's insurance carrier would always be primary for them. So, for instance in the case of a married couple who each carry their own insurance and each have their spouses on their policies as well, the employee's own insurance would be primary for them, and their spouse's insurance would be secondary. So, let's say Mary and Bob are married and each carry insurance through their employers. Mary carries Blue Cross for herself and her husband, and Bob carries Blue Shield for them both. Mary's account should read Blue Cross prime (her employer's health coverage) and Blue Shield as secondary (her spouse's coverage). Bob's account would read just the opposite. It should have Blue Shield as prime (his employer's health coverage) and Blue Cross as second (his spouse's coverage).

These rules do not apply in the case of an individual policy though. Let's say Mary and Bob don't work, but rather pay for their Blue Cross and Blue Shield policies privately, with both persons covered on each policy. The prime coverage would revert to the policy that is in effect the longest. Let's say the Blue Cross coverage was picked up 1/1/2002, and the Blue Shield coverage became effective 5/1/2003. Blue Cross would be prime due to the effective dates of the policies. Each policy would only cover the persons listed on the policy.

In the event that a person has two employer group health plans (if the person is working two jobs with benefits), then the primary payer would be the policy in effect the longest. An employer group health plan is always prime over an individual policy.

Any state Medicaid or county social welfare program will automatically be last in the line of insurance priorities.

In the case of children, the rules change yet again. There is now in place "the birthday rule," which states that when children are covered by more than one parent, the parent whose birthday comes first in the year is prime for those children. Mary's birthday is 6/2, and Bob's is 7/9. Mary's birthday is first in the year (not who is older—year of birth does not matter) so her coverage will be primary for her children. This rule was established to balance out liability within the insurance industry. Decades ago it was the rule that the father's insurance was always primary for any children and the mother's, if any, was secondary. It was determined that certain industries, like construction, were being unduly burdened with the cost and care for children's healthcare, so the birthday rule was established. This rule does not come into play for stepchildren. Children are covered through court order by either one or both natural parents. In the case where both natural parents still carry coverage for the child, then the birthday rule would apply, just not to the stepparent.

CHILDREN'S INSURANCE COVERAGE IN DIVORCED FAMILIES AND STEPFAMILIES

In the case of a divorce, things can get very tricky. It may be necessary to consult the parent's marital settlement agreement to determine who is prime and who the responsible carrier is. It is not always true that both parties will be 50 percent responsible for insurance costs. I have seen cases where both divorced parents carry the children on their policies, in which case the birthday rule described above would still apply to determine who is prime. If, however, one parent is prohibited from taking out health insurance due to cost, the children can be covered only by one parent with the other parent splitting 50 percent of the out of pocket expenses. Before you bill any parent for any co-pays or out of pocket expenses, be sure you know their legal situation.

Since insurance coverage in a divorced setting can be complicated, it is appropriate to ask for that section of the court documents to be accurate in your billing. In cases where there is a nasty divorce, one parent might try to use the child's medical expenses to extort money from the other parent, thinking they will not know any better. If a non-custodial parent approaches you to find out what his or her portion of the out of pocket expenses would be, consult their legal documents before making payment arrangements. If they indeed are liable for a portion of the bill, collect only that portion from them and no more. Make sure they are still a legal parent, entitled to financial information as documented in the court filings. Remember further that medical information is confidential and cannot be shared with any party not entitled to it. If there is any kind of restraining order, or court order keeping an estranged parent from a child who is a patient of yours, or if that parent has lost custody for any reason, you cannot share information. If they are still a legal and partial custodial parent, then they have a right to that information. If you have any questions at all regarding this, I would advise you to consult your attorney

THIRD-PARTY LIABILITY

In the case of an injured patient at the responsibility of another party (i.e. an accident or injury that was another's fault, let's say a fall down the stairs at a friend's house), the claim falls under the heading of Third Party Liability. These cases are generally paid as a lump sum settlement for all services provided. Usually, the carrier will wait until all bills are received before any settlement is offered so that the true extent of the damage can be accurately assessed. If you take a TPL case, you run the risk of not getting paid at all, or having it carried out for a very long time. If a case is disputed, as in a workers' compensation case, a court case will ensue, tying up compensation for some time.

If a patient is covered by both TPL insurance and private insurance, it is perfectly acceptable to bill the private insurance until the TPL insurance pays, then reimburse the private insurance company after payment is received. This is knows as a "conditional payment." If the TPL insurance payment is less than the contracted rate for that carrier, then you may keep up to the contract rate, but not over, if the insurance companies coordinate benefits.

ELIGIBILITY

It is the responsibility of each physician's office to verify the patient's eligibility at the time of service. This can be done by either checking the Internet or your current patient roster from the insurance company for current and up-to-date information regarding this specific patient (if available to you), or by making a phone call to the insurance company. Eligibility generally runs from month to month and will continue as long as the patient continues uninterrupted employment within the same company. Since employee group health benefits are paid in advance, it is possible you would not be notified right away that a patient is no longer covered by their previous carrier. Eligibility should be re-verified whenever a job situation changes or during any open enrollment period when an employee has the option of changing their insurance choices. If an employee chooses to leave their current employment situation, thereby terminating their insurance, and these charges are subsequently denied as "coverage terminated," you are then able to bill the patient directly for these charges. Re-verify any new insurance coverage for effective date prior to re-billing these charges to a new carrier, as many employers have a waiting period for benefits for new employees.

Many major insurance carriers will allow you to check eligibility via the Internet. This will be a secure web site that you must register for using your client's provider number, tax ID number, and any other identifying information the insurance company deems necessary to keep the site secure and identify who is accessing their information. This is a safe and effective tool in determining eligibility and primacy for your patients. You must, however, do your part in keeping the site secure by never sharing your password or provider ID number. If you become aware of any abuse of the system, you must report it immediately to protect your patients' confidentiality.

SECONDARY CLAIMS

It is common for people to be covered by more than one insurance company. For example, you can have your Employer Group Health Plan (EGHP) that insures you while you are working. When you retire and become eligible for Medicare, your EGHP then becomes your secondary policy. After Medicare makes their payment, the balance can then be billed to the secondary insurance company. These are also known as cross-over or supplemental claims. Many of these claims are now being done electronically. Medicare will automatically and electronically file these claims with the payment information already being reported.

If they are not done electronically, it will be your responsibility to file these claims manually. Another claim form for the specific service will need to be generated. You will need to attach to that claim the Explanation of Benefits (EOB) from the primary carrier, showing how much they paid, what the contracted write-off amount is, and how much is the patient liability. Secondary carriers will only be responsible for the patient liability portion. They are not responsible (if they are contracted carriers) for the write-off portion of the bill.

AUDITS

Audits are commonplace these days in order to ensure that the claims are being paid at the correct rate. Just as you will follow up on your unpaid claims, the insurance company will review the overpaid claims and request reimbursement. If a claim is found to be overpaid, a refund will be requested from your office, and you will be given a period of time to comply. If you disagree with their findings, an appeal will need to be written explaining what the problem is and why you disagree with it. If they deny your appeal and you do not refund the overpayment, they will deduct the overpayment from future claim checks, also known as a claim recoupment. Occasionally companies will ask for the entire payment back stating that the claim should never have been paid in the first place. They can cite eligibility termination, the claim being received beyond the billing limitation, or any number of other reasons for requesting the money back. If they are correct and the claim should not have been paid, then interest and penalties can be applied if you do not refund their money in a timely fashion. Make sure to keep up on this correspondence and follow through as soon as possible to avoid problems and expense later on. The auditors must provide complete documentation and justification for their request, and allow you a reasonable amount of time to respond.

APPEALS

Let's say that you have followed all the examples and rules listed above and your reimbursement fell short of what your contract states it should. You will then need to file a written appeal for additional payment. An appeal is a business letter written from your office to the insurance company explaining the situation to the best of your understanding. All documentation to date needs to be attached (original claim form, copy of contract clause showing the underpayment, copy of incorrect EOB, prior authorization, any previous letters written about this claim, etc.). The letter should contain the following:

- The first paragraph tells who you are and why you are writing the appeal. It must state the phrase "This is a first level appeal for additional payment for the account of (patient's name)." All identifying patient information should be included here (i.e. identification number, date of service, where the patient was seen, what they were seen for, etc.).
- The second paragraph should contain a detailed explanation of the problem including reference to all documentation showing where the error has occurred.
- And the third paragraph should state what you want the insurance company to do about the problem. List a specific solution to the problem at hand. If they owe you more money, include your figures showing how you arrived at that dollar amount. Also, remember to include a phone number and e-mail address so they can get back to you if they need to. Make sure and keep additional copies in your files for your own reference. Give them an adequate amount of time to respond to your request before calling to inquire about the status of additional payment. Usually sixty to ninety days is adequate, although some companies do take longer.

Here is an example of an appeal letter:

A. Doctor, M.D.
12340 Medical Lane
Small Town, CA 94847
(917) 777-0001

December 8, 2008

Health Carriers Insurance
P.O. Box 111111111
Large Town, CA 94949

RE: Mary Smith
ID: 111000099999
DOS: 11/14/2005
Charges: $1500.00
Account #: 001-03

Dear Gentlemen/Ladies:

This letter is a first level appeal for the account of Ms. Mary Smith, ID number referenced above. This claim has been paid incorrectly, resulting in an underpayment of $50.00.

Per our contract, the service that Ms. Smith was provided should be paid at $750.00. The payment that was received was only for $700.00. The write-off portion was $750.00, leaving a balance of $50.00. Since this amount was not applied to the patient liability, that leaves an underpayment on your part for the remaining $50.00.

Please remit this underpayment as soon as possible. All documentation (original claim, EOB, contract, correspondence, patient's insurance card showing eligibility) is attached. I can be reached at the address and number listed on the letterhead for any question. You can also reach me at betty. biller@drsoffice.com . If there are circumstances of which I am not aware for the processing of this claim, please contact me immediately so we can clear up this matter. Thank you, in advance, for you time and help in this matter.

Sincerely,
Betty Jo Biller
Collections Representative
Offices of A. Doctor. M.D.

There are generally three levels of appeals. The first, detailed above, will be processed through the claims center. There are very specific time limits on when to file appeals, so make sure to follow these rules closely or your appeal will be denied for untimely filing reasons.

The second level appeal will be the same process, except that you will include the denial and all documentation from your first appeal with your filing. The second level appeal will generally go to the medical review level within the insurance company. This is a more intensive review with more highly trained professional personnel than the appeal within the local claims process. If your second level appeal is denied, you have only one option left.

The third level appeal, or provider grievance process, is your last resort. If your claim has been denied twice previously, again write an appeal letter with all appropriate documentation, including the contract clause showing why the claim was denied in error or underpaid in error. If the claim is denied at this level, you have exhausted all efforts within the insurance system and the claim should be written off.

There are some cases where providers have taken things a step further and actually filed suit in court for compensation at this level, and several of these cases have actually been won, but at a cost. When the provider's contract came due, the option to renew was not picked up by the insurance company, and in the long run the physician ended up losing more money in the loss of business. This is an option that should be carefully weighed before pursuing, as there could be a much higher cost involved than just collection of the bill.

ELECTRONIC BILLING

When you consider electronic billing, there are several different types of technical hook-ups that are available. Each is a different setup with limited availability in various areas. The first, and most widely available, is called Direct Data Entry (DDE). This is when your computer connects directly with another insurance company computer and your information is entered straight into their system with no middle-man. Electronic Data Interchange (EDI) is the next type. This is more of a networking system, where your system is online with the interchange company all the time, and they are responsible for seeing your information transferred on appropriately. EFT stands for Electronic Funds Transfer and is an online bookkeeping system, like your banking system, where funds are transferred back and forth between accounts, but no checks are actually written. You will receive a notice from the insurance company as to what is being deposited, and an Explanation of Benefits (EOB) will be sent to you detailing out how the claim was paid and why. It will also detail out any write-off portion and patient liability. The last type of electronic information transfer is through what is known as a clearinghouse. A clearinghouse is a private company that will contract with insurance companies to process and transfer information to their systems. They keep up on technological issues and keep connections with multiple insurance companies, so you need only connect to them. They will take the claims from multiple providers, split and re-batch them with other providers, and transfer claims directly to the insurance companies for you. There is a charge for this service, generally being a per claim charge.

ASSIGNMENT OF BENEFITS: ASSIGNED CLAIMS VS. NON-ASSIGNMENT OF CLAIMS

Assignment of a claim refers to the provider accepting the contracted rate, or usual and customary rate that the insurance will pay, in return for having the claim payment sent directly to their office. If a claim is not assigned, and in the case of a non-contracting payer, the payment for that claim would then go directly to the patient and the provider would be responsible for collecting the payment from them. While the payment would be less than total charges, it is generally more advantageous to have the payment sent directly to your office and write off a small portion of the bill rather than trying to collect from a patient that may not understand that the money does not belong to them. Remember these are seriously ill and sometimes elderly patients. Sick and old are not a good combination when trying to explain sometimes complicated financial matters. Also, there are cases where well-meaning family members have taken charge of their family member's finances and they have no idea that those payments do not belong to the patient. Assigned claims will avoid these and many other pitfalls and guarantee payment, albeit somewhat less than your total charge.

EOB
(EXPLANATION OF BENEFITS EXAMPLE)

Blue Shield
P.O. Box 885758
Los Alameidos, CA 90050-6000

Patient Name	ID #	DOS	Total Charge	Amount Allowed	Patient Liability	Amount paid
James Smith	948474849	1/1/01	$209.00	$165.00	$10.00	$155.00
Claim Totals			$209.00	$165.00	$10.00	$155.00

When examining the figures on an explanation of benefits, we must review all of the figures individually to determine what they mean together. There are two calculations involved to be able to completely understand what all of the figures together mean.

The total charges represent the total amount charged for that specific day's services.

The amount allowed represents the contract rate for that service. This amount can be reconciled to the contract that you signed with the insurance company. It can be either a flat rate for that service, a percentage, or other calculation (DRG). Review your individual contract to ensure that this payment rate is correct.

The difference between the total charges and the contract amount is your contractual write-off amount. This will be your first calculation. This amount cannot be billed to the patient and must be written off. If there is no contract between you and the insurance company, then this amount can be passed on to the patient, but only under that circumstance.

The patient liability amount is what you can bill the patient for. This is the second calculation. If this is not specifically spelled out on the EOB, it can be calculated by subtracting the difference between the contract amount and the paid amount. This amount is the only portion that can be billed to the patient for a contracting payer. If this is a non-contracting payer, this amount can be added with the difference between the total charges and the amount allowed and the patient billed for the full difference.

The amount paid is the actual amount that the insurance company cuts you a check for.

Let's try some questions.

BILLING EXERCISES

BILLING EXERCISE 1

Assuming all insurance companies mentioned are contracted payers, making these all assigned claims, answer the following questions:

1. A patient has Medicare as their primary insurance and Blue Shield as their second.
    Billed: $150.00
    Allowed: $75.00
    Medicare paid: $53.00
    Pt Liability: $22.00
    How much would you bill Blue Shield for?
    What is your write-off amount?

2. A patient has Blue Cross insurance
    Billed: $300.00
    Allowed: $250.00
    Blue Cross paid: $250.00
    What is your write-off amount?
    How much would you bill the patient for?

3. A Healthnet managed-care capitated patient was seen in your office for a routine office visit. This patient has a $10.00 co-pay.
    Total charges: $538.00
    How much would you bill the insurance company for?
    How much would you bill the patient for?
    How much is your write-off amount?

4. You have a Medi-Medi patient. (What does Medi-Medi stand for?)
    Billed amount: $378.00
    Allowed amount: $278.00
    Medicare paid: $210.00
    Patient liability: $68.00
    What is your write-off amount?
    How much would you bill the patient for?
    Who would you bill as second?

5. You have a UFCW patient.
    Billed amount: $62.00
    Allowed: $50.00
    Write-off amount: $12.00
    UFCW paid: $50.00
    How much would you bill the patient for?

6. You have a Medicare patient.
    Billed amount: $458.00
    Allowed amount: $458.00
    Medicare paid: $432.00
    How much would you bill the patient for?
    What is your write-off amount?
    Who would you bill as secondary?

7. You have a Blue Cross patient.
    Billed amount: $325.00
    Allowed amount: $275.00
    Blue Cross paid: $260.00
    What is your write-off amount?
    What is your patient liability?

8. For a non-contracted insurance company without accepting assignment.
    Billed amount: $5,000.00
    Insurance paid: $3,500.00
    Patient deductible: $500.00
    How much is your write-off portion?
    How much can you bill the patient for?

(See answers in Section V)

Here's another exercise in billing.

BILLING EXERCISE 2

Assuming that these are all contracting payers accepting assignment on these claims, answer the following questions.

1. You have a Blue Cross patient.
   Billed charges: $887.00
   Allowed: $230.00
   B/C paid: $185.00
   What is your write-off amount?
   How much would you bill the patient for?

2. You have a patient with Medicare prime and Blue Cross second.
   Billed charges: $545.00
   Allowed: $540.00
   Medicare paid: $350.00
   How much would you bill the patient for?
   What is your write-off amount?
   Who is responsible for $190.00?

3. You have a managed-care Mercy capitated patient with a $10.00 co-pay.
   Billed charges: $625.00
   What would you bill the insurance company for?
   How much would you bill the patient for?
   What is your write-off amount?

4. You have a Healthnet patient.
   Billed charges: $3,686.00
   Allowed: $25.00
   Healthnet paid: $0.00
   What is your write-off amount?
   How much will you bill the patient for?
   What action would you take on this claim?

5. You have a Pacificare managed care patient who opted for an out of network physician.
   Total charges: $5,000.00
   Pacificare allowed: $0.00
   Pacificare paid: $0.00
   How much would you write off and why?
   How much would you bill the patient for?

6. You have a Western Health Advantage patient.
   Billed charges: $368.00
   Allowed: $350.00
   WHA paid: $325.00
   What is your write-off amount?
   How much would you bill the patient for?

7. You have a Medi-Caid patient.
   Total charges: $5,268.00
   Allowed: $150.00

Medi-Caid paid: $150.00
What is your write-off amount?
How much would you bill the patient for?

8. You have a Blue Shield patient.
    Total charges: $350.00
    Non-covered: $25.00
    Allowed: $300.00
    B/S paid: $225.00
    What is your write-off amount?
    What would you bill the patient for?

9. You have a UFCW patient.
    Total charges: $1,500.00
    Allowed: $1,500.00
    UFCW paid: $1,000.00
    Patient deductible: $500.00
    What is your write-off amount?
    How much would you bill the patient for?

10. You have a UFCW patient.
    Total charges: $3,000.00
    Allowed: $2,500.00
    UFCW paid: $1,000.00
    Patient deductible: $500.00
    What is your write-off amount?
    How much would you bill the patient for?

11. You have a patient in an automobile accident. He has no health insurance; you are not contracted
    with his automobile insurance.
    Total charges: $150.00
    Auto Insurance allowed: $75.00
    Auto Insurance paid: $75.00
    What is your write-off amount?
    How much would you bill the patient for?

12. You have a patient in an automobile accident and are not contracted with the auto insurance
    company. This patient is also covered by Healthnet.
    Total billed: $575.00
    Allowed: $500.00
    Insurance paid: $450.00
    Who is prime?
    Who is second?
    What is your write-off amount?
    How much would you bill the patient for?
    Who would you bill as second?

(See answers in Section V)

For additional exercises, please see the Medical Billing, Coding, and Reimbursement Supplemental
Workbook.

HCFA-1500

The HCFA-1500 form is the universally accepted form for billing professional fees (the doctor's portion for services provided). Appearing as red ink on a white background, it allows for the receiving company to scan the document and pick up the items that you have filled in without picking up the background boxes into their system. Scanners can be programmed not to pick up the color red. You will notice on some of the attached sample forms, the type has been intentionally misaligned in the boxes. This is an example to illustrate that the type in the boxes need not be perfectly aligned since the background (red) information won't be picked up by the receiving company, only your typed information. Exact alignment is not necessary. Try to get the type as close as you can when filling out these forms, but don't waste time and forms if it is not perfect. The scanner will do the work for you. If you have to make an addition or correction to a form, it should always be done in either blue or black ink, never red. Even if you use electronic billing, all of the same information will have to be entered into your system for electronic transfer to either the clearinghouse or the insurance company. If any of the information is not applicable, leave the space blank. Do not enter things such as N/A or Does Not Apply. Complete instructions appear on the back of the form itself. The following boxes and descriptions appear on the form's front side.

Box 1	Type of health insurance; check the appropriate box: Medicare, Medicaid, Champus, ChampVA, Group Health, Black Lung, Other.
Box 1a	Enter the patient's Health Insurance Claim number (ID #).
Box 2	Enter the patient's full name as it appears on their ID card. (Beware of nicknames. The names should match exactly.)
Box 3	Enter the patient's full date of birth MM/DD/CCYY and sex (check the box for male or female).
Box 4	Enter the insured's full name as it appears on the ID card. This may be different than the patient. (Beware of nicknames. The names should match exactly.)
Box 5	Enter the patient's address.
Box 6	Check the box for the patient's relationship to the insured.
Box 7	Enter the insured's address.
Box 8	Enter the marital status and employment status for the patient by checking the appropriate boxes here.
Box 9	Enter the name of any secondary insurance policy the patient may be covered under.
Box 9a	Enter the other insurance policy (if applicable).
Box 9b	Enter the other insured's date of birth and sex (if applicable).

Box 9c	Enter the employer's name for the secondary insurance policy.
Box 9d	Enter the insurance plan name for the secondary policy.
Box 10 a–c	Check the boxes that apply regarding the patient's employment, auto accident, or other accident.
Box 11	Enter the insured's policy or group number for the primary insurance.
Box 11a	Enter the insured's date of birth and sex for the primary policy.
Box 11b	Enter the employer's name for the primary policy.
Box 11c	Enter the insurance company or plan name for the primary policy.
Box 11d	Is there another benefit plan (referring to secondary insurance)? If yes, then answer boxes 9-9d. If not, then skip.
Box 12	Patient or Guardian signature. You can enter "Signature on File" if you have the patient's original signature on file at your office. Enter the date.
Box 13	Insured's signature.
Box 14	Enter the first date of the current illness or injury. For instance, if this is ongoing treatment due to a car accident, enter the date of the accident here. If it due to an illness, enter the date of the onset of the illness.
Box 15	If the patient has had the same or similar illness, enter date. For instance, if the patient has cancer and has been in remission, enter the date the cancer was first diagnosed here.
Box 16	Enter the dates the patient is unable to work, i.e. disabled from work due to illness or injury.
Box 17	Name of referring physician or other source.
Box 17a	ID number of referring physician. (Call the office of that physician for this information.)
Box 17b	Referring Provider NPI.
Box 18	Hospitalization dates (if applicable).
Box 19	Reserved for local use—leave blank unless instructed by an insurance company to use this field for specific information.
Box 20	Outside Lab? Mark yes only of you sent a specimen to a lab you are not associated with for processing. Also enter the charges for this service.
Box 21	Enter the diagnosis for the patient. This will be the ICD-9 code, not the description. You can enter up to four diagnoses.
Box 22	Medicaid resubmission code—reserve this space specifically for Medicaid patient resubmissions.
Box 23	Enter the prior authorization number, if necessary, that you received before you saw the patient, if required by the insurance company.
Box 24a	Enter the date of service.
Box 24b	Enter the place of service (see Appendices Section for approved list).
Box 24c	Enter the type of service.
Box 24d	Enter the CPT procedure codes for the services provided.

Billing

85

Box 24e	Enter the diagnosis code, referencing the ICD-9 code in Box 21. For instance, if this procedure refers to the diagnosis code in the #2 spot, enter a 2 here.
Box 24f	Enter the charges.
Box 24g	Enter the days or units.
Box 24h	Enter if this is related to family planning (birth control).
Box 24i	ID Qual.
Box 24j	Rendering physician ID and NPI.
Box 24k	Reserved for local use—leave blank unless instructed to use this field by an insurance carrier.
Box 25	Enter your Federal Tax ID# and indicate whether it is a Social Security number of a Federal Tax ID #.
Box 26	Enter your Patient Account Number.
Box 27	Accept Assignment for this claim? Check Yes or No.
Box 28	Enter the total charges for this claim.
Box 29	Enter the amount paid by the primary carrier, if this is a claim to the secondary payer.
Box 30	Enter the balance due if this is a claim to the secondary payer.
Box 31	Enter the physician's signature here. A rubber stamp is acceptable but "Signature on File" is generally not.
Box 32	Enter the name and address of the facility where the services are rendered. If this is an office visit, enter your office address.
Box 32a	Enter Provider's License #.
Box 32b	Enter Provider's NPI.
Box 33	Enter the physician's billing name (if a corporation, enter the corp. name), address, phone number, provider ID#, and NPI #.

Copies of the Billing Form HCFA-1500 may be ordered from:

Superintendent of Documents   or   American Medical Assoc.
U.S. Government Printing Office   P.O. Box 109050
Washington, D.C. 20402   Chicago, Illinois 60610
(202) 783-3238   Attn: Order Department
(800) 621-8335

One of the things you will need to clarify with the doctor's office up front is how to sign the claims. Will they be returned to the office for the doctor to sign or will you sign them? You can sign your own name, with a letter of permission from the doctor stating that you are his representative and are able to do this. You can also sign the doctor's name, but again, only with expressed written and legal permission (Power of Attorney). A signature stamp is similarly acceptable; however, it must be kept under lock and key, as it is a valid signature and can be used for checks, credit card purchases, etc. The easiest and least intrusive thing for all parties to do is to have you sign your own name with a letter of permission from the physician. Individual insurers may have their own form for you to use for this as well. Make sure to check with each insurance company directly for their own requirements.

Based on the following scenarios, let's fill out some HCFA-1500 forms. Each patient will have a patient information sheet with all of the patient's information and a superbill from the doctor, showing all of the doctor's charge and diagnostic information.

The patient information sheet typically will contain the following information.

Patient Information Sheet

Today's date; name of patient; patient account number; patient social security number; patient's address; patient's phone number (home and work); patient's occupation; primary insurance company name and address; primary insurance company phone number; employer; subscriber/relationship; subscriber ID#; subscriber DOB; secondary insurance company name and address; Secondary insurance company phone number; employer; subscriber/relationship; subscriber ID#; and subscriber DOB.

For the purposes of exercises in this manual, here is a sample of the patient information sheet we will be using.

New Patient Information Sheet

Account #:
Patient Name:
Patient Address:
Patient Phone Number:
Date of Birth:
Social Security Number:

Primary Insurance

Subscriber Name:
Subscriber ID#:
Subscriber Date of Birth:
Group Number/Relationship:
Insurance Company Name:
Insurance Company Address:
Insurance Phone Number:
Employer Name:
Employer Address and Phone Number:

Secondary Insurance

Subscriber Name:
Subscriber ID#:
Subscriber Date of Birth:
Group Number/Relationship:
Insurance Company Name:
Insurance Company Address:

Insurance Company Phone Number:
Employer:
Employer Address and Phone Number:

Auto Insurance

Auto Insurance Carrier Name and Address:
Subscriber:
Subscriber's Address:
Phone Number:
Policy ID#:
Date of Injury:

SUPERBILL (CHARGE SHEET)

A superbill, or charge sheet, will typically contain the following information: Patient's name; patient's account number; patient social security number; date patient is seen (Date of Service); patient's diagnosis (list up to four); service codes/charge; name of referring physician; ID# of referring physician; Hospitalization dates; outside lab; family planning; EMG; COB; prior auth #; disability dates; date of first injury, illness, or onset; place of service; type of service; name and address of treating physician; name and address where services were rendered; physician TIN#; and license #/provider #.

For the purposes of exercises in this manual, here is a sample of the superbill we will be using.

John Smith, M.D.
123340 Doctor Lane,
Modesto, CA 94577
(530) 530-5330
CA State License Number: D9580698
NPI Number: 123456789

Superbill Sample

Patient Name:
Account Number:
Date of Service:

Procedure Performed (Description) and CPT Code:

1.

2.

3.

4.

5.

Procedure CPT Code/Charges:

1.

2.

3.

4.

5.

Diagnosis (Description):

1.

2.

3.

4.

5.

Diagnosis (ICD-9 code):

1.

2.

3.

4.

5.

Authorization:
Auto Accident:
Work Related:
DOI/Onset Date:
Family Planning:
Coordination of Benefits:
Emergency Services:

Let's try a sample form. Using the sample Patient Information Sheet, fill out the top portion (patient information section) of the HCFA-1500 form. See page 93 for an example of how the completed section should look.)

NEW PATIENT INFORMATION SHEET

Date: November 20, 2008
Account #: 067-14
Patient Name: Kelly Johns
Patient Address: 40596 Smith Lane, Oroville, CA 09098
Patient Phone Number: (919) 938-4049
Date of Birth: 01/01/1910
Social Security Number: 00A-01-7D75

Primary Insurance

Subscriber Name: Kelly Johns
Subscriber ID#: 0019-94949849
Subscriber Date of Birth: 01/01/1910
Group Number/Relationship: self
Insurance Company Name: Pacific Insurers
Insurance Company Address: 10 Pacific Coast Hwy, Malibu, CA 95989
Phone Number: (888) 900-4847
Employer: Beauty Boutique

Secondary Insurance

Subscriber Name:
Subscriber ID#:
Subscriber Date of Birth:
Group Number/Relationship:
Insurance Company Name:
Insurance Company Address:
Phone Number:
Employer:

Auto Insurance

Auto Insurance Carrier Name and Address:
Subscriber:
Subscriber's Address:
Phone Number:
Policy ID#:
Date of Injury:

1500

HEALTH INSURANCE CLAIM FORM

APPROVED BY NATIONAL UNIFORM CLAIM COMMITTEE 08/05

CARRIER

☐ PICA   PICA ☐

1. MEDICARE	MEDICAID	TRICARE CHAMPUS	CHAMPVA	GROUP HEALTH PLAN	FECA BLK LUNG	OTHER	1a. INSURED'S I.D. NUMBER	(For Program in Item 1)
☐ (Medicare #)	☐ (Medicaid #)	☐ (Sponsor's SSN)	☐ (Member ID#)	☐ (SSN or ID)	☐ (SSN)	☐ (ID)		

2. PATIENT'S NAME (Last Name, First Name, Middle Initial)

3. PATIENT'S BIRTH DATE   MM | DD | YY   SEX   M ☐   F ☐

4. INSURED'S NAME (Last Name, First Name, Middle Initial)

5. PATIENT'S ADDRESS (No., Street)

6. PATIENT RELATIONSHIP TO INSURED   Self ☐   Spouse ☐   Child ☐   Other ☐

7. INSURED'S ADDRESS (No., Street)

CITY   STATE

8. PATIENT STATUS   Single ☐   Married ☐   Other ☐

CITY   STATE

ZIP CODE   TELEPHONE (Include Area Code) ( )

Employed ☐   Full-Time Student ☐   Part-Time Student ☐

ZIP CODE   TELEPHONE (Include Area Code) ( )

9. OTHER INSURED'S NAME (Last Name, First Name, Middle Initial)

10. IS PATIENT'S CONDITION RELATED TO:

11. INSURED'S POLICY GROUP OR FECA NUMBER

a. OTHER INSURED'S POLICY OR GROUP NUMBER

a. EMPLOYMENT? (Current or Previous)   ☐ YES   ☐ NO

a. INSURED'S DATE OF BIRTH   MM | DD | YY   SEX   M ☐   F ☐

b. OTHER INSURED'S DATE OF BIRTH   MM | DD | YY   SEX   M ☐   F ☐

b. AUTO ACCIDENT?   PLACE (State)   ☐ YES   ☐ NO ___

b. EMPLOYER'S NAME OR SCHOOL NAME

c. EMPLOYER'S NAME OR SCHOOL NAME

c. OTHER ACCIDENT?   ☐ YES   ☐ NO

c. INSURANCE PLAN NAME OR PROGRAM NAME

d. INSURANCE PLAN NAME OR PROGRAM NAME

10d. RESERVED FOR LOCAL USE

d. IS THERE ANOTHER HEALTH BENEFIT PLAN?   ☐ YES   ☐ NO   *If yes*, return to and complete item 9 a-d.

READ BACK OF FORM BEFORE COMPLETING & SIGNING THIS FORM.

12. PATIENT'S OR AUTHORIZED PERSON'S SIGNATURE I authorize the release of any medical or other information necessary to process this claim. I also request payment of government benefits either to myself or to the party who accepts assignment below.

SIGNED _____   DATE _____

13. INSURED'S OR AUTHORIZED PERSON'S SIGNATURE I authorize payment of medical benefits to the undersigned physician or supplier for services described below.

SIGNED _____

PATIENT AND INSURED INFORMATION

14. DATE OF CURRENT: MM | DD | YY   ◄ ILLNESS (First symptom) OR INJURY (Accident) OR PREGNANCY(LMP)

15. IF PATIENT HAS HAD SAME OR SIMILAR ILLNESS. GIVE FIRST DATE   MM | DD | YY

16. DATES PATIENT UNABLE TO WORK IN CURRENT OCCUPATION   MM | DD | YY   FROM   TO   MM | DD | YY

17. NAME OF REFERRING PROVIDER OR OTHER SOURCE

17a.
17b. NPI

18. HOSPITALIZATION DATES RELATED TO CURRENT SERVICES   MM | DD | YY   FROM   TO   MM | DD | YY

19. RESERVED FOR LOCAL USE

20. OUTSIDE LAB?   ☐ YES   ☐ NO $ CHARGES

21. DIAGNOSIS OR NATURE OF ILLNESS OR INJURY (Relate Items 1, 2, 3 or 4 to Item 24E by Line)

1. |___.___| 3. |___.___|

2. |___.___| 4. |___.___|

22. MEDICAID RESUBMISSION CODE   ORIGINAL REF. NO.

23. PRIOR AUTHORIZATION NUMBER

24. A. DATE(S) OF SERVICE						B. PLACE OF SERVICE	C. EMG	D. PROCEDURES, SERVICES, OR SUPPLIES (Explain Unusual Circumstances)		E. DIAGNOSIS POINTER	F. $ CHARGES	G. DAYS OR UNITS	H. EPSDT Family Plan	I. ID QUAL.	J. RENDERING PROVIDER ID. #
From MM	DD	YY	To MM	DD	YY			CPT/HCPCS	MODIFIER						
1														NPI	
2														NPI	
3														NPI	
4														NPI	
5														NPI	
6														NPI	

25. FEDERAL TAX I.D. NUMBER   ☐ SSN ☐ EIN

26. PATIENT'S ACCOUNT NO.

27. ACCEPT ASSIGNMENT? (For govt. claims, see back)   ☐ YES   ☐ NO

28. TOTAL CHARGE $

29. AMOUNT PAID $

30. BALANCE DUE $

31. SIGNATURE OF PHYSICIAN OR SUPPLIER INCLUDING DEGREES OR CREDENTIALS (I certify that the statements on the reverse apply to this bill and are made a part thereof.)

SIGNED _____   DATE _____

32. SERVICE FACILITY LOCATION INFORMATION

a.   b.

33. BILLING PROVIDER INFO & PH # ( )

a.   b.

PHYSICIAN OR SUPPLIER INFORMATION

1500

HEALTH INSURANCE CLAIM FORM
APPROVED BY NATIONAL UNIFORM CLAIM COMMITTEE 08/05

| | PICA | | | | | | PICA | | |

CARRIER

1. MEDICARE (Medicare #) | MEDICAID (Medicaid #) | TRICARE CHAMPUS (Sponsor's SSN) | CHAMPVA (Medicaid #) | GROUP HEALTH PLAN (SSN or ID) | FECA BLK LUNG (SSN) | OTHER ☒ (ID) | **1a. INSURED'S I.D. NUMBER** (FOR PROGRAM IN ITEM 1)
0019-94949849

2. PATIENT'S NAME (Last Name, First Name, Middle Initial)
Johns   Kelly

3. PATIENT'S BIRTH DATE MM DD YY **01/01/1910** M SEX F ☒

4. INSURED'S NAME (Last Name, First Name, Middle Initial)
Johns   Kelly

5. PATIENT'S ADDRESS (No., Street)
40596 Smith Lane

6. PATIENT RELATIONSHIP TO INSURED
Self ☒ Spouse ☐ Child ☐ Other ☐

7. INSURED'S ADDRESS (No., Street)
40596 Smith Lane

CITY **Oroville** STATE **CA**

8. PATIENT STATUS
Single ☒ Married ☐ Other ☐
Employed ☒ Full-Time Student ☐ Part-Time Student ☐

CITY **Oroville** STATE **CA**

ZIP CODE **09098** TELEPHONE (Include Area Code) **919-938-4049**

ZIP CODE **09098** TELEPHONE (Include Area Code) **919-938-4049**

9. OTHER INSURED'S NAME (Last Name, First Name, Middle Initial)

10. IS PATIENT'S CONDITION RELATED TO:

11. INSURED'S POLICY GROUP OR FECA NUMBER
001

a. OTHER INSURED'S POLICY OR GROUP NUMBER

a. EMPLOYMENT? (CURRENT OR PREVIOUS) YES ☐ NO ☒

a. INSURED'S DATE OF BIRTH MM DD YY **01/01/1910** M ☐ SEX F ☒

b. OTHER INSURED'S DATE OF BIRTH MM DD YY M ☐ F ☐

b. AUTO ACCIDENT? YES ☐ NO ☒ PLACE (State)

b. EMPLOYER'S NAME OR SCHOOL NAME
Beauty Boutique

c. EMPLOYER'S NAME OR SCHOOL NAME

c. OTHER ACCIDENT? YES ☐ NO ☒

c. INSURANCE PLAN NAME OR PROGRAM NAME
Pacific Insurers

d. INSURANCE PLAN NAME OR PROGRAM NAME

10d. RESERVED FOR LOCAL USE

d. IS THERE ANOTHER HEALTH BENEFIT PLAN?
YES ☐ NO ☒ If yes, return to and complete item 9 a-d.

READ BACK OF FORM BEFORE COMPLETING & SIGNING THIS FORM.
12. PATIENT'S OR AUTHORIZED PERSON'S SIGNATURE I authorize the release of any medical or other information necessary to process this claim. I also request payment of government benefits either to myself or to the party who accepts assignment below.

SIGNED _____ DATE _____

13. INSURED'S OR AUTHORIZED PERSON'S SIGNATURE I authorize payment of medical benefits to the undersigned physician or supplier for services described below.

SIGNED _____

PATIENT AND INSURED INFORMATION

14. DATE OF CURRENT: MM DD YY ILLNESS (First symptom) OR INJURY (Accident) OR PREGNANCY(LMP)

15. IF PATIENT HAS HAD SAME OR SIMILAR ILLNESS GIVE FIRST DATE MM DD YY

16. DATES PATIENT UNABLE TO WORK IN CURRENT OCCUPATION MM DD YY FROM TO MM DD YY

17. NAME OF REFERRING PROVIDER OR OTHER SOURCE
17a.
17b. NPI

18. HOSPITALIZATION DATES RELATED TO CURRENT SERVICES MM DD YY FROM TO MM DD YY

19. RESERVED FOR LOCAL USE

20. OUTSIDE LAB? YES ☐ NO ☐ $ CHARGES

21. DIAGNOSIS OR NATURE OF ILLNESS OR INJURY. (RELATE ITEMS 1,2,3 OR 4 TO ITEM 24E BY LINE)
1. _____ 3. _____
2. _____ 4. _____

22. MEDICAID RESUBMISSION CODE ORIGINAL REF. NO.

23. PRIOR AUTHORIZATION NUMBER

24. A. DATE(S) OF SERVICE From MM DD YY	To MM DD YY	B. Place of Service	C. EMG	D. PROCEDURES, SERVICES, OR SUPPLIES (Explain Unusual Circumstances) CPT/HCPCS	MODIFIER	E. DIAGNOSIS POINTER	F. $ CHARGES	G. DAYS OR UNITS	H. EPSDT Family Plan	I. ID QUAL.	J. RENDERING PROVIDER ID. #
1										NPI	
2										NPI	
3										NPI	
4										NPI	
5										NPI	
6										NPI	

25. FEDERAL TAX I.D. NUMBER SSN ☐ EIN ☐

26. PATIENT'S ACCOUNT NO.

27. ACCEPT ASSIGNMENT? (For govt. claims, see back) YES ☐ NO ☐

28. TOTAL CHARGE $

29. AMOUNT PAID $

30. BALANCE DUE $

31. SIGNATURE OF PHYSICIAN OR SUPPLIER INCLUDING DEGREES OR CREDENTIALS (I certify that the statements on the reverse apply to this bill and are made a part thereof.)
SIGNED _____ DATE _____

32. SERVICE FACILITY LOCATION INFORMATION
a. b.

33. BILLING PROVIDER INFO & PH # ( )
a. b.

PHYSICIAN OR SUPPLIER INFORMATION

Now let's look at the superbill for this same patient and then add the charges and diagnosis information at the bottom. Remember to look up the place of service codes and type of service codes in the addendum chapter at the back of the book.

See page 124 for an example of what a completed form should look like.

John Smith, M.D.
123340 Doctor Lane
Modesto, CA 94577
(530) 530-5330
CA State License Number: D9580698
NPI Number: 123456789

Superbill Sample

Patient Name: Kelly Johns
Account Number: 067-14
Date of Service: November 20, 2008

Procedure Performed (Description) and CPT Code:

1. Office Visit New Patient Comprehensive

2.

3.

4.

5.

Procedure CPT Code/Charges:

1. 99204

2.

3.

4.

5.

Diagnosis (Description):

1. Kohler's Disease (osteochondrosis)

2.

3.

4.

5.

Diagnosis (ICD-9 code):

1. 7352.5

2.

3.

4.

5.

Authorization:
Auto Accident:
Work Related:
DOI/Onset Date:
Family Planning:
Coordination of Benefits:
Emergency Services:

1500

HEALTH INSURANCE CLAIM FORM

APPROVED BY NATIONAL UNIFORM CLAIM COMMITTEE 08/05

| | PICA | | | | | | PICA | |

1. MEDICARE (Medicare #) | **MEDICAID** (Medicaid #) | **TRICARE CHAMPUS** (Sponsor's SSN) | **CHAMPVA** (Medicaid #) | **GROUP HEALTH PLAN** (SSN or ID) | **FECA BLK LUNG** (SSN) | **OTHER** [X] (ID)

1a. INSURED'S I.D. NUMBER (FOR PROGRAM IN ITEM 1)
0019-94949849

2. PATIENT'S NAME (Last Name, First Name, Middle Initial)
Johns   Kelly

3. PATIENT'S BIRTH DATE MM DD YY
01/01/1910   M [ ]   **SEX** F [X]

4. INSURED'S NAME (Last Name, First Name, Middle Initial)
Johns   Kelly

5. PATIENT'S ADDRESS (No., Street)
40596 Smith Lane

6. PATIENT RELATIONSHIP TO INSURED
Self [X]   Spouse [ ]   Child [ ]   Other [ ]

7. INSURED'S ADDRESS (No., Street)
40596 Smith Lane

CITY Oroville   **STATE** CA

8. PATIENT STATUS
Single [X]   Married [ ]   Other [ ]

CITY Oroville   **STATE** CA

ZIP CODE 09098   **TELEPHONE** (Include Area Code) 919-938-4049

Employed [X]   Full-Time Student [ ]   Part-Time Student [ ]

ZIP CODE 09098   **TELEPHONE** (Include Area Code) 919-938-4049

9. OTHER INSURED'S NAME (Last Name, First Name, Middle Initial)

10. IS PATIENT'S CONDITION RELATED TO:

11. INSURED'S POLICY GROUP OR FECA NUMBER
001

a. OTHER INSURED'S POLICY OR GROUP NUMBER

a. EMPLOYMENT? (CURRENT OR PREVIOUS)
YES [ ]   NO [X]

a. INSURED'S DATE OF BIRTH MM DD YY
01/01/1910   M [ ]   **SEX** F [X]

b. OTHER INSURED'S DATE OF BIRTH MM DD YY   **SEX** M [ ] F [ ]

b. AUTO ACCIDENT?   PLACE (State)
YES [ ]   NO [X]

b. EMPLOYER'S NAME OR SCHOOL NAME
Beauty Boyutique

c. EMPLOYER'S NAME OR SCHOOL NAME

c. OTHER ACCIDENT?
YES [ ]   NO [X]

c. INSURANCE PLAN NAME OR PROGRAM NAME
Pacific Insurers

d. INSURANCE PLAN NAME OR PROGRAM NAME

10d. RESERVED FOR LOCAL USE

d. IS THERE ANOTHER HEALTH BENEFIT PLAN?
YES [ ]   NO [X]   **If yes,** return to and complete item 9 a-d.

READ BACK OF FORM BEFORE COMPLETING & SIGNING THIS FORM.

12. PATIENT'S OR AUTHORIZED PERSON'S SIGNATURE I authorize the release of any medical or other information necessary to process this claim. I also request payment of government benefits either to myself or to the party who accepts assignment below.

SIGNED _____   DATE _____

13. INSURED'S OR AUTHORIZED PERSON'S SIGNATURE I authorize payment of medical benefits to the undersigned physician or supplier for services described below.

SIGNED _____

14. DATE OF CURRENT: MM DD YY   ILLNESS (First symptom) OR INJURY (Accident) OR PREGNANCY(LMP)

15. IF PATIENT HAS HAD SAME OR SIMILAR ILLNESS. GIVE FIRST DATE MM DD YY

16. DATES PATIENT UNABLE TO WORK IN CURRENT OCCUPATION FROM MM DD YY   TO MM DD YY

17. NAME OF REFERRING PROVIDER OR OTHER SOURCE

17a.
17b. NPI

18. HOSPITALIZATION DATES RELATED TO CURRENT SERVICES FROM MM DD YY   TO MM DD YY

19. RESERVED FOR LOCAL USE

20. OUTSIDE LAB? $ CHARGES
YES [ ]   NO [ ]

21. DIAGNOSIS OR NATURE OF ILLNESS OR INJURY. (RELATE ITEMS 1,2,3 OR 4 TO ITEM 24E BY LINE)
1. 732.5
2.
3.
4.

22. MEDICAID RESUBMISSION CODE   ORIGINAL REF. NO.

23. PRIOR AUTHORIZATION NUMBER

24. A. DATE(S) OF SERVICE From MM DD YY	To MM DD YY	B. Place of Service	C. EMG	D. PROCEDURES, SERVICES, OR SUPPLIES (Explain Unusual Circumstances) CPT/HCPCS	MODIFIER	E. DIAGNOSIS POINTER	F. $ CHARGES	G. DAYS OR UNITS	H. EPSDT Family Plan	I. ID QUAL.	J. RENDERING PROVIDER ID. #
1 11/20/08	11/20/08	11	1	99204		1	105.00			NPI	123456789
2										NPI	
3										NPI	
4										NPI	
5										NPI	
6										NPI	

25. FEDERAL TAX I.D. NUMBER   SSN [ ] EIN [X]
94-0000000

26. PATIENT'S ACCOUNT NO.
067-14

27. ACCEPT ASSIGNMENT? (For govt. claims, see back)
YES [X]   NO [ ]

28. TOTAL CHARGE $ 105.00

29. AMOUNT PAID $ 0.00

30. BALANCE DUE $ 105.00

31. SIGNATURE OF PHYSICIAN OR SUPPLIER INCLUDING DEGREES OR CREDENTIALS (I certify that the statements on the reverse apply to this bill and are made a part thereof.)

SIGNED _____   DATE _____

32. SERVICE FACILITY LOCATION INFORMATION
John Smith MD
123340 Dr Ln, Modesto, CA 94577
a. D9580698   b. 123456789

33. BILLING PROVIDER INFO & PH # (530) 530-5330
John Smith MD
123340 Dr Ln, Modesto CA 94577
a. D9580698   b. 123456789

NUCC Instruction Manual available at: www.nucc.org

OMB No. 1215-0055
Expires: 10/31/2009

HCFA-1500 EXERCISES

Let's try some more examples. Attached are six more patients records with corresponding charges. Fill out the HCFA-1500 forms with the information provided on both the Patient Information Sheets and corresponding superbills. Make sure to watch for multiple superbills from multiple providers for some patients. Examples of the completed forms are at the end of the section for comparison purposes. Please review your entries against the completed form to see how well you did.

There are some extra blank forms in the appendix section at the end of the book should you need them.

NEW PATIENT INFORMATION SHEET

Date: October 19, 2008
Account #: 001-01
Patient Name: James Smith, Jr.
Patient Address: 12340 Sunny Lane, Sacramento, CA 95846
Patient Phone Number: 916-111-1111
Date of Birth: 01/01/2001
Social Security Number: 11X-11-1Y11

Primary Insurance

Subscriber Name: Mary Smith
Subscriber Date of Birth: 11/07/1968
Subscriber ID#: 666-55-4440-02
Group Number/Relationship: 46389
Insurance Company Name: Pacificare
Insurance Company Address: P.O. Box 8888, San Leandro, CA 18181
Phone Number: 800-800-8000
Employer: Safeway

Secondary Insurance

Subscriber Name: James Smith, Sr.
Subscriber ID#: 12893-1289
Subscriber Date of Birth: 12/24/1965
Group Number/Relationship: 43380/Father
Insurance Company Name: Blue Cross
Insurance Company Address: P.O. Box 65789, Rancho Cordova, CA 95777
Phone Number: 800-700-7000
Employer: Blue Cross

Auto Insurance

Auto Insurance Carrier Name and Address:
Subscriber:
Subscriber's Address:
Phone Number:
Policy ID#:
Date of Injury:

John Smith, M.D.
123340 Doctor Lane
Modesto, CA 94577
(530) 530-5330
CA State License Number: D9580698
NPI Number: 123456789

Superbill Sample

Patient Name: James Smith
Account Number: 001-01
Date of Service: 4/6/08

Procedure Performed (Description) and CPT Code:

1. Office Visit, established patient, minimal services

2.

3.

4.

5.

Procedure CPT Code/Charges:

1. 99211/$55.00

2.

3.

4.

5.

Diagnosis (Description):

1. Bronchitis

2.

3.

4.

5.

Diagnosis (ICD-9 Code):

1. 490

2.

3.

4.

5.

Authorization: no
Auto Accident: no
Work Related: no
DOI/Onset Date: n/a
Family Planning: no
Coordination of Benefits: no
Emergency Services: no

1500

HEALTH INSURANCE CLAIM FORM

APPROVED BY NATIONAL UNIFORM CLAIM COMMITTEE 08/05

CARRIER →

☐☐ PICA   PICA ☐☐☐

1. MEDICARE   MEDICAID   TRICARE CHAMPUS   CHAMPVA   GROUP HEALTH PLAN   FECA BLK LUNG   OTHER   1a. INSURED'S I.D. NUMBER   (For Program in Item 1)

☐ (Medicare #) ☐ (Medicaid #) ☐ (Sponsor's SSN) ☐ (Member ID#) ☐ (SSN or ID) ☐ (SSN) ☐ (ID)

2. PATIENT'S NAME (Last Name, First Name, Middle Initial)

3. PATIENT'S BIRTH DATE   MM   DD   YY   SEX   M ☐   F ☐

4. INSURED'S NAME (Last Name, First Name, Middle Initial)

5. PATIENT'S ADDRESS (No., Street)

6. PATIENT RELATIONSHIP TO INSURED   Self ☐   Spouse ☐   Child ☐   Other ☐

7. INSURED'S ADDRESS (No., Street)

CITY   STATE

8. PATIENT STATUS   Single ☐   Married ☐   Other ☐

CITY   STATE

ZIP CODE   TELEPHONE (Include Area Code)   ( )

Employed ☐   Full-Time Student ☐   Part-Time Student ☐

ZIP CODE   TELEPHONE (Include Area Code)   ( )

9. OTHER INSURED'S NAME (Last Name, First Name, Middle Initial)

10. IS PATIENT'S CONDITION RELATED TO:

11. INSURED'S POLICY GROUP OR FECA NUMBER

a. OTHER INSURED'S POLICY OR GROUP NUMBER

a. EMPLOYMENT? (Current or Previous)   ☐ YES   ☐ NO

a. INSURED'S DATE OF BIRTH   MM   DD   YY   SEX   M ☐   F ☐

b. OTHER INSURED'S DATE OF BIRTH   MM   DD   YY   SEX   M ☐   F ☐

b. AUTO ACCIDENT?   PLACE (State)   ☐ YES   ☐ NO

b. EMPLOYER'S NAME OR SCHOOL NAME

c. EMPLOYER'S NAME OR SCHOOL NAME

c. OTHER ACCIDENT?   ☐ YES   ☐ NO

c. INSURANCE PLAN NAME OR PROGRAM NAME

d. INSURANCE PLAN NAME OR PROGRAM NAME

10d. RESERVED FOR LOCAL USE

d. IS THERE ANOTHER HEALTH BENEFIT PLAN?   ☐ YES   ☐ NO   *If yes*, return to and complete item 9 a-d.

READ BACK OF FORM BEFORE COMPLETING & SIGNING THIS FORM.

12. PATIENT'S OR AUTHORIZED PERSON'S SIGNATURE I authorize the release of any medical or other information necessary to process this claim. I also request payment of government benefits either to myself or to the party who accepts assignment below.

SIGNED_____ DATE_____

13. INSURED'S OR AUTHORIZED PERSON'S SIGNATURE I authorize payment of medical benefits to the undersigned physician or supplier for services described below.

SIGNED_____

14. DATE OF CURRENT: MM   DD   YY   ◀ ILLNESS (First symptom) OR INJURY (Accident) OR PREGNANCY(LMP)

15. IF PATIENT HAS HAD SAME OR SIMILAR ILLNESS. GIVE FIRST DATE   MM   DD   YY

16. DATES PATIENT UNABLE TO WORK IN CURRENT OCCUPATION   MM   DD   YY   FROM   TO   MM   DD   YY

17. NAME OF REFERRING PROVIDER OR OTHER SOURCE

17a.

17b. NPI

18. HOSPITALIZATION DATES RELATED TO CURRENT SERVICES   MM   DD   YY   FROM   TO   MM   DD   YY

19. RESERVED FOR LOCAL USE

20. OUTSIDE LAB?   ☐ YES   ☐ NO $ CHARGES

21. DIAGNOSIS OR NATURE OF ILLNESS OR INJURY (Relate Items 1, 2, 3 or 4 to Item 24E by Line)

1. |___.___|

2. |___.___|

3. |___.___|

4. |___.___|

22. MEDICAID RESUBMISSION CODE   ORIGINAL REF. NO.

23. PRIOR AUTHORIZATION NUMBER

24. A	DATE(S) OF SERVICE				B. PLACE OF SERVICE	C. EMG	D. PROCEDURES, SERVICES, OR SUPPLIES (Explain Unusual Circumstances)		E. DIAGNOSIS POINTER	F. $ CHARGES	G. DAYS OR UNITS	H. EPSDT Family Plan	I. ID QUAL.	J. RENDERING PROVIDER ID. #
	From MM DD YY		To MM DD YY				CPT/HCPCS	MODIFIER						
1														NPI
2														NPI
3														NPI
4														NPI
5														NPI
6														NPI

25. FEDERAL TAX I.D. NUMBER   SSN ☐ EIN ☐

26. PATIENT'S ACCOUNT NO.

27. ACCEPT ASSIGNMENT? (For govt. claims, see back)   ☐ YES   ☐ NO

28. TOTAL CHARGE $

29. AMOUNT PAID $

30. BALANCE DUE $

31. SIGNATURE OF PHYSICIAN OR SUPPLIER INCLUDING DEGREES OR CREDENTIALS (I certify that the statements on the reverse apply to this bill and are made a part thereof.)

SIGNED_____ DATE_____

32. SERVICE FACILITY LOCATION INFORMATION

a. NPI   b.

33. BILLING PROVIDER INFO & PH #   ( )

a. NPI   b.

PHYSICIAN OR SUPPLIER INFORMATION   PATIENT AND INSURED INFORMATION

New Patient Information Sheet

Date: October 19, 2008
Account #: 002-04
Patient Name: Joe Schmoe
Patient Address: 14389 Wickland Dr., Rancho Cordova CA 95777
Patient Phone Number: 916-619-9119
Date of Birth: 11/21/1962
Social Security Number: 01C-01-0U01

Primary Insurance

Subscriber Name: Joe Schmoe
Subscriber ID#: 1438962
Subscriber Date of Birth: 11/21/1962
Group Number/Relationship: 8765432/Self
Insurance Company Name: Hometown Health
Insurance Company Address: P.O. Box 1414111, Reno, NV 89511
Phone Number: 789-541-0162
Employer: Copy Mart

Secondary Insurance

Subscriber Name:
Subscriber ID#:
Subscriber Date of Birth:
Group Number/Relationship:
Insurance Company Name:
Insurance Company Address:
Phone Number:
Employer:

Auto Insurance

Auto Insurance Carrier Name and Address:
Subscriber:
Subscriber's Address:
Phone Number:
Policy ID#:
Date of Injury:

John Smith, M.D.
123340 Doctor Lane
Modesto, CA 94577
(530) 530-5330
CA State License Number: D9580698
NPI Number: 123456789

Superbill Sample

Patient Name: Joe Schmoe
Account Number: 002-04
Date of Service: 6/12/08

Procedure Performed (Description) and CPT Code:

1. Consult, new patient, detailed

2.

3.

4.

5.

Procedure CPT Code/Charges:

1. 99243/$195.00

2.

3.

4.

5.

Diagnosis (Description):

1. Anxiety

2. Depression

3.

4.

5.

Diagnosis (ICD-9 code):

1. 300.00

2. 311

3.

4.

5.

Authorization: no
Auto Accident: no
Work Related: no
DOI/Onset Date: n/a
Family Planning: no
Coordination of Benefits: no
Emergency Services: no

CARRIER →

1500

HEALTH INSURANCE CLAIM FORM

APPROVED BY NATIONAL UNIFORM CLAIM COMMITTEE 08/05

PICA   PICA

1. MEDICARE (Medicare #)	MEDICAID (Medicaid #)	TRICARE CHAMPUS (Sponsor's SSN)	CHAMPVA (Member ID#)	GROUP HEALTH PLAN (SSN or ID)	FECA BLK LUNG (SSN)	OTHER (ID)	1a. INSURED'S I.D. NUMBER (For Program in Item 1)

2. PATIENT'S NAME (Last Name, First Name, Middle Initial)

3. PATIENT'S BIRTH DATE   MM   DD   YY   SEX   M ☐   F ☐

4. INSURED'S NAME (Last Name, First Name, Middle Initial)

5. PATIENT'S ADDRESS (No., Street)

6. PATIENT RELATIONSHIP TO INSURED   Self ☐   Spouse ☐   Child ☐   Other ☐

7. INSURED'S ADDRESS (No., Street)

CITY   STATE

8. PATIENT STATUS   Single ☐   Married ☐   Other ☐

CITY   STATE

ZIP CODE   TELEPHONE (Include Area Code) ( )

Employed ☐   Full-Time Student ☐   Part-Time Student ☐

ZIP CODE   TELEPHONE (Include Area Code) ( )

9. OTHER INSURED'S NAME (Last Name, First Name, Middle Initial)

10. IS PATIENT'S CONDITION RELATED TO:

11. INSURED'S POLICY GROUP OR FECA NUMBER

a. OTHER INSURED'S POLICY OR GROUP NUMBER

a. EMPLOYMENT? (Current or Previous)   ☐ YES   ☐ NO

a. INSURED'S DATE OF BIRTH   MM   DD   YY   SEX   M ☐   F ☐

b. OTHER INSURED'S DATE OF BIRTH   MM   DD   YY   SEX   M ☐   F ☐

b. AUTO ACCIDENT?   ☐ YES   ☐ NO   PLACE (State)

b. EMPLOYER'S NAME OR SCHOOL NAME

c. EMPLOYER'S NAME OR SCHOOL NAME

c. OTHER ACCIDENT?   ☐ YES   ☐ NO

c. INSURANCE PLAN NAME OR PROGRAM NAME

d. INSURANCE PLAN NAME OR PROGRAM NAME

10d. RESERVED FOR LOCAL USE

d. IS THERE ANOTHER HEALTH BENEFIT PLAN?   ☐ YES   ☐ NO   *If yes*, return to and complete item 9 a-d.

READ BACK OF FORM BEFORE COMPLETING & SIGNING THIS FORM.

12. PATIENT'S OR AUTHORIZED PERSON'S SIGNATURE I authorize the release of any medical or other information necessary to process this claim. I also request payment of government benefits either to myself or to the party who accepts assignment below.

SIGNED _____ DATE _____

13. INSURED'S OR AUTHORIZED PERSON'S SIGNATURE I authorize payment of medical benefits to the undersigned physician or supplier for services described below.

SIGNED _____

← PATIENT AND INSURED INFORMATION

14. DATE OF CURRENT: MM   DD   YY   ILLNESS (First symptom) OR INJURY (Accident) OR PREGNANCY(LMP)

15. IF PATIENT HAS HAD SAME OR SIMILAR ILLNESS. GIVE FIRST DATE   MM   DD   YY

16. DATES PATIENT UNABLE TO WORK IN CURRENT OCCUPATION   MM   DD   YY   FROM   TO   MM   DD   YY

17. NAME OF REFERRING PROVIDER OR OTHER SOURCE   17a.   17b. NPI

18. HOSPITALIZATION DATES RELATED TO CURRENT SERVICES   MM   DD   YY   FROM   TO   MM   DD   YY

19. RESERVED FOR LOCAL USE

20. OUTSIDE LAB?   ☐ YES   ☐ NO $ CHARGES

21. DIAGNOSIS OR NATURE OF ILLNESS OR INJURY (Relate Items 1, 2, 3 or 4 to Item 24E by Line)

1. |___.___   3. |___.___

2. |___.___   4. |___.___

22. MEDICAID RESUBMISSION CODE   ORIGINAL REF. NO.

23. PRIOR AUTHORIZATION NUMBER

24. A. DATE(S) OF SERVICE						B. PLACE OF SERVICE	C. EMG	D. PROCEDURES, SERVICES, OR SUPPLIES (Explain Unusual Circumstances)		E. DIAGNOSIS POINTER	F. $ CHARGES	G. DAYS OR UNITS	H. EPSDT Family Plan	I. ID QUAL	J. RENDERING PROVIDER ID. #
From MM	DD	YY	To MM	DD	YY			CPT/HCPCS	MODIFIER						
1														NPI	
2														NPI	
3														NPI	
4														NPI	
5														NPI	
6														NPI	

25. FEDERAL TAX I.D. NUMBER   SSN ☐ EIN ☐

26. PATIENT'S ACCOUNT NO.

27. ACCEPT ASSIGNMENT? (For govt. claims, see back)   ☐ YES   ☐ NO

28. TOTAL CHARGE $

29. AMOUNT PAID $

30. BALANCE DUE $

31. SIGNATURE OF PHYSICIAN OR SUPPLIER INCLUDING DEGREES OR CREDENTIALS (I certify that the statements on the reverse apply to this bill and are made a part thereof.)

SIGNED _____ DATE _____

32. SERVICE FACILITY LOCATION INFORMATION

a. NPI   b.

33. BILLING PROVIDER INFO & PH # ( )

a. NPI   b.

← PHYSICIAN OR SUPPLIER INFORMATION

New Patient Information Sheet

Date: October 19, 2008
Account #: 001-03
Patient Name: Bobby O'Neil (Robert)
Patient Address: P.O. Box 6089, San Francisco, CA 94140
Patient Phone Number: 215-001-0002
Date of Birth: 03/14/1925
Social Security Number: 0N1-32-32B1

Primary Insurance

Subscriber Name: Robert O'Neil
Subscriber ID#: 003468901-01
Subscriber Date of Birth: 03/14/1925
Group Number/Relationship: 32061/Self
Insurance Company Name: Blue Shield
Insurance Company Address: P.O. Box 1474, Shingle Springs, CA 95682
Phone Number: 800-801-1010
Employer: Tires R Us

Secondary Insurance

Subscriber Name:
Subscriber ID#:
Subscriber Date of Birth:
Group Number/Relationship:
Insurance Company Name:
Insurance Company Address:
Phone Number:
Employer:

Auto Insurance

Auto Insurance Carrier Name and Address:
Subscriber:
Subscriber's Address:
Phone Number:
Policy ID#:
Date of Injury:

John Smith, M.D.
123340 Doctor Lane
Modesto, CA 94577 (530) 530-5330
CA State License Number: D9580698
NPI Number: 123456789

Superbill Sample

Patient Name: Bobby O'Neil
Account Number: 001-03
Date of Service: 3/1/08

Procedure Performed (Description) and CPT Code:

1. Office visit, new patient, comprehensive

2. Prescription refill

3.

4.

5.

Procedure CPT Code/Charges:

1. 99205/$159.00

2.

3.

4.

5.

Diagnosis (Description):

1. Asthma

2. High blood pressure

3. Diabetes

4.

5.

Diagnosis (ICD-9 code):

1. 493.9

2. 401.9

3. 250.0

4.

5.

Authorization: no
Auto Accident: no
Work Related: no
DOI/Onset Date: 7/19/1980
Family Planning: no
Coordination of Benefits: no
Emergency Services: no

1500

HEALTH INSURANCE CLAIM FORM

APPROVED BY NATIONAL UNIFORM CLAIM COMMITTEE 08/05

CARRIER

| | PICA | | | | | | | | PICA | |

1. MEDICARE	MEDICAID	TRICARE CHAMPUS	CHAMPVA	GROUP HEALTH PLAN	FECA BLK LUNG	OTHER	1a. INSURED'S I.D. NUMBER	(For Program in Item 1)
(Medicare #)	(Medicaid #)	(Sponsor's SSN)	(Member ID#)	(SSN or ID)	(SSN)	(ID)		

2. PATIENT'S NAME (Last Name, First Name, Middle Initial)

3. PATIENT'S BIRTH DATE   MM   DD   YY   SEX   M □   F □

4. INSURED'S NAME (Last Name, First Name, Middle Initial)

5. PATIENT'S ADDRESS (No., Street)

6. PATIENT RELATIONSHIP TO INSURED   Self □   Spouse □   Child □   Other □

7. INSURED'S ADDRESS (No., Street)

CITY   STATE

8. PATIENT STATUS   Single □   Married □   Other □

CITY   STATE

ZIP CODE   TELEPHONE (Include Area Code) (   )

Employed □   Full-Time Student □   Part-Time Student □

ZIP CODE   TELEPHONE (Include Area Code) (   )

9. OTHER INSURED'S NAME (Last Name, First Name, Middle Initial)

10. IS PATIENT'S CONDITION RELATED TO:

11. INSURED'S POLICY GROUP OR FECA NUMBER

a. OTHER INSURED'S POLICY OR GROUP NUMBER

a. EMPLOYMENT? (Current or Previous)   □ YES   □ NO

a. INSURED'S DATE OF BIRTH   MM   DD   YY   SEX   M □   F □

b. OTHER INSURED'S DATE OF BIRTH   MM   DD   YY   SEX   M □   F □

b. AUTO ACCIDENT?   PLACE (State)   □ YES   □ NO

b. EMPLOYER'S NAME OR SCHOOL NAME

c. EMPLOYER'S NAME OR SCHOOL NAME

c. OTHER ACCIDENT?   □ YES   □ NO

c. INSURANCE PLAN NAME OR PROGRAM NAME

d. INSURANCE PLAN NAME OR PROGRAM NAME

10d. RESERVED FOR LOCAL USE

d. IS THERE ANOTHER HEALTH BENEFIT PLAN?   □ YES   □ NO   *If yes*, return to and complete item 9 a-d.

READ BACK OF FORM BEFORE COMPLETING & SIGNING THIS FORM.

12. PATIENT'S OR AUTHORIZED PERSON'S SIGNATURE I authorize the release of any medical or other information necessary to process this claim. I also request payment of government benefits either to myself or to the party who accepts assignment below.

SIGNED _____   DATE _____

13. INSURED'S OR AUTHORIZED PERSON'S SIGNATURE I authorize payment of medical benefits to the undersigned physician or supplier for services described below.

SIGNED _____

PATIENT AND INSURED INFORMATION

14. DATE OF CURRENT: MM   DD   YY   ILLNESS (First symptom) OR INJURY (Accident) OR PREGNANCY(LMP)

15. IF PATIENT HAS HAD SAME OR SIMILAR ILLNESS. GIVE FIRST DATE   MM   DD   YY

16. DATES PATIENT UNABLE TO WORK IN CURRENT OCCUPATION   MM   DD   YY   FROM   TO   MM   DD   YY

17. NAME OF REFERRING PROVIDER OR OTHER SOURCE

17a.

17b. NPI

18. HOSPITALIZATION DATES RELATED TO CURRENT SERVICES   MM   DD   YY   FROM   TO   MM   DD   YY

19. RESERVED FOR LOCAL USE

20. OUTSIDE LAB?   □ YES   □ NO $ CHARGES

21. DIAGNOSIS OR NATURE OF ILLNESS OR INJURY (Relate Items 1, 2, 3 or 4 to Item 24E by Line)

1. L___ . ___   3. L___ . ___

2. L___ . ___   4. L___ . ___

22. MEDICAID RESUBMISSION CODE   ORIGINAL REF. NO.

23. PRIOR AUTHORIZATION NUMBER

24. A. DATE(S) OF SERVICE						B. PLACE OF SERVICE	C. EMG	D. PROCEDURES, SERVICES, OR SUPPLIES (Explain Unusual Circumstances)		E. DIAGNOSIS POINTER	F. $ CHARGES	G. DAYS OR UNITS	H. EPSDT Family Plan	I. ID QUAL.	J. RENDERING PROVIDER ID. #
From			To					CPT/HCPCS	MODIFIER						
MM	DD	YY	MM	DD	YY										
1														NPI	
2														NPI	
3														NPI	
4														NPI	
5														NPI	
6														NPI	

25. FEDERAL TAX I.D. NUMBER   SSN □ EIN □

26. PATIENT'S ACCOUNT NO.

27. ACCEPT ASSIGNMENT? (For govt. claims, see back)   □ YES   □ NO

28. TOTAL CHARGE $

29. AMOUNT PAID $

30. BALANCE DUE $

31. SIGNATURE OF PHYSICIAN OR SUPPLIER INCLUDING DEGREES OR CREDENTIALS (I certify that the statements on the reverse apply to this bill and are made a part thereof.)

SIGNED _____   DATE _____

32. SERVICE FACILITY LOCATION INFORMATION

a. NPI   b.

33. BILLING PROVIDER INFO & PH # (   )

a. NPI   b.

PHYSICIAN OR SUPPLIER INFORMATION

NUCC Instruction Manual available at: www.nucc.org

APPROVED OMB-0938-0999 FORM CMS-1500 (08-05)

New Patient Information Sheet

Date: October 19, 2008
Account #: 001-02
Patient Name: Norma Jones
Patient Address: 12340 14th Ave., Davis, CA 96060
Patient Phone Number: 916-333-1111
Date of Birth: 11/18/1957
Social Security Number: 5M5-55-55H1

Primary Insurance

Subscriber Name: Norma Jones
Subscriber ID#: 187432-06
Subscriber Date of Birth: 11/18/1957
Group Number/Relationship: 003/Self
Insurance Company Name: Healthnet
Insurance Company Address: P.O. Box 6060,   San Francisco, CA 91420
Phone Number: 800-600-0006
Employer:

Secondary Insurance

Subscriber Name:
Subscriber ID#:
Subscriber Date of Birth:
Group Number/Relationship:
Insurance Company Name:
Insurance Company Address:
Phone Number:
Employer:

Auto Insurance

Auto Insurance Carrier Name and Address: Farmers, POB 00001 Fresno, CA 95821
Subscriber: Jacob Allen
Subscriber's Address: 12340 14th Ave., Davis, CA 96060
Phone Number: 800-421-2121
Policy ID#: 0303030
Date of Injury: 05/08/08

John Smith, M.D.
123340 Doctor Lane
Modesto, CA 94577
(530) 530-5330
CA State License Number: D9580698
NPI Number: 123456789

Superbill Sample

Patient Name: Norma Jones
Account Number: 001-02
Date of Service: 5/9/08

Procedure Performed (Description) and CPT Code:

1. Office visit, established patient, comprehensive

2. Referral out for head, chest, and neck X-rays

3. Referral out for blood draw—chemistry panel

4. Referral out for urinalysis

5.

Procedure CPT Code/Charges:

1. 99215/$105.00

2.

3.

4.

5.

Diagnosis (Description):

1. Head injury

2. Neck injury

3. Headache

4.

5.

Diagnosis (ICD-9 Code):

1. 959.01

2. 959.09

3. 784.0

4.

5.

Authorization: no
Auto Accident: yes
Work Related: no
DOI/Onset Date: 5/8/08
Family Planning: no
Coordination of Benefits: yes
Emergency Services: yes

Professional Pathology and Lab

123355 Doctor Lane
Modesto, CA 94577
(530) 888-8888
CA State License Number: L0505050
NPI Number: 111223456

Superbill Sample

Patient Name: Norma Jones
Account Number: 001-02
Date of Service: 5/9/08

Procedure Performed (Description) and CPT Code:

1. Head X-ray (1 view)

2. Neck X-ray (1 view)

3. Chest X-ray (4 views)

4. General Health Chemistry Blood Panel

5. Routine Urinalysis

Procedure CPT Code/Charges:

1. 70350/$78.00

2. 70360/$68.00

3. 71034/$54.00 each x 4

4. 80050/$48.50

5. 81002/$37.50

Diagnosis (Description):

1. Head injury

2. Neck injury

3. Headache

4.

5.

Diagnosis (ICD-9 Code):

1. 959.01

2. 959.09

3. 784.0

4.

5.

Authorization: no
Auto Accident: yes
Work Related: no
DOI/Onset Date: 5/8/08
Family Planning: no
Coordination of Benefits: yes
Emergency Services: no

1500

HEALTH INSURANCE CLAIM FORM

APPROVED BY NATIONAL UNIFORM CLAIM COMMITTEE 08/05

CARRIER

☐☐ PICA   PICA ☐☐

1. MEDICARE MEDICAID TRICARE CHAMPUS CHAMPVA GROUP HEALTH PLAN FECA BLK LUNG OTHER	1a. INSURED'S I.D. NUMBER (For Program in Item 1)
☐ (Medicare #) ☐ (Medicaid #) ☐ (Sponsor's SSN) ☐ (Member ID#) ☐ (SSN or ID) ☐ (SSN) ☐ (ID)	

2. PATIENT'S NAME (Last Name, First Name, Middle Initial)	3. PATIENT'S BIRTH DATE SEX	4. INSURED'S NAME (Last Name, First Name, Middle Initial)
	MM DD YY M ☐ F ☐	

5. PATIENT'S ADDRESS (No., Street)	6. PATIENT RELATIONSHIP TO INSURED	7. INSURED'S ADDRESS (No., Street)
	Self ☐ Spouse ☐ Child ☐ Other ☐	

CITY STATE	8. PATIENT STATUS	CITY STATE
	Single ☐ Married ☐ Other ☐	
ZIP CODE TELEPHONE (Include Area Code) ( )	Employed ☐ Full-Time Student ☐ Part-Time Student ☐	ZIP CODE TELEPHONE (Include Area Code) ( )

9. OTHER INSURED'S NAME (Last Name, First Name, Middle Initial)	10. IS PATIENT'S CONDITION RELATED TO:	11. INSURED'S POLICY GROUP OR FECA NUMBER
a. OTHER INSURED'S POLICY OR GROUP NUMBER	a. EMPLOYMENT? (Current or Previous) ☐ YES ☐ NO	a. INSURED'S DATE OF BIRTH SEX MM DD YY M ☐ F ☐
b. OTHER INSURED'S DATE OF BIRTH SEX MM DD YY M ☐ F ☐	b. AUTO ACCIDENT? PLACE (State) ☐ YES ☐ NO	b. EMPLOYER'S NAME OR SCHOOL NAME
c. EMPLOYER'S NAME OR SCHOOL NAME	c. OTHER ACCIDENT? ☐ YES ☐ NO	c. INSURANCE PLAN NAME OR PROGRAM NAME
d. INSURANCE PLAN NAME OR PROGRAM NAME	10d. RESERVED FOR LOCAL USE	d. IS THERE ANOTHER HEALTH BENEFIT PLAN? ☐ YES ☐ NO If yes, return to and complete item 9 a-d.

READ BACK OF FORM BEFORE COMPLETING & SIGNING THIS FORM.

12. PATIENT'S OR AUTHORIZED PERSON'S SIGNATURE I authorize the release of any medical or other information necessary to process this claim. I also request payment of government benefits either to myself or to the party who accepts assignment below.	13. INSURED'S OR AUTHORIZED PERSON'S SIGNATURE I authorize payment of medical benefits to the undersigned physician or supplier for services described below.
SIGNED_____ DATE_____	SIGNED_____

PATIENT AND INSURED INFORMATION

14. DATE OF CURRENT: ILLNESS (First symptom) OR INJURY (Accident) OR PREGNANCY(LMP) MM DD YY	15. IF PATIENT HAS HAD SAME OR SIMILAR ILLNESS. GIVE FIRST DATE MM DD YY	16. DATES PATIENT UNABLE TO WORK IN CURRENT OCCUPATION MM DD YY MM DD YY FROM TO
17. NAME OF REFERRING PROVIDER OR OTHER SOURCE	17a. ____ 17b. NPI	18. HOSPITALIZATION DATES RELATED TO CURRENT SERVICES MM DD YY MM DD YY FROM TO
19. RESERVED FOR LOCAL USE		20. OUTSIDE LAB? ☐ YES ☐ NO $ CHARGES
21. DIAGNOSIS OR NATURE OF ILLNESS OR INJURY (Relate Items 1, 2, 3 or 4 to Item 24E by Line) 1. ____ 3. ____ 2. ____ 4. ____		22. MEDICAID RESUBMISSION CODE ORIGINAL REF. NO.
		23. PRIOR AUTHORIZATION NUMBER

24. A. DATE(S) OF SERVICE		B. PLACE OF SERVICE	C. EMG	D. PROCEDURES, SERVICES, OR SUPPLIES (Explain Unusual Circumstances)		E. DIAGNOSIS POINTER	F. $ CHARGES	G. DAYS OR UNITS	H. EPSDT Family Plan	I. ID QUAL.	J. RENDERING PROVIDER ID. #
From MM DD YY	To MM DD YY			CPT/HCPCS	MODIFIER						
1										NPI	
2										NPI	
3										NPI	
4										NPI	
5										NPI	
6										NPI	

25. FEDERAL TAX I.D. NUMBER SSN EIN ☐ ☐	26. PATIENT'S ACCOUNT NO.	27. ACCEPT ASSIGNMENT? (For govt. claims, see back) ☐ YES ☐ NO	28. TOTAL CHARGE $	29. AMOUNT PAID $	30. BALANCE DUE $

31. SIGNATURE OF PHYSICIAN OR SUPPLIER INCLUDING DEGREES OR CREDENTIALS (I certify that the statements on the reverse apply to this bill and are made a part thereof.) SIGNED_____ DATE_____	32. SERVICE FACILITY LOCATION INFORMATION a. NPI b.	33. BILLING PROVIDER INFO & PH # ( ) a. NPI b.

PHYSICIAN OR SUPPLIER INFORMATION

1500

HEALTH INSURANCE CLAIM FORM

APPROVED BY NATIONAL UNIFORM CLAIM COMMITTEE 08/05

PICA | | | | | | | PICA

| 1. MEDICARE (Medicare #) | MEDICAID (Medicaid #) | TRICARE CHAMPUS (Sponsor's SSN) | CHAMPVA (Member ID#) | GROUP HEALTH PLAN (SSN or ID) | FECA BLK LUNG (SSN) | OTHER (ID) | 1a. INSURED'S I.D. NUMBER (For Program in Item 1) |

2. PATIENT'S NAME (Last Name, First Name, Middle Initial)

3. PATIENT'S BIRTH DATE MM DD YY   SEX   M □ F □

4. INSURED'S NAME (Last Name, First Name, Middle Initial)

5. PATIENT'S ADDRESS (No., Street)

6. PATIENT RELATIONSHIP TO INSURED
Self □ Spouse □ Child □ Other □

7. INSURED'S ADDRESS (No., Street)

CITY   STATE

8. PATIENT STATUS
Single □ Married □ Other □

CITY   STATE

ZIP CODE   TELEPHONE (Include Area Code) ( )

Employed □ Full-Time Student □ Part-Time Student □

ZIP CODE   TELEPHONE (Include Area Code) ( )

9. OTHER INSURED'S NAME (Last Name, First Name, Middle Initial)

10. IS PATIENT'S CONDITION RELATED TO:

11. INSURED'S POLICY GROUP OR FECA NUMBER

a. OTHER INSURED'S POLICY OR GROUP NUMBER

a. EMPLOYMENT? (Current or Previous)
□ YES □ NO

a. INSURED'S DATE OF BIRTH MM DD YY   SEX   M □ F □

b. OTHER INSURED'S DATE OF BIRTH MM DD YY   SEX   M □ F □

b. AUTO ACCIDENT?   PLACE (State)
□ YES □ NO

b. EMPLOYER'S NAME OR SCHOOL NAME

c. EMPLOYER'S NAME OR SCHOOL NAME

c. OTHER ACCIDENT?
□ YES □ NO

c. INSURANCE PLAN NAME OR PROGRAM NAME

d. INSURANCE PLAN NAME OR PROGRAM NAME

10d. RESERVED FOR LOCAL USE

d. IS THERE ANOTHER HEALTH BENEFIT PLAN?
□ YES □ NO   *If yes*, return to and complete item 9 a-d.

READ BACK OF FORM BEFORE COMPLETING & SIGNING THIS FORM.
12. PATIENT'S OR AUTHORIZED PERSON'S SIGNATURE I authorize the release of any medical or other information necessary to process this claim. I also request payment of government benefits either to myself or to the party who accepts assignment below.

SIGNED _____ DATE _____

13. INSURED'S OR AUTHORIZED PERSON'S SIGNATURE I authorize payment of medical benefits to the undersigned physician or supplier for services described below.

SIGNED _____

14. DATE OF CURRENT: MM DD YY ILLNESS (First symptom) OR INJURY (Accident) OR PREGNANCY(LMP)

15. IF PATIENT HAS HAD SAME OR SIMILAR ILLNESS. GIVE FIRST DATE MM DD YY

16. DATES PATIENT UNABLE TO WORK IN CURRENT OCCUPATION MM DD YY FROM   TO

17. NAME OF REFERRING PROVIDER OR OTHER SOURCE

17a.
17b. NPI

18. HOSPITALIZATION DATES RELATED TO CURRENT SERVICES MM DD YY FROM   TO

19. RESERVED FOR LOCAL USE

20. OUTSIDE LAB? $ CHARGES
□ YES □ NO

21. DIAGNOSIS OR NATURE OF ILLNESS OR INJURY (Relate Items 1, 2, 3 or 4 to Item 24E by Line)

1. _____ . _____   3. _____ . _____

2. _____ . _____   4. _____ . _____

22. MEDICAID RESUBMISSION CODE   ORIGINAL REF. NO.

23. PRIOR AUTHORIZATION NUMBER

24. A. DATE(S) OF SERVICE						B. PLACE OF SERVICE	C. EMG	D. PROCEDURES, SERVICES, OR SUPPLIES (Explain Unusual Circumstances)		E. DIAGNOSIS POINTER	F. $ CHARGES	G. DAYS OR UNITS	H. EPSDT Family Plan	I. ID. QUAL.	J. RENDERING PROVIDER ID. #
From MM	DD	YY	To MM	DD	YY			CPT/HCPCS	MODIFIER						
1														NPI	
2														NPI	
3														NPI	
4														NPI	
5														NPI	
6														NPI	

25. FEDERAL TAX I.D. NUMBER   SSN EIN □ □

26. PATIENT'S ACCOUNT NO.

27. ACCEPT ASSIGNMENT? (For govt. claims, see back)
□ YES □ NO

28. TOTAL CHARGE $

29. AMOUNT PAID $

30. BALANCE DUE $

31. SIGNATURE OF PHYSICIAN OR SUPPLIER INCLUDING DEGREES OR CREDENTIALS (I certify that the statements on the reverse apply to this bill and are made a part thereof.)

SIGNED _____ DATE _____

32. SERVICE FACILITY LOCATION INFORMATION

a. NPI   b.

33. BILLING PROVIDER INFO & PH # ( )

a. NPI   b.

CARRIER

PATIENT AND INSURED INFORMATION

PHYSICIAN OR SUPPLIER INFORMATION

NEW PATIENT INFORMATION SHEET

Date: October 19, 2008
Account #: 003-06
Patient Name: Wilbur James
Patient Address: 44849 State Street, Colfax, CA 90060
Patient Phone Number: 916-530-0060
Date of Birth: 01/22/1957
Social Security Number: S30-00-0K01

Primary Insurance

Subscriber Name: Wilbur James
Subscriber ID#: 183741
Subscriber Date of Birth: 01/22/1957
Group Number/Relationship: 14389/Self
Insurance Company Name: Western Health Advantage
Insurance Company Address: 4900 Garden Highway, Sacramento, CA 95655
Phone Number: 800-008-8080
Employer: ABC Nursery

Secondary Insurance

Subscriber Name:
Subscriber ID#:
Subscriber Date of Birth:
Group Number/Relationship:
Insurance Company Name:
Insurance Company Address:
Phone Number:
Employer:

Auto Insurance

Auto Insurance Carrier Name and Address:
Subscriber:
Subscriber's Address:
Phone Number:
Policy ID#:
Date of Injury:

John Smith, M.D.
123340 Doctor Lane
Modesto, CA 94577
(530) 530-5330
CA State License Number: D9580698
NPI Number: 123456789

Superbill Sample

Patient Name: Wilbur James
Account Number: 003-06
Date of Service: 6/29/08

Procedure Performed (Description) and CPT Code:

1. Office visit, established patient

2.

3.

4.

5.

Procedure CPT Code/Charges:

1. 99211

2.

3.

4.

5.

Diagnosis (Description):

1. Head cold

2. Rhinitis

3. Headache

4.

5.

Diagnosis (ICD-9 Code):

1. 460

2. 472.0

3. 784.0

4.

5.

Authorization: no
Auto Accident: no
Work Related: no
DOI/Onset Date: n/a
Family Planning: no
Coordination of Benefits: no
Emergency Services: no

1500

HEALTH INSURANCE CLAIM FORM

APPROVED BY NATIONAL UNIFORM CLAIM COMMITTEE 08/05

| | | PICA | | | | | PICA | | |

CARRIER

1. MEDICARE MEDICAID TRICARE CHAMPVA GROUP FECA OTHER	1a. INSURED'S I.D. NUMBER (For Program in Item 1)
CHAMPUS HEALTH PLAN BLK LUNG	
(Medicare #) (Medicaid #) (Sponsor's SSN) (Member ID#) (SSN or ID) (SSN) (ID)	

| 2. PATIENT'S NAME (Last Name, First Name, Middle Initial) | 3. PATIENT'S BIRTH DATE SEX | 4. INSURED'S NAME (Last Name, First Name, Middle Initial) |
| | MM DD YY M F | |

| 5. PATIENT'S ADDRESS (No., Street) | 6. PATIENT RELATIONSHIP TO INSURED | 7. INSURED'S ADDRESS (No., Street) |
| | Self Spouse Child Other | |

| CITY STATE | 8. PATIENT STATUS Single Married Other | CITY STATE |

| ZIP CODE TELEPHONE (Include Area Code) ( ) | Full-Time Part-Time Employed Student Student | ZIP CODE TELEPHONE (Include Area Code) ( ) |

| 9. OTHER INSURED'S NAME (Last Name, First Name, Middle Initial) | 10. IS PATIENT'S CONDITION RELATED TO: | 11. INSURED'S POLICY GROUP OR FECA NUMBER |

| a. OTHER INSURED'S POLICY OR GROUP NUMBER | a. EMPLOYMENT? (Current or Previous) YES NO | a. INSURED'S DATE OF BIRTH SEX MM DD YY M F |

| b. OTHER INSURED'S DATE OF BIRTH SEX MM DD YY M F | b. AUTO ACCIDENT? PLACE (State) YES NO | b. EMPLOYER'S NAME OR SCHOOL NAME |

| c. EMPLOYER'S NAME OR SCHOOL NAME | c. OTHER ACCIDENT? YES NO | c. INSURANCE PLAN NAME OR PROGRAM NAME |

| d. INSURANCE PLAN NAME OR PROGRAM NAME | 10d. RESERVED FOR LOCAL USE | d. IS THERE ANOTHER HEALTH BENEFIT PLAN? YES NO **If yes**, return to and complete item 9 a-d. |

PATIENT AND INSURED INFORMATION

READ BACK OF FORM BEFORE COMPLETING & SIGNING THIS FORM.

12. PATIENT'S OR AUTHORIZED PERSON'S SIGNATURE I authorize the release of any medical or other information necessary to process this claim. I also request payment of government benefits either to myself or to the party who accepts assignment below.

SIGNED _____ DATE _____

13. INSURED'S OR AUTHORIZED PERSON'S SIGNATURE I authorize payment of medical benefits to the undersigned physician or supplier for services described below.

SIGNED _____

| 14. DATE OF CURRENT: ILLNESS (First symptom) OR MM DD YY INJURY (Accident) OR PREGNANCY(LMP) | 15. IF PATIENT HAS HAD SAME OR SIMILAR ILLNESS. GIVE FIRST DATE MM DD YY | 16. DATES PATIENT UNABLE TO WORK IN CURRENT OCCUPATION MM DD YY MM DD YY FROM TO |

| 17. NAME OF REFERRING PROVIDER OR OTHER SOURCE | 17a. 17b. NPI | 18. HOSPITALIZATION DATES RELATED TO CURRENT SERVICES MM DD YY MM DD YY FROM TO |

| 19. RESERVED FOR LOCAL USE | 20. OUTSIDE LAB? $ CHARGES YES NO |

21. DIAGNOSIS OR NATURE OF ILLNESS OR INJURY (Relate Items 1, 2, 3 or 4 to Item 24E by Line)	22. MEDICAID RESUBMISSION CODE ORIGINAL REF. NO.
1. _____ . _____ 3. _____ . _____	
2. _____ . _____ 4. _____ . _____	23. PRIOR AUTHORIZATION NUMBER

24. A. DATE(S) OF SERVICE						B. PLACE OF SERVICE	C. EMG	D. PROCEDURES, SERVICES, OR SUPPLIES (Explain Unusual Circumstances) CPT/HCPCS MODIFIER	E. DIAGNOSIS POINTER	F. $ CHARGES	G. DAYS OR UNITS	H. EPSDT Family Plan	I. ID. QUAL	J. RENDERING PROVIDER ID. #
	From			To											
	MM	DD	YY	MM	DD	YY									
1														NPI	
2														NPI	
3														NPI	
4														NPI	
5														NPI	
6														NPI	

| 25. FEDERAL TAX I.D. NUMBER SSN EIN | 26. PATIENT'S ACCOUNT NO. | 27. ACCEPT ASSIGNMENT? (For govt. claims, see back) YES NO | 28. TOTAL CHARGE $ | 29. AMOUNT PAID $ | 30. BALANCE DUE $ |

| 31. SIGNATURE OF PHYSICIAN OR SUPPLIER INCLUDING DEGREES OR CREDENTIALS (I certify that the statements on the reverse apply to this bill and are made a part thereof.) SIGNED DATE | 32. SERVICE FACILITY LOCATION INFORMATION a. NPI b. | 33. BILLING PROVIDER INFO & PH # ( ) a. NPI b. |

PHYSICIAN OR SUPPLIER INFORMATION

NUCC Instruction Manual available at: www.nucc.org

APPROVED OMB-0938-0999 FORM CMS-1500 (08-05)

NEW PATIENT INFORMATION SHEET

Date: October 19, 2008
Account #: 004-11
Patient Name: Nikki Jacoby
Patient Address: 14187 Quail Ridge Drive, Carson, NV 89111
Patient Phone Number: 775-775-7775
Date of Birth: 05/31/1983
Social Security Number: L60-6I-66K0

Primary Insurance

Subscriber Name: Raymond Jacoby
Subscriber ID#: 14874432160
Subscriber Date of Birth: 10/19/1952
Group Number/Relationship: 16849/Father
Insurance Company Name: Health Options
Insurance Company Address: P.O. Box 689420, Reno, NV 89111
Phone Number: 800-600-4000
Employer: Top Notch Investors

Secondary Insurance

Subscriber Name: Loretta Jacoby-Jenkins
Subscriber ID#: 83742106897143
Subscriber Date of Birth: 12/29/1963
Group Number/Relationship: 16121/Mother
Insurance Company Name: American Fiction Writers Health and Welfare Plan
Insurance Company Address: P.O. Box 83629, Rancho Cordova, CA 95655
Phone Number: 800-111-2222
Employer: Self-employed

Auto Insurance

Auto Insurance Carrier Name and Address:
Subscriber:
Subscriber's Address:
Phone Number:
Policy ID#:
Date of Injury:

John Smith, M.D
123340 Doctor Lane
Modesto, CA 94577
(530) 530-5330
CA State License Number: D9580698
NPI Number: 123456789

Superbill Sample

Patient Name: Nikki Jacoby
Account Number: 004-11
Date of Service: 8/16/2008

Procedure Performed (Description) and CPT Code:

1. Office visit, established patient

2. Flu shot

3.

4.

5.

Procedure CPT Code/Charges:

1. 99211

2. 90645

3.

4.

5.

Diagnosis (Description):

1. Flu vaccination, influenza b

2.

3.

4.

5.

Diagnosis (ICD-9 Code):

1. V04.8

2.

3.

4.

5.

Authorization: no
Auto Accident: no
Work Related: no
DOI/Onset Date: n/a
Family Planning: no
Coordination of Benefits: no
Emergency Services: no

1500

HEALTH INSURANCE CLAIM FORM

APPROVED BY NATIONAL UNIFORM CLAIM COMMITTEE 08/05

☐☐ PICA
                                                                                    PICA ☐☐

| 1. MEDICARE ☐ (Medicare #) | MEDICAID ☐ (Medicaid #) | TRICARE CHAMPUS ☐ (Sponsor's SSN) | CHAMPVA ☐ (Member ID#) | GROUP HEALTH PLAN ☐ (SSN or ID) | FECA BLK LUNG ☐ (SSN) | OTHER ☐ (ID) | 1a. INSURED'S I.D. NUMBER | (For Program in Item 1) |

2. PATIENT'S NAME (Last Name, First Name, Middle Initial)

3. PATIENT'S BIRTH DATE MM ¦ DD ¦ YY   SEX   M ☐   F ☐

4. INSURED'S NAME (Last Name, First Name, Middle Initial)

5. PATIENT'S ADDRESS (No., Street)

6. PATIENT RELATIONSHIP TO INSURED   Self ☐   Spouse ☐   Child ☐   Other ☐

7. INSURED'S ADDRESS (No., Street)

CITY   STATE

8. PATIENT STATUS   Single ☐   Married ☐   Other ☐

CITY   STATE

ZIP CODE   TELEPHONE (Include Area Code) ( )

Employed ☐   Full-Time Student ☐   Part-Time Student ☐

ZIP CODE   TELEPHONE (Include Area Code) ( )

9. OTHER INSURED'S NAME (Last Name, First Name, Middle Initial)

10. IS PATIENT'S CONDITION RELATED TO:

11. INSURED'S POLICY GROUP OR FECA NUMBER

a. OTHER INSURED'S POLICY OR GROUP NUMBER

a. EMPLOYMENT? (Current or Previous)   YES ☐   NO ☐

a. INSURED'S DATE OF BIRTH MM ¦ DD ¦ YY   SEX   M ☐   F ☐

b. OTHER INSURED'S DATE OF BIRTH MM ¦ DD ¦ YY   SEX   M ☐   F ☐

b. AUTO ACCIDENT?   PLACE (State)   YES ☐   NO ☐

b. EMPLOYER'S NAME OR SCHOOL NAME

c. EMPLOYER'S NAME OR SCHOOL NAME

c. OTHER ACCIDENT?   YES ☐   NO ☐

c. INSURANCE PLAN NAME OR PROGRAM NAME

d. INSURANCE PLAN NAME OR PROGRAM NAME

10d. RESERVED FOR LOCAL USE

d. IS THERE ANOTHER HEALTH BENEFIT PLAN?   YES ☐   NO ☐   *If yes*, return to and complete item 9 a-d.

READ BACK OF FORM BEFORE COMPLETING & SIGNING THIS FORM.
12. PATIENT'S OR AUTHORIZED PERSON'S SIGNATURE I authorize the release of any medical or other information necessary to process this claim. I also request payment of government benefits either to myself or to the party who accepts assignment below.

SIGNED _____ DATE _____

13. INSURED'S OR AUTHORIZED PERSON'S SIGNATURE I authorize payment of medical benefits to the undersigned physician or supplier for services described below.

SIGNED _____

14. DATE OF CURRENT: MM ¦ DD ¦ YY ILLNESS (First symptom) OR INJURY (Accident) OR PREGNANCY(LMP)

15. IF PATIENT HAS HAD SAME OR SIMILAR ILLNESS. GIVE FIRST DATE MM ¦ DD ¦ YY

16. DATES PATIENT UNABLE TO WORK IN CURRENT OCCUPATION MM ¦ DD ¦ YY   FROM ____ TO MM ¦ DD ¦ YY

17. NAME OF REFERRING PROVIDER OR OTHER SOURCE

17a.
17b. NPI

18. HOSPITALIZATION DATES RELATED TO CURRENT SERVICES MM ¦ DD ¦ YY   FROM ____ TO MM ¦ DD ¦ YY

19. RESERVED FOR LOCAL USE

20. OUTSIDE LAB?   YES ☐   NO ☐ $ CHARGES

21. DIAGNOSIS OR NATURE OF ILLNESS OR INJURY (Relate Items 1, 2, 3 or 4 to Item 24E by Line)

1. |___ . ___| 3. |___ . ___|
2. |___ . ___| 4. |___ . ___|

22. MEDICAID RESUBMISSION CODE ___ ORIGINAL REF. NO. ___

23. PRIOR AUTHORIZATION NUMBER

24. A. DATE(S) OF SERVICE						B. PLACE OF SERVICE	C. EMG	D. PROCEDURES, SERVICES, OR SUPPLIES (Explain Unusual Circumstances) CPT/HCPCS ¦ MODIFIER	E. DIAGNOSIS POINTER	F. $ CHARGES	G. DAYS OR UNITS	H. EPSDT Family Plan	I. ID. QUAL	J. RENDERING PROVIDER ID. #
From MM	DD	YY	To MM	DD	YY									
1													NPI	
2													NPI	
3													NPI	
4													NPI	
5													NPI	
6													NPI	

25. FEDERAL TAX I.D. NUMBER   SSN ☐ EIN ☐

26. PATIENT'S ACCOUNT NO.

27. ACCEPT ASSIGNMENT? (For govt. claims, see back)   YES ☐   NO ☐

28. TOTAL CHARGE $

29. AMOUNT PAID $

30. BALANCE DUE $

31. SIGNATURE OF PHYSICIAN OR SUPPLIER INCLUDING DEGREES OR CREDENTIALS (I certify that the statements on the reverse apply to this bill and are made a part thereof.)

SIGNED _____ DATE _____

32. SERVICE FACILITY LOCATION INFORMATION

a. NPI   b.

33. BILLING PROVIDER INFO & PH # ( )

a. NPI   b.

NUCC Instruction Manual available at: www.nucc.org   APPROVED OMB-0938-0999 FORM CMS-1500 (08-05)

CARRIER

PATIENT AND INSURED INFORMATION

PHYSICIAN OR SUPPLIER INFORMATION

1500

HEALTH INSURANCE CLAIM FORM
APPROVED BY NATIONAL UNIFORM CLAIM COMMITTEE 08/05

CARRIER

☐☐ PICA   PICA

1.	MEDICARE	MEDICAID	TRICARE CHAMPUS	CHAMPVA	GROUP HEALTH PLAN (SSN or ID)	FECA BLK LUNG (SSN)	OTHER	1a. INSURED'S I.D. NUMBER	(FOR PROGRAM IN ITEM 1)
	☐ (Medicare #)	☐ (Medicaid #)	☐ (Sponsor's SSN)	☐ (Medicaid #)	☐	☐	☒ (ID)	666-55-4440-02	

2. PATIENT'S NAME (Last Name, First Name, Middle Initial)	3. PATIENT'S BIRTH DATE MM DD YY	SEX	4. INSURED'S NAME (Last Name, First Name, Middle Initial)
Smith James	01/01/2001	M ☒ F ☐	Smith Mary

5. PATIENT'S ADDRESS (No., Street)	6. PATIENT RELATIONSHIP TO INSURED	7. INSURED'S ADDRESS (No., Street)
12340 Sunny Lane	Self ☒ Spouse ☐ Child ☐ Other ☐	12340 Sunny Lane

CITY	STATE	8. PATIENT STATUS	CITY	STATE
Sac.	CA	Single ☐ Married ☐ Other ☐	Sac.	CA

ZIP CODE	TELEPHONE (Include Area Code)		ZIP CODE	TELEPHONE (Include Area Code)
95846	916-111-1111	Employed ☐ Full-Time Student ☐ Part-Time Student ☐	95846	916-111-1111

9. OTHER INSURED'S NAME (Last Name, First Name, Middle Initial)	10. IS PATIENT'S CONDITION RELATED TO:	11. INSURED'S POLICY GROUP OR FECA NUMBER
Smith James Sr.		46389

a. OTHER INSURED'S POLICY OR GROUP NUMBER	a. EMPLOYMENT? (CURRENT OR PREVIOUS)	a. INSURED'S DATE OF BIRTH MM DD YY	SEX
43390	☐ YES ☒ NO	11/07/1968	M ☐ F ☒

b. OTHER INSURED'S DATE OF BIRTH MM DD YY	SEX	b. AUTO ACCIDENT?	PLACE (State)	b. EMPLOYER'S NAME OR SCHOOL NAME
12/24/1965	M ☒ F ☐	☐ YES ☒ NO		Safeway

c. EMPLOYER'S NAME OR SCHOOL NAME	c. OTHER ACCIDENT?	c. INSURANCE PLAN NAME OR PROGRAM NAME
Blue Cross	☐ YES ☒ NO	Pacificare

d. INSURANCE PLAN NAME OR PROGRAM NAME	10d. RESERVED FOR LOCAL USE	d. IS THERE ANOTHER HEALTH BENEFIT PLAN?
Blue Cross		☒ YES ☐ NO **If yes**, return to and complete item 9 a-d.

READ BACK OF FORM BEFORE COMPLETING & SIGNING THIS FORM.

12. PATIENT'S OR AUTHORIZED PERSON'S SIGNATURE I authorize the release of any medical or other information necessary to process this claim. I also request payment of government benefits either to myself or to the party who accepts assignment below.

SIGNED _____   DATE _____

13. INSURED'S OR AUTHORIZED PERSON'S SIGNATURE I authorize payment of medical benefits to the undersigned physician or supplier for services described below.

SIGNED _____

PATIENT AND INSURED INFORMATION

14. DATE OF CURRENT: MM DD YY	ILLNESS (First symptom) OR INJURY (Accident) OR PREGNANCY(LMP)	15. IF PATIENT HAS HAD SAME OR SIMILAR ILLNESS. GIVE FIRST DATE. MM DD YY	16. DATES PATIENT UNABLE TO WORK IN CURRENT OCCUPATION MM DD YY
			FROM ____ TO ____

17. NAME OF REFERRING PROVIDER OR OTHER SOURCE	17a.	18. HOSPITALIZATION DATES RELATED TO CURRENT SERVICES MM DD YY
	17b. NPI	FROM ____ TO ____

19. RESERVED FOR LOCAL USE	20. OUTSIDE LAB?	$ CHARGES
	☐ YES ☐ NO	

21. DIAGNOSIS OR NATURE OF ILLNESS OR INJURY. (RELATE ITEMS 1,2,3 OR 4 TO ITEM 24E BY LINE)

1. 490   3.

2. ____   4.

22. MEDICAID RESUBMISSION CODE	ORIGINAL REF. NO.

23. PRIOR AUTHORIZATION NUMBER

24. A. DATE(S) OF SERVICE From MM DD YY	To MM DD YY	B. Place of Service	C. EMG	D. PROCEDURES, SERVICES, OR SUPPLIES (Explain Unusual Circumstances) CPT/HCPCS	MODIFIER	E. DIAGNOSIS POINTER	F. $ CHARGES	G. DAYS OR UNITS	H. EPSDT Family Plan	I. ID QUAL.	J. RENDERING PROVIDER ID. #
1	04/06/08	04/06/08	11	1	99211		1	55.00				123456789
											NPI	
2											NPI	
3											NPI	
4											NPI	
5											NPI	
6											NPI	

PHYSICIAN OR SUPPLIER INFORMATION

25. FEDERAL TAX I.D. NUMBER	SSN EIN	26. PATIENT'S ACCOUNT NO.	27. ACCEPT ASSIGNMENT? (For govt. claims, see back)	28. TOTAL CHARGE	29. AMOUNT PAID	30. BALANCE DUE
94-0000000	☐ ☒	001-01	☒ YES ☐ NO	$ 55.00	$ 0.00	$ 55.00

31. SIGNATURE OF PHYSICIAN OR SUPPLIER INCLUDING DEGREES OR CREDENTIALS (I certify that the statements on the reverse apply to this bill and are made a part thereof.)	32. SERVICE FACILITY LOCATION INFORMATION	33. BILLING PROVIDER INFO & PH # (530) 530-5330
	John Smith MD	John Smith MD
	123340 Dr Ln, Modesto, CA 94577	123340 Dr Ln, Modesto CA 94577
SIGNED ____ DATE ____	a. D9580698 b. 123456789	a. D9580698 b. 123456789

1500

HEALTH INSURANCE CLAIM FORM

APPROVED BY NATIONAL UNIFORM CLAIM COMMITTEE 08/05

CARRIER

PICA | | | | | | | | PICA

| 1. MEDICARE (Medicare #) | MEDICAID (Medicaid #) | TRICARE CHAMPUS (Sponsor's SSN) | CHAMPVA (Medicaid #) | GROUP HEALTH PLAN (SSN or ID) | FECA BLK LUNG (SSN) | OTHER ☒ (ID) | 1a. INSURED'S I.D. NUMBER (FOR PROGRAM IN ITEM 1) 1438962 |

| 2. PATIENT'S NAME (Last Name, First Name, Middle Initial) Schmoe Joe | 3. PATIENT'S BIRTH DATE MM DD YY 11/21/1962 SEX M ☒ F ☐ | 4. INSURED'S NAME (Last Name, First Name, Middle Initial) Schmoe Joe |

| 5. PATIENT'S ADDRESS (No., Street) 14389 Wickland Dr | 6. PATIENT RELATIONSHIP TO INSURED Self ☒ Spouse ☐ Child ☐ Other ☐ | 7. INSURED'S ADDRESS (No., Street) 14389 Wickland Dr |

| CITY Rancho Cordova STATE CA | 8. PATIENT STATUS Single ☒ Married ☐ Other ☐ | CITY Rancho Cordova STATE CA |

| ZIP CODE 99982 TELEPHONE (Include Area Code) 916-619-9119 | Employed ☒ Full-Time Student ☐ Part-Time Student ☐ | ZIP CODE 99982 TELEPHONE (Include Area Code) 916-619-9119 |

PATIENT AND INSURED INFORMATION

| 9. OTHER INSURED'S NAME (Last Name, First Name, Middle Initial) | 10. IS PATIENT'S CONDITION RELATED TO: | 11. INSURED'S POLICY GROUP OR FECA NUMBER 8765432 |

| a. OTHER INSURED'S POLICY OR GROUP NUMBER | a. EMPLOYMENT? (CURRENT OR PREVIOUS) YES ☐ NO ☐ | a. INSURED'S DATE OF BIRTH MM DD YY 11/21/1962 SEX M ☒ F ☐ |

| b. OTHER INSURED'S DATE OF BIRTH MM DD YY SEX M ☐ F ☐ | b. AUTO ACCIDENT? PLACE (State) YES ☐ NO ☐ | b. EMPLOYER'S NAME OR SCHOOL NAME Copy Mart |

| c. EMPLOYER'S NAME OR SCHOOL NAME | c. OTHER ACCIDENT? YES ☐ NO ☐ | c. INSURANCE PLAN NAME OR PROGRAM NAME Hometown Health |

| d. INSURANCE PLAN NAME OR PROGRAM NAME | 10d. RESERVED FOR LOCAL USE | d. IS THERE ANOTHER HEALTH BENEFIT PLAN? YES ☐ NO ☒ If yes, return to and complete item 9 a-d. |

READ BACK OF FORM BEFORE COMPLETING & SIGNING THIS FORM.

12. PATIENT'S OR AUTHORIZED PERSON'S SIGNATURE I authorize the release of any medical or other information necessary to process this claim. I also request payment of government benefits either to myself or to the party who accepts assignment below.

SIGNED _____ DATE _____

13. INSURED'S OR AUTHORIZED PERSON'S SIGNATURE I authorize payment of medical benefits to the undersigned physician or supplier for services described below.

SIGNED _____

| 14. DATE OF CURRENT: MM DD YY ◄ ILLNESS (First symptom) OR INJURY (Accident) OR PREGNANCY(LMP) | 15. IF PATIENT HAS HAD SAME OR SIMILAR ILLNESS. GIVE FIRST DATE MM DD YY | 16. DATES PATIENT UNABLE TO WORK IN CURRENT OCCUPATION MM DD YY FROM TO MM DD YY |

| 17. NAME OF REFERRING PROVIDER OR OTHER SOURCE | 17a. 17b. NPI | 18. HOSPITALIZATION DATES RELATED TO CURRENT SERVICES MM DD YY FROM TO MM DD YY |

| 19. RESERVED FOR LOCAL USE | | 20. OUTSIDE LAB? YES ☐ NO ☐ $ CHARGES |

| 21. DIAGNOSIS OR NATURE OF ILLNESS OR INJURY (RELATE ITEMS 1,2,3 OR 4 TO ITEM 24E BY LINE) 1. 300.00 3. 2. 311 4. | 22. MEDICAID RESUBMISSION CODE ORIGINAL REF. NO. 23. PRIOR AUTHORIZATION NUMBER |

PHYSICIAN OR SUPPLIER INFORMATION

24. A. DATE(S) OF SERVICE From MM DD YY	To MM DD YY	B. Place of Service	C. EMG	D. PROCEDURES, SERVICES, OR SUPPLIES (Explain Unusual Circumstances) CPT/HCPCS	MODIFIER	E. DIAGNOSIS POINTER	F. $ CHARGES	G. DAYS OR UNITS	H. EPSDT Family Plan	I. ID QUAL.	J. RENDERING PROVIDER ID. #
1	06/12/08	06/12/08	11	1	99243		1,2	195.00			NPI	123456789
2											NPI	
3											NPI	
4											NPI	
5											NPI	
6											NPI	

| 25. FEDERAL TAX I.D. NUMBER 94-0000000 SSN ☐ EIN ☒ | 26. PATIENT'S ACCOUNT NO. 002-04 | 27. ACCEPT ASSIGNMENT? (For govt. claims, see back) YES ☒ NO ☐ | 28. TOTAL CHARGE $ 195.00 | 29. AMOUNT PAID $ 0.00 | 30. BALANCE DUE $ 195.00 |

| 31. SIGNATURE OF PHYSICIAN OR SUPPLIER INCLUDING DEGREES OR CREDENTIALS (I certify that the statements on the reverse apply to this bill and are made a part thereof.) SIGNED _____ DATE _____ | 32. SERVICE FACILITY LOCATION INFORMATION John Smith MD 123340 Dr Ln, Modesto, CA 94577 a. D9580698 b. 123456789 | 33. BILLING PROVIDER INFO & PH # (530) 530-5330 John Smith, MD 123340 Dr Ln, Modesto CA 94577 a. D9580698 b. 123456789 |

1500

HEALTH INSURANCE CLAIM FORM
APPROVED BY NATIONAL UNIFORM CLAIM COMMITTEE 08/05

CARRIER

PICA

1. MEDICARE	MEDICAID	TRICARE CHAMPUS	CHAMPVA	GROUP HEALTH PLAN	FECA BLK LUNG	OTHER	1a. INSURED'S I.D. NUMBER (FOR PROGRAM IN ITEM 1)
(Medicare #)	(Medicaid #)	(Sponsor's SSN)	(Medicaid #)	(SSN or ID)	(SSN)	☒ (ID)	003468901-01

2. PATIENT'S NAME (Last Name, First Name, Middle Initial)
ONeil   Robert

3. PATIENT'S BIRTH DATE MM/DD/YY 03/14/1925 SEX M ☒ F

4. INSURED'S NAME (Last Name, First Name, Middle Initial)
ONeil   Robert

5. PATIENT'S ADDRESS (No., Street)
P.O. Box 6089

6. PATIENT RELATIONSHIP TO INSURED
Self ☒ Spouse Child Other

7. INSURED'S ADDRESS (No., Street)
P.O. Box 6089

CITY San Francisco STATE CA

8. PATIENT STATUS
Single ☒ Married Other

CITY San Francisco STATE CA

ZIP CODE 94140 TELEPHONE (Include Area Code) 215-001-0002

Employed ☒ Full-Time Student Part-Time Student

ZIP CODE 94140 TELEPHONE (Include Area Code) 215-001-0002

9. OTHER INSURED'S NAME (Last Name, First Name, Middle Initial)

10. IS PATIENT'S CONDITION RELATED TO:

11. INSURED'S POLICY GROUP OR FECA NUMBER
32061

a. OTHER INSURED'S POLICY OR GROUP NUMBER

a. EMPLOYMENT? (CURRENT OR PREVIOUS) YES ☒ NO

a. INSURED'S DATE OF BIRTH MM/DD/YY 03/14/1925 SEX M ☒ F

b. OTHER INSURED'S DATE OF BIRTH MM DD YY SEX M F

b. AUTO ACCIDENT? YES ☒ NO PLACE (State)

b. EMPLOYER'S NAME OR SCHOOL NAME
Tires R Us

c. EMPLOYER'S NAME OR SCHOOL NAME

c. OTHER ACCIDENT? YES ☒ NO

c. INSURANCE PLAN NAME OR PROGRAM NAME
Blue Shield

d. INSURANCE PLAN NAME OR PROGRAM NAME

10d. RESERVED FOR LOCAL USE

d. IS THERE ANOTHER HEALTH BENEFIT PLAN?
YES ☒ NO If yes, return to and complete item 9 a-d.

READ BACK OF FORM BEFORE COMPLETING & SIGNING THIS FORM.
12. PATIENT'S OR AUTHORIZED PERSON'S SIGNATURE I authorize the release of any medical or other information necessary to process this claim. I also request payment of government benefits either to myself or to the party who accepts assignment below.

SIGNED   DATE

13. INSURED'S OR AUTHORIZED PERSON'S SIGNATURE I authorize payment of medical benefits to the undersigned physician or supplier for services described below.

SIGNED

14. DATE OF CURRENT: MM DD YY ILLNESS (First symptom) OR INJURY (Accident) OR PREGNANCY(LMP)

15. IF PATIENT HAS HAD SAME OR SIMILAR ILLNESS. GIVE FIRST DATE MM DD YY

16. DATES PATIENT UNABLE TO WORK IN CURRENT OCCUPATION FROM MM DD YY TO MM DD YY

17. NAME OF REFERRING PROVIDER OR OTHER SOURCE

17a.
17b. NPI

18. HOSPITALIZATION DATES RELATED TO CURRENT SERVICES FROM MM DD YY TO MM DD YY

19. RESERVED FOR LOCAL USE

20. OUTSIDE LAB? YES NO $ CHARGES

21. DIAGNOSIS OR NATURE OF ILLNESS OR INJURY. (RELATE ITEMS 1,2,3 OR 4 TO ITEM 24E BY LINE)
1. 493.9   3. 250.0
2. 401.9   4.

22. MEDICAID RESUBMISSION CODE ORIGINAL REF. NO.

23. PRIOR AUTHORIZATION NUMBER

24. A. DATE(S) OF SERVICE From MM DD YY	To MM DD YY	B. Place of Service	C. EMG	D. PROCEDURES, SERVICES, OR SUPPLIES (Explain Unusual Circumstances) CPT/HCPCS	MODIFIER	E. DIAGNOSIS POINTER	F. $ CHARGES	G. DAYS OR UNITS	H. EPSDT Family Plan	I. ID QUAL.	J. RENDERING PROVIDER ID. #
1 03/01/2008	03/01/2008	11	1	99205		1,2,3	159.00			NPI	123456789
2										NPI	
3										NPI	
4										NPI	
5										NPI	
6										NPI	

25. FEDERAL TAX I.D. NUMBER SSN EIN ☒
94-0000000

26. PATIENT'S ACCOUNT NO.
001-03

27. ACCEPT ASSIGNMENT? (For govt. claims, see back) ☒ YES NO

28. TOTAL CHARGE $ 159.00
29. AMOUNT PAID $ 0.00
30. BALANCE DUE $ 159.00

31. SIGNATURE OF PHYSICIAN OR SUPPLIER INCLUDING DEGREES OR CREDENTIALS (I certify that the statements on the reverse apply to this bill and are made a part thereof.)

SIGNED   DATE

32. SERVICE FACILITY LOCATION INFORMATION
John Smith MD
123340 Dr Ln, Modesto, CA 94577
a. D9580698   b. 123456789

33. BILLING PROVIDER INFO & PH # (530) 530-5330
John Smith MD
123340 Dr Ln Modesto CA 94577
a. D9580698   b. 123456789

PATIENT AND INSURED INFORMATION / PHYSICIAN OR SUPPLIER INFORMATION

NUCC Instruction Manual available at: www.nucc.org

OMB No. 1215-0055
Expires: 10/31/2009

1500

HEALTH INSURANCE CLAIM FORM

APPROVED BY NATIONAL UNIFORM CLAIM COMMITTEE 08/05

| | PICA | | | | | | | | | | PICA | |

1. MEDICARE (Medicare #) ☐ **MEDICAID** (Medicaid #) ☐ **TRICARE CHAMPUS** (Sponsor's SSN) ☐ **CHAMPVA** (Medicaid #) ☐ **GROUP HEALTH PLAN** (SSN or ID) ☐ **FECA BLK LUNG** (SSN) ☐ **OTHER** (ID) ☒

1a. INSURED'S I.D. NUMBER (FOR PROGRAM IN ITEM 1)
0303030

2. PATIENT'S NAME (Last Name, First Name, Middle Initial)
Jones   Norma

3. PATIENT'S BIRTH DATE MM DD YY
11/18/1957   **SEX** M ☐ F ☒

4. INSURED'S NAME (Last Name, First Name, Middle Initial)
Allen   Jacob

5. PATIENT'S ADDRESS (No., Street)
12340 14th Ave

6. PATIENT RELATIONSHIP TO INSURED
Self ☐ Spouse ☐ Child ☐ Other ☒

7. INSURED'S ADDRESS (No., Street)
1420 C Street

CITY
Davis   **STATE** CA

8. PATIENT STATUS
Single ☒ Married ☐ Other ☐
Employed ☒ Full-Time Student ☐ Part-Time Student ☐

CITY
Sacramento   **STATE** CA

ZIP CODE
96060   **TELEPHONE (Include Area Code)**
916-333-1111

ZIP CODE
95814   **TELEPHONE (Include Area Code)**
916-682-1111

9. OTHER INSURED'S NAME (Last Name, First Name, Middle Initial)
Jones   Norma

10. IS PATIENT'S CONDITION RELATED TO:

11. INSURED'S POLICY GROUP OR FECA NUMBER
0303030

a. OTHER INSURED'S POLICY OR GROUP NUMBER
003

a. EMPLOYMENT? (CURRENT OR PREVIOUS)
YES ☐ NO ☒

a. INSURED'S DATE OF BIRTH MM DD YY
11/18/1957   **SEX** M ☒ F ☐

b. OTHER INSURED'S DATE OF BIRTH MM DD YY
11/18/1957   **SEX** M ☐ F ☒

b. AUTO ACCIDENT?   **PLACE (State)**
YES ☒ NO ☐ CA

b. EMPLOYER'S NAME OR SCHOOL NAME

c. EMPLOYER'S NAME OR SCHOOL NAME
Meadowlark Mall

c. OTHER ACCIDENT?
YES ☐ NO ☒

c. INSURANCE PLAN NAME OR PROGRAM NAME

d. INSURANCE PLAN NAME OR PROGRAM NAME
Healthnet

10d. RESERVED FOR LOCAL USE

d. IS THERE ANOTHER HEALTH BENEFIT PLAN?
YES ☒ NO ☐ If yes, return to and complete item 9 a-d

READ BACK OF FORM BEFORE COMPLETING & SIGNING THIS FORM.

12. PATIENT'S OR AUTHORIZED PERSON'S SIGNATURE I authorize the release of any medical or other information necessary to process this claim. I also request payment of government benefits either to myself or to the party who accepts assignment below.

SIGNED _____ DATE _____

13. INSURED'S OR AUTHORIZED PERSON'S SIGNATURE I authorize payment of medical benefits to the undersigned physician or supplier for services described below.

SIGNED _____

14. DATE OF CURRENT: MM DD YY
05/08/08   ILLNESS (First symptom) OR INJURY (Accident) OR PREGNANCY(LMP)

15. IF PATIENT HAS HAD SAME OR SIMILAR ILLNESS. GIVE FIRST DATE MM DD YY

16. DATES PATIENT UNABLE TO WORK IN CURRENT OCCUPATION
FROM MM DD YY   TO MM DD YY

17. NAME OF REFERRING PROVIDER OR OTHER SOURCE

17a.
17b. NPI

18. HOSPITALIZATION DATES RELATED TO CURRENT SERVICES
FROM MM DD YY   TO MM DD YY

19. RESERVED FOR LOCAL USE

20. OUTSIDE LAB?
YES ☐ NO ☐   **$ CHARGES**

21. DIAGNOSIS OR NATURE OF ILLNESS OR INJURY. (RELATE ITEMS 1,2,3 OR 4 TO ITEM 24E BY LINE)
1. 959.01
2. 959.09
3. 784.00
4.

22. MEDICAID RESUBMISSION CODE   **ORIGINAL REF. NO.**

23. PRIOR AUTHORIZATION NUMBER

24. A. DATE(S) OF SERVICE						B. Place of Service	C. EMG	D. PROCEDURES, SERVICES, OR SUPPLIES (Explain Unusual Circumstances)		E. DIAGNOSIS POINTER	F. $ CHARGES	G. DAYS OR UNITS	H. EPSDT Family Plan	I. ID QUAL.	J. RENDERING PROVIDER ID. #
	From MM DD YY			To MM DD YY				CPT/HCPCS	MODIFIER						
1	05/09/08			5/09/08		11	1	99215		1,2,3	105.00			NPI	123456789
2														NPI	
3														NPI	
4														NPI	
5														NPI	
6														NPI	

25. FEDERAL TAX I.D. NUMBER   SSN ☐ EIN ☒
94-0000000

26. PATIENT'S ACCOUNT NO.
001-02

27. ACCEPT ASSIGNMENT? (For govt. claims, see back)
YES ☒ NO ☐

28. TOTAL CHARGE
$ 105.00

29. AMOUNT PAID
$ 0.00

30. BALANCE DUE
$ 105.00

31. SIGNATURE OF PHYSICIAN OR SUPPLIER INCLUDING DEGREES OR CREDENTIALS (I certify that the statements on the reverse apply to this bill and are made a part thereof.)

SIGNED _____ DATE _____

32. SERVICE FACILITY LOCATION INFORMATION
John Smith MD
123340 Dr Ln Modesto CA 94577
a. D9580698   b. 123456789

33. BILLING PROVIDER INFO & PH # (530) 530-5330
John Smith MD
123340 Dr Ln Modesto   CA   94577
a. D9580698   b. 123456789

CARRIER — PATIENT AND INSURED INFORMATION — PHYSICIAN OR SUPPLIER INFORMATION

1500

HEALTH INSURANCE CLAIM FORM
APPROVED BY NATIONAL UNIFORM CLAIM COMMITTEE 08/05

☐☐☐ PICA ☐   PICA ☐☐☐

1. MEDICARE ☐ (Medicare #)	MEDICAID ☐ (Medicaid #)	TRICARE CHAMPUS ☐ (Sponsor's SSN)	CHAMPVA ☐ (Medicaid #)	GROUP HEALTH PLAN ☐ (SSN or ID)	FECA BLK LUNG ☐ (SSN)	OTHER ☒ (ID)	1a. INSURED'S I.D. NUMBER (FOR PROGRAM IN ITEM 1)
							0303030

2. PATIENT'S NAME (Last Name, First Name, Middle Initial)	3. PATIENT'S BIRTH DATE MM DD YY / SEX	4. INSURED'S NAME (Last Name, First Name, Middle Initial)
Jones Norma	11/18/1957 M ☐ F ☒	Allen Jacob

5. PATIENT'S ADDRESS (No., Street)	6. PATIENT RELATIONSHIP TO INSURED	7. INSURED'S ADDRESS (No., Street)
12340 14th Ave	Self ☐ Spouse ☐ Child ☐ Other ☒	1420 C Street

CITY	STATE	8. PATIENT STATUS	CITY	STATE
Davis	CA	Single ☒ Married ☐ Other ☐	Sacramento	CA

ZIP CODE	TELEPHONE (Include Area Code)		ZIP CODE	TELEPHONE (Include Area Code)
96060	916-333-1111	Employed ☒ Full-Time Student ☐ Part-Time Student ☐	95814	916-682-1111

9. OTHER INSURED'S NAME (Last Name, First Name, Middle Initial)	10. IS PATIENT'S CONDITION RELATED TO:	11. INSURED'S POLICY GROUP OR FECA NUMBER
Jones Norma		0303030

a. OTHER INSURED'S POLICY OR GROUP NUMBER	a. EMPLOYMENT? (CURRENT OR PREVIOUS)	a. INSURED'S DATE OF BIRTH MM DD YY / SEX
003	YES ☐ NO ☒	M ☒ F ☐

b. OTHER INSURED'S DATE OF BIRTH MM DD YY / SEX	b. AUTO ACCIDENT? PLACE (State)	b. EMPLOYER'S NAME OR SCHOOL NAME
11/18/1957 M ☐ F ☒	YES ☒ NO ☐ CA	

c. EMPLOYER'S NAME OR SCHOOL NAME	c. OTHER ACCIDENT?	c. INSURANCE PLAN NAME OR PROGRAM NAME
Meadowlark Mall	YES ☐ NO ☒	

d. INSURANCE PLAN NAME OR PROGRAM NAME	10d. RESERVED FOR LOCAL USE	d. IS THERE ANOTHER HEALTH BENEFIT PLAN?
Healthnet		☒ YES ☐ NO If yes, return to and complete item 9 a-d.

READ BACK OF FORM BEFORE COMPLETING & SIGNING THIS FORM.

12. PATIENT'S OR AUTHORIZED PERSON'S SIGNATURE I authorize the release of any medical or other information necessary to process this claim. I also request payment of government benefits either to myself or to the party who accepts assignment below.

SIGNED _____ DATE _____

13. INSURED'S OR AUTHORIZED PERSON'S SIGNATURE I authorize payment of medical benefits to the undersigned physician or supplier for services described below.

SIGNED _____

14. DATE OF CURRENT: MM DD YY ILLNESS (First symptom) OR INJURY (Accident) OR PREGNANCY(LMP)	15. IF PATIENT HAS HAD SAME OR SIMILAR ILLNESS. GIVE FIRST DATE MM DD YY	16. DATES PATIENT UNABLE TO WORK IN CURRENT OCCUPATION MM DD YY / MM DD YY
05/08/08		FROM ____ TO ____

17. NAME OF REFERRING PROVIDER OR OTHER SOURCE	17a.	18. HOSPITALIZATION DATES RELATED TO CURRENT SERVICES MM DD YY / MM DD YY
	17b. NPI	FROM ____ TO ____

19. RESERVED FOR LOCAL USE	20. OUTSIDE LAB? ☐ YES ☐ NO $ CHARGES

21. DIAGNOSIS OR NATURE OF ILLNESS OR INJURY. (RELATE ITEMS 1,2,3 OR 4 TO ITEM 24E BY LINE)	22. MEDICAID RESUBMISSION CODE ORIGINAL REF. NO.
1. 959.01 3. 784.00	
2. 959.09 4.	23. PRIOR AUTHORIZATION NUMBER

24. A. DATE(S) OF SERVICE From MM DD YY	To MM DD YY	B. Place of Service	C. EMG	D. PROCEDURES, SERVICES, OR SUPPLIES (Explain Unusual Circumstances) CPT/HCPCS	MODIFIER	E. DIAGNOSIS POINTER	F. $ CHARGES	G. DAYS OR UNITS	H. EPSDT Family Plan	I. ID QUAL.	J. RENDERING PROVIDER ID. #
1	05/09/08	05/09/08	49	1	70358		1,2,3	78.00	1		NPI	111223456
2	05/09/08	05/09/08	49	1	70360		1,2,3	68.00	1		NPI	111223456
3	05/09/08	05/09/08	49	1	71034		1,2,3	216.00	4		NPI	111223456
4	05/09/08	05/09/08	49	1	80050		1,2,3	48.50	1		NPI	111223456
5	05/09/08	05/09/08	49	1	81002		1,2,3	37.50	1		NPI	111223456
6										NPI	

25. FEDERAL TAX I.D. NUMBER SSN EIN	26. PATIENT'S ACCOUNT NO.	27. ACCEPT ASSIGNMENT? (For govt. claims, see back)	28. TOTAL CHARGE	29. AMOUNT PAID	30. BALANCE DUE
94-0000001 ☐ ☒	001-02	☒ YES ☐ NO	$ 448.00	$ 0.00	$ 448.00

31. SIGNATURE OF PHYSICIAN OR SUPPLIER INCLUDING DEGREES OR CREDENTIALS (I certify that the statements on the reverse apply to this bill and are made a part thereof.)	32. SERVICE FACILITY LOCATION INFORMATION	33. BILLING PROVIDER INFO & PH # (530) 530-5330
	Prof. Pathology Lab	Prof. Pathology Lab
	123355 Dr Ln, Modesto CA 94577	123355 Dr Ln Modesto CA 94577
SIGNED _____ DATE _____	a. L0505050 b. 11223456	a. L0505050 b. 11223456

CARRIER

PATIENT AND INSURED INFORMATION

PHYSICIAN OR SUPPLIER INFORMATION

NUCC Instruction Manual available at: www.nucc.org

OMB No. 1215-0055
Expires: 10/31/2009

(1500)

HEALTH INSURANCE CLAIM FORM
APPROVED BY NATIONAL UNIFORM CLAIM COMMITTEE 08/05

| | PICA | | | | | | | | | | PICA | |

| 1. MEDICARE ☐ (Medicare #) | MEDICAID ☐ (Medicaid #) | TRICARE CHAMPUS ☐ (Sponsor's SSN) | CHAMPVA ☐ (Medicaid #) | GROUP HEALTH PLAN ☐ (SSN or ID) | FECA BLK LUNG ☐ (SSN) | OTHER ☒ (ID) | 1a. INSURED'S I.D. NUMBER [FOR PROGRAM IN ITEM 1] 183741 |

2. PATIENT'S NAME (Last Name, First Name, Middle Initial)
James Wilbur

3. PATIENT'S BIRTH DATE MM DD YY 01/22/1957 SEX M ☒ F ☐

4. INSURED'S NAME (Last Name, First Name, Middle Initial)
James Wilbur

5. PATIENT'S ADDRESS (No., Street)
44849 State Street

6. PATIENT RELATIONSHIP TO INSURED
Self ☒ Spouse ☐ Child ☐ Other ☐

7. INSURED'S ADDRESS (No., Street)
44849 State Street

CITY Colfax STATE CA

8. PATIENT STATUS
Single ☒ Married ☐ Other ☐
Employed ☒ Full-Time Student ☐ Part-Time Student ☐

CITY Colfax STATE CA

ZIP CODE 90060 TELEPHONE (Include Area Code) 916-530-0060

ZIP CODE 90060 TELEPHONE (Include Area Code) 916-530-0060

9. OTHER INSURED'S NAME (Last Name, First Name, Middle Initial)

10. IS PATIENT'S CONDITION RELATED TO:

11. INSURED'S POLICY GROUP OR FECA NUMBER
14389

a. OTHER INSURED'S POLICY OR GROUP NUMBER

a. EMPLOYMENT? (CURRENT OR PREVIOUS) ☐ YES ☒ NO

a. INSURED'S DATE OF BIRTH MM DD YY 01/22/1957 SEX M ☒ F ☐

b. OTHER INSURED'S DATE OF BIRTH MM DD YY — SEX M ☐ F ☐

b. AUTO ACCIDENT? PLACE (State) ☐ YES ☒ NO

b. EMPLOYER'S NAME OR SCHOOL NAME
ABC Nursery

c. EMPLOYER'S NAME OR SCHOOL NAME

c. OTHER ACCIDENT? ☐ YES ☒ NO

c. INSURANCE PLAN NAME OR PROGRAM NAME
WHA

d. INSURANCE PLAN NAME OR PROGRAM NAME

10d. RESERVED FOR LOCAL USE

d. IS THERE ANOTHER HEALTH BENEFIT PLAN? ☐ YES ☒ NO If yes, return to and complete item 9 a-d.

READ BACK OF FORM BEFORE COMPLETING & SIGNING THIS FORM.
12. PATIENT'S OR AUTHORIZED PERSON'S SIGNATURE I authorize the release of any medical or other information necessary to process this claim. I also request payment of government benefits either to myself or to the party who accepts assignment below.

SIGNED _____ DATE _____

13. INSURED'S OR AUTHORIZED PERSON'S SIGNATURE I authorize payment of medical benefits to the undersigned physician or supplier for services described below.

SIGNED _____

14. DATE OF CURRENT: MM DD YY ILLNESS (First symptom) OR INJURY (Accident) OR PREGNANCY(LMP)

15. IF PATIENT HAS HAD SAME OR SIMILAR ILLNESS GIVE FIRST DATE MM DD YY

16. DATES PATIENT UNABLE TO WORK IN CURRENT OCCUPATION MM DD YY FROM TO MM DD YY

17. NAME OF REFERRING PROVIDER OR OTHER SOURCE

17a.
17b. NPI

18. HOSPITALIZATION DATES RELATED TO CURRENT SERVICES MM DD YY FROM TO MM DD YY

19. RESERVED FOR LOCAL USE

20. OUTSIDE LAB? ☐ YES ☐ NO $ CHARGES

21. DIAGNOSIS OR NATURE OF ILLNESS OR INJURY. (RELATE ITEMS 1,2,3 OR 4 TO ITEM 24E BY LINE)

1. 460   3. 784.0
2. 472.0   4.

22. MEDICAID RESUBMISSION CODE ORIGINAL REF. NO.

23. PRIOR AUTHORIZATION NUMBER

24. A. DATE(S) OF SERVICE From MM DD YY	To MM DD YY	B. Place of Service	C. EMG	D. PROCEDURES, SERVICES, OR SUPPLIES (Explain Unusual Circumstances) CPT/HCPCS	MODIFIER	E. DIAGNOSIS POINTER	F. $ CHARGES	G. DAYS OR UNITS	H. EPSDT Family Plan	I. ID QUAL.	J. RENDERING PROVIDER ID. #
1 06/29/2008	06/29/2008	11	1	99211		1,2,3	69.00			NPI	123456789
2										NPI	
3										NPI	
4										NPI	
5										NPI	
6										NPI	

25. FEDERAL TAX I.D. NUMBER 94-0000000 SSN ☐ EIN ☒

26. PATIENT'S ACCOUNT NO. 003-06

27. ACCEPT ASSIGNMENT? (For govt. claims, see back) YES ☒ NO ☐

28. TOTAL CHARGE $ 69.00

29. AMOUNT PAID $ 0.00

30. BALANCE DUE $ 69.00

31. SIGNATURE OF PHYSICIAN OR SUPPLIER INCLUDING DEGREES OR CREDENTIALS (I certify that the statements on the reverse apply to this bill and are made a part thereof.)

SIGNED _____ DATE _____

32. SERVICE FACILITY LOCATION INFORMATION
John Smith MD
123340 Dr Ln Modesto, CA 94577
a. D9580698   b. 123456789

33. BILLING PROVIDER INFO & PH # (530) 530-5330
John Smith MD
123340 Dr Ln Modesto CA 94577
a. D9580698   b. 123456789

NUCC Instruction Manual available at: www.nucc.org

OMB No. 1215-0055
Expires: 10/31/2009

1500

HEALTH INSURANCE CLAIM FORM

APPROVED BY NATIONAL UNIFORM CLAIM COMMITTEE 08/05

CARRIER

PICA | | PICA

1. MEDICARE (Medicare #) / **MEDICAID** (Medicaid #) / **TRICARE CHAMPUS** (Sponsor's SSN) / **CHAMPVA** (Medicaid #) / **GROUP HEALTH PLAN** (SSN or ID) / **FECA BLK LUNG** (SSN) / **OTHER** [X] (ID)

1a. INSURED'S I.D. NUMBER (FOR PROGRAM IN ITEM 1): 14874432160

2. PATIENT'S NAME (Last Name, First Name, Middle Initial): Jacoby Nikki

3. PATIENT'S BIRTH DATE: 05/31/1983   SEX: M [ ] F [X]

4. INSURED'S NAME (Last Name, First Name, Middle Initial): Jacoby Raymond

5. PATIENT'S ADDRESS (No., Street): 14187 Quail Ridge Rd

6. PATIENT RELATIONSHIP TO INSURED: Self [ ] Spouse [ ] Child [X] Other [ ]

7. INSURED'S ADDRESS (No., Street): 14187 Quail Ridge Dr

CITY: Carson   STATE: NV

8. PATIENT STATUS: Single [X] Married [ ] Other [ ] ; Employed [ ] Full-Time Student [ ] Part-Time Student [ ]

CITY: Carson   STATE: NV

ZIP CODE: 89511   TELEPHONE: 775-775-7775

ZIP CODE: 89511   TELEPHONE: 775-775-7775

9. OTHER INSURED'S NAME (Last Name, First Name, Middle Initial): Jacoby-Jenkins Loretta

10. IS PATIENT'S CONDITION RELATED TO:

11. INSURED'S POLICY GROUP OR FECA NUMBER: 16849

a. OTHER INSURED'S POLICY OR GROUP NUMBER: 16121

a. EMPLOYMENT? (CURRENT OR PREVIOUS): YES [ ] NO [X]

a. INSURED'S DATE OF BIRTH: 10/19/1952   SEX: M [X] F [ ]

b. OTHER INSURED'S DATE OF BIRTH: 12/29/1963   SEX: M [ ] F [X]

b. AUTO ACCIDENT?: YES [ ] NO [X]   PLACE (State)

b. EMPLOYER'S NAME OR SCHOOL NAME: Top Notch Investors

c. EMPLOYER'S NAME OR SCHOOL NAME: self-employed

c. OTHER ACCIDENT?: YES [ ] NO [X]

c. INSURANCE PLAN NAME OR PROGRAM NAME: Health Options

d. INSURANCE PLAN NAME OR PROGRAM NAME: American Fiction Writers

10d. RESERVED FOR LOCAL USE

d. IS THERE ANOTHER HEALTH BENEFIT PLAN?: [X] YES [ ] NO   If yes, return to and complete item 9 a-d.

READ BACK OF FORM BEFORE COMPLETING & SIGNING THIS FORM.

12. PATIENT'S OR AUTHORIZED PERSON'S SIGNATURE I authorize the release of any medical or other information necessary to process this claim. I also request payment of government benefits either to myself or to the party who accepts assignment below.

SIGNED   DATE

13. INSURED'S OR AUTHORIZED PERSON'S SIGNATURE I authorize payment of medical benefits to the undersigned physician or supplier for services described below.

SIGNED

14. DATE OF CURRENT: ILLNESS (First symptom) OR INJURY (Accident) OR PREGNANCY(LMP)

15. IF PATIENT HAS HAD SAME OR SIMILAR ILLNESS. GIVE FIRST DATE

16. DATES PATIENT UNABLE TO WORK IN CURRENT OCCUPATION: FROM ___ TO ___

17. NAME OF REFERRING PROVIDER OR OTHER SOURCE: 17a.   17b. NPI

18. HOSPITALIZATION DATES RELATED TO CURRENT SERVICES: FROM ___ TO ___

19. RESERVED FOR LOCAL USE

20. OUTSIDE LAB?: YES [ ] NO [ ] $ CHARGES

21. DIAGNOSIS OR NATURE OF ILLNESS OR INJURY. (RELATE ITEMS 1,2,3 OR 4 TO ITEM 24E BY LINE)

1. V04.8   3.
2.   4.

22. MEDICAID RESUBMISSION CODE   ORIGINAL REF. NO.

23. PRIOR AUTHORIZATION NUMBER

24. A. DATE(S) OF SERVICE From	To	B. Place of Service	C. EMG	D. PROCEDURES CPT/HCPCS	MODIFIER	E. DIAGNOSIS POINTER	F. $ CHARGES	G. DAYS OR UNITS	H. EPSDT Family Plan	I. ID QUAL.	J. RENDERING PROVIDER ID. #
1 08/16/2008	08/16/2008	11	1	99211		1	89.00			NPI	123456789
2 08/16/2008	08/16/2008	11	1	90645		1	16.00			NPI	123456789
3										NPI	
4										NPI	
5										NPI	
6										NPI	

25. FEDERAL TAX I.D. NUMBER: 94-0000000   SSN [ ] EIN [X]

26. PATIENT'S ACCOUNT NO.: 004-11

27. ACCEPT ASSIGNMENT?: YES [X] NO [ ]

28. TOTAL CHARGE: $ 105.00

29. AMOUNT PAID: $ 0.00

30. BALANCE DUE: $ 105.00

31. SIGNATURE OF PHYSICIAN OR SUPPLIER INCLUDING DEGREES OR CREDENTIALS (I certify that the statements on the reverse apply to this bill and are made a part thereof.)

SIGNED   DATE

32. SERVICE FACILITY LOCATION INFORMATION: John Smith MD   123340 Dr Ln Modesto CA 94577   a. D9580698   b. 123456789

33. BILLING PROVIDER INFO & PH #: (530) 530-5330   John Smith MD   123340 Dr Ln Modesto CA 94577   a. D9580698   b. 123456789

NUCC Instruction Manual available at: www.nucc.org

OMB No. 1215-0055 Expires: 10/31/2009

UB-04

Like the HCFA-1500, the UB-04 form is the universally accepted form for billing facility fees (hospital or clinic portion). Again, appearing as red ink on a white background, it allows for the receiving company to scan the document and pick up the items that you have filled in, without picking up the background boxes into their system. Scanners can be programmed not to pick up the color red.

You will notice once again, on some of the attached sample forms, the type has been intentionally misaligned in the boxes. This is another example to illustrate that the type in the boxes need not be perfectly aligned since the background (red) information won't be picked up by the receiving company, only your typed information. Exact alignment is not necessary. Try to get the type as close as you can when filling out these forms, but don't waste time and forms if it is not perfect. The scanner will do the work for you. If you have to make an addition or correction to a form, it should always be done in either blue or black ink, never red. Even if you use electronic billing, all of the same information will have to be entered into your system for electronic transfer to either the clearinghouse or the insurance company. If any of the information is not applicable, leave the space blank. Do not enter things such as N/A or Does Not Apply.

The most notable difference between the UB-04 and the HCFA-1500 is the number of boxes the forms contain. The HCFA-1500 has thirty-three boxes, and the UB-04 has eighty-one. The reason for this difference is that the nature of the UB-04 is much more in-depth. The form is designed for inpatient billing, and outpatient facility charges. Technical charges and contracts have a much higher degree of information that needs to be transferred back and forth to the insurance company, necessitating the need for the greater number of information fields.

The UB-04 will be used for both inpatient claims and outpatient hospital or clinic based services. The most notable difference here is that on an outpatient claim, all HCPCS codes must be individually listed line by line on the UB-04, and on an inpatient claim, there will be a summary by revenue code and an attached itemized listing. This is due to the large number of billable items listed on an inpatient claim as opposed to a single day outpatient claim. Also on an inpatient claim, there are fields requiring date and time of admit, condition on admit, and number of billable days in addition to the individual charges.

When first entering the hospital, either through the emergency room, or the non-emergency registration office, a Hospital Admittance Request, or HAR will be filled out. This is the equivalent to the Patient Information Form that the patient will fill out in the doctor's office. In addition to all of the outpatient information, the form will also contain fields such as time presented at hospital, time admitted to room, room number assigned, chief complaint, condition on admittance, and admitting diagnosis. The reason for these extra fields is the necessity to convey to the insurance company, through codes, the patient's exact condition upon presentation at the hospital. For example, if the patient has been in a car accident (E819) and presents in an unconscious state (780.09), through transport by ambulance to the ER, condition codes and the additional diagnoses would reflect that. In this case, the chief complaint (the reason why the patient presented at the ER that day) would be unconscious state NEC; but after examination by the physician, the patient may be found to have broken bones, head injury, or other more serious injuries. The admitting diagnosis, like the primary diagnosis for a professional fee, is the main reason that the patient presented at the facility that day.

Code the symptoms only, if an exact diagnosis hasn't yet been determined. If, after the patient has been seen at your facility, a more precise diagnosis is determined, then it should be added behind the admitting diagnosis in Box 67a-q on the form. New on the UB-04 is the POA (Present on Admission) Indicator. In the small box next to each diagnosis, a Y or N is required to show if that symptom or diagnosis was present when the patient was first admitted to the facility. This is used for inpatient claims only. Also new on the UB-04 are the Taxomony codes required for field #81. These are government assigned codes indicating the specialty of the provider. Each medical specialty is assigned a code which must be reported in addition to the providers NPI number. If the Taxonomy code for a given specialty does not match the specialty on file for an assigned NPI number, the claim will be denied. If you have a physician or provider that can render services under different specialties, care must be taken to endure that the correct NPI and the correct taxonomy codes are applied to each claim.

The reason for the time of arrival and the time of admittance is for contract purposes. Many insurance contracts have a clause that states if the patient is there for less than twenty-four hours, it must be billed as an outpatient observation procedure, rather than an inpatient hospital stay charge. On the other hand, there is also generally a clause that states if the patient is there under observation for more than twenty-four hours, charges should be billed as an inpatient procedure, even if the patient never occupied a hospital bed during that time. The patient could spend the entire twenty-four hour period in the observation or recovery bays, but still be able to be charged for a room charge due to the extended period of time the patient stayed at the facility. These days and times are important in determining the correct reimbursement for charges billed.

The following boxes and descriptions appear on the UB-04 form.

UB-04 Form Locator Box #	Field Name and Description
Box 1	Provider name, City, State, Zip, phone and fax
Box 2	Pay-to Name, Address, and secondary identification
Box 3a	Patient Control Number
Box 3b	Medical/Health Record Number
Box 4	Type of Bill (alphanumeric)
Box 5	Federal Tax ID #
Box 6	Statement Covers Period
Box 7	Unlabeled - not used
Box 8	Patient Name
Box 9	Patient Address
Box 10	Patient's Birth Date
Box 11	Patient's Sex
Box 12	Admission Date
Box 13	Admission Hour
Box 14	Type of Admission/Visit
Box 15	Point of Origin for Admission/Visit
Box 16	Discharge Hour
Box 17	Patient Status
Box 18-28	Condition Codes
Box 29	Accident State - not used

Box 30	Unlabeled - not used
Box 31-34	Occurrence Code and Date
Box 35-36	Occurrence Span Code/from thru dates
Box 37	unlabeled - not used
Box 38	Responsible Party Name and Address - not required
Box 39-41	Value Codes and Amounts
Box 42	Revenue Code
Box 43	Revenue Description
Box 44	HCPCS/Rates/HIPPS Rate Codes
Box 45	Service Date
Box 46	Units of Service
Box 47	Total Charges
Box 48	Non-covered Charges
Box 49	Unlabeled - not used
Box 50a-c	Payer Identification
Box 51a-c	Health Plan ID
Box 52a-c	Release of Information Certification Indicator
Box 53a-c	Assignment of Benefits
Box 54a-c	Prior Payments
Box 55a-c	Estimated Amount Due
Box 56	Billing Provider NPI
Box 57	Other Provider ID
Box 58a-c	Insured's Name
Box 59a-c	Patient's Relationship to Insured
Box 60a-c	Insured ID number
Box 61a-c	Insurance Group Name
Box 62a-c	Insurance Group Number
Box 63a-c	Treatment Authorization Number
Box 64a-c	Document Control Number
Box 65a-c	Employer Name
Box 66a-q	Diagnosis and Procedure Code Qualifier
Box 67	Principal Diagnosis Codes
Box 67a-q	Other Diagnosis Codes
Box 68	Unlabeled - not used
Box 69	Admitting Diagnosis
Box 70a-c	Patient Reason for Visit (for outpatient claims)
Box 71	Prospective Payment System Code (PPS)

Box 72	External Cause of Injury Codes (ECI) - not used
Box 73	Unlabeled - not used
Box 74	Principle Procedure Code/Date (Inpatient procedure performed)
Box 74a-e	Other Procedure Code/Date
Box 75	Unlabeled - not used
Box 76	Attending Provider and Identifiers (NPI)
Box 77	Operating Provider Name and NPI
Box 78-79	Other Provider Name and NPI
Box 80	Remarks - enter information necessary for billing that is not shown elsewhere on the form
Box 81	Code Qualifiers Field (Local, National, and Taxonomy Codes)

In addition to the UB-04, an itemized listing breaking down the charges for each revenue code should be attached to the claims as well, listing all charges by date. So, for instance, if you have charges for three days, there should be an itemized listing with a total for each separate day, then the UB-04 will have the total charges for all days combined. Please see the attached sample.

Certain charges do not have CPT codes. These will include some miscellaneous supplies and inpatient room charges. They will be charged by an itemized listing and revenue code only. Also, remember to look for HCPCS codes as well. These will appear in the CPT column and will generally begin with a letter, followed by four numbers. There is no difference in billing these charges. Simply put the HCPCS code anywhere the CPT code should go.

When working either in or for a large inpatient facility, there may or may not be a superbill showing all of the patient's charges. Generally speaking, the charges are entered into the computer on a daily basis, as they are incurred. You may need to produce your own itemized listing, either from a computer printout from your facility or from individual charge slips for each item that is used. Either way, an itemization, printed on blank paper (no special form is needed), is required to attach to the UB-04. The final page for each claim should be a summary total, whose totals will be then carried forward to the UB-04 claim form. Please see the attached sample.

Here is a sample of a HAR that might be used at a local hospital.

HAR (Hospital Admittance Request)

Hospital Admittance Request Form

Today's Date:

Name of Patient:

Patient Account number:

Patient Social Security Number:

Patient's Address:

Patient's Phone Number (Home and Work):

Patient's Occupation:

Sex:

Marital Status:

Primary Insurance Company Name and Address:

Primary Insurance Company Phone Number:

Employer:

Employer's Address and Phone Number:

Subscriber/Relationship:

Subscriber ID#:

Subscriber DOB:

Secondary Insurance Company Name and Address:

Secondary Insurance Company Phone Number:

Subscriber/Relationship:

Subscriber ID#:

Subscriber DOB:

Date Patient Is Seen (Date of Service):

Chief Complaint:

Condition on Admission:

Admitting Diagnosis:

Time Presented at Hospital:

Time Admitted to Room:

Room Number Assigned:

Name and ID# of Referring Physician:

Hospitalization Dates:

Outside Lab:

Family Planning:

EMG:

COB:

Prior Auth #:

Disability Dates:

Date of First Injury, Illness, or Onset:

Place of Service:

Type of Service:

Name and Address of Treating Physician:

Name and Address Where Services Were Rendered:

Physician Lic. #:

Provider #:

Tax ID #:

HAR EXERCISES

Let's try some exercises. This first claim will be for outpatient ER services. Use the information from this sample HAR and the attached charge sheets to fill out the UB-04 claim form. A completed form will follow for comparison purposes. Please review your entries against the completed form (on page 174) to see how well you did.

HOSPITAL ADMITTANCE REQUEST FORM

Today's Date: 12/7/08
Name of Patient: Audrey Jones
Patient Account number: 98018823726
Patient Social Security Number: 55A-05-6L60
Patient's Address: P.O. Box 684321, Bend, OR 60101-0101
Patient's Phone Number (Home and Work): (801) 108-0000
Patient's Occupation: Truck Driver
Sex: F
Marital Status: M
Primary Insurance Company Name and Address: Blue Shield, P.O. Box 6900016, Red Bluff, CA 90060
Primary Insurance Company Phone Number: (818) 181-8181
Employer: County Library
Employer's Address and Phone Number: 1918 Reading Lane, Sacramento, CA 91818
Subscriber/Relationship: Self
Subscriber ID#: 898747474747474
Subscriber DOB: 12/29/1959
Secondary Insurance Company Name and Address: ABC Ins., 4212 Ins. Lane, Sacramento, CA 95959
Secondary Insurance Company Phone Number: (800) 888-0000
Subscriber/Relationship: John Jones/spouse
Employer: ABC Trucking
Employer's Address and Phone Number: 1234 Truck Lane, Sacramento, CA 95814
Subscriber ID#: 99383-02982918
Subscriber DOB: 11/14/1959
Date Patient Is Seen (Date of Service): 12/7/2008
Service: Emergency Room visit, new patient; $850.00, 99281; Revenue Code 450
Chief Complaint: right foot pain, 729.5
Condition on Admission: conscious, alert
Admitting Diagnosis: Fracture right fifth metatarsal, 825.25
Time Presented at Hospital: 11:39 P.M.
Time Admitted to Room: n/a

Room Number Assigned: n/a
Name and ID# of Referring Physician: none
Hospitalization Dates: 12/7/2008
Outside Lab: no
Family Planning: no
EMG: yes

COB: yes
Prior Auth #: no
Disability dates: Undetermined
Date of First Injury, Illness, or Onset: 12/7/2008
Place of Service: OP Hospital
Type of Service: Medical

Name and Address of Treating Physician: John Smith, M.D.
Physician License #: CA8475948, NPI 111111111
Name and Address Where Services Were Rendered: Main Hospital, 15594 Main St., Davis, CA 94444
NPI Number: 987654321
Physician TIN#: 94-9383834

ITEMIZED LISTING

Patient Name: Audrey Jones
Admit Date: 12/7/08
Provider: Main Hospital

Account Number: 98018823726
Discharge Date: 12/7/08
Service Date: 12/7/08

CPT Code	Rev Code	Service Date	Description	Category	Qty	Charge (ea unit)	Total Charge
99281	450	12/7/08	ER Visit	ER	1	$850.00	$850.00

ITEMIZED LISTING SUMMARY TOTALS

Patient Name: Audrey Jones　　　　Account Number: 98018823726
Admit Date: 12/7/08　　　　　　　Discharge Date: 12/7/08
Provider: Main Hospital　　　　　Service Date: 12/7/08

Date:　　　　　　　　　　　　　　Total Charges
12/7/08　　　　　　　　　　　　　$850.00
Grand Totals:　　　　　　　　$850.00

Rev Codes:	Desc.	Units:	Total Charges:
450	ER Visit	1	$850.00
Grand Total:		1	$850.00

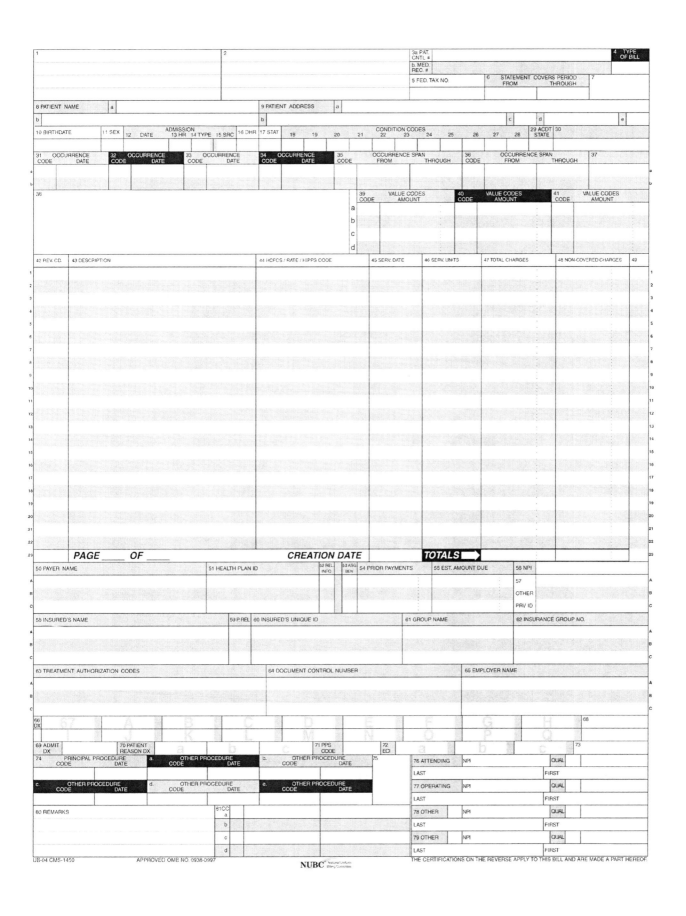

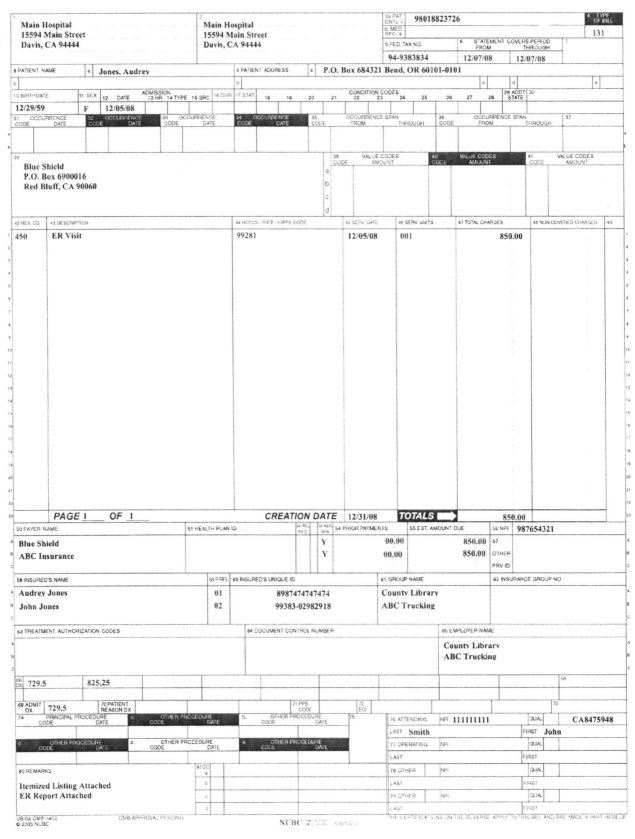

REVENUE CODES (FOR USE WITH UB-04 INPATIENT AND OUTPATIENT FACILITY CHARGE BILLING):

Quick Reference Guide for General Revenue Code Headings

001X	Reserved for Internal Payer Use
002X	Health Insurance-Prospective Payment System
010X	All-Inclusive Rate
011X	Room and Board-Private
012X	Room and Board-Semi-private (two-bed)
013X	Room and Board-Three and four bed
014X	Room and Board-Private Deluxe
015X	Room and Board-Ward Medical-General
016X	Room and Board-Other
017X	Room and Board-Nursery
018X	Leave of Absence
019X	Subacute Care
020X	Intensive Care
021X	Coronary Care
022X	Special Charges
023X	Incremental Nursing Charge
024X	All-inclusive Ancillary
025X	Pharmacy (See also 063X)
026X	IV Therapy
027X	Medical/Surgical Supplies and Devices (See also 062X)
028X	Oncology
029X	Durable Medical Equipment (Other than rental)
030X	Laboratory
031X	Laboratory-Pathology
032X	Radiology-Diagnostic
033X	Radiology-Therapeutic and/or Chemotherapy Administration
034X	Nuclear Medicine
035X	CT Scan
036X	Operating Room Services
037X	Anesthesia
038X	Blood
039X	Blood and Blood Component Administration, Processing, and Storage
040X	Other Imaging Services
041X	Respiratory Services
042X	Physical Therapy
043X	Occupational Therapy
044X	Speech-Language Pathology
045X	Emergency Room
046X	Pulmonary Function
047X	Audiology
048X	Cardiology
049X	Ambulatory Surgical Care
050X	Outpatient Services
051X	Clinic
052X	Free Standing Clinic

053X	Osteopathic Services
054X	Ambulance
055X	Skilled Nursing
056X	Medical Social Services
057X	Home Health Aide (Home Health)
058X	Other Visits (Home Health)
059X	Units of Service (Home Health)
060X	Oxygen Home Health
061X	MRT (Magnetic Resonance Technology)
062X	Medical Surgical Supplies (See also 027X)
063X	Drugs Requiring Specific Identification (See also 025X)
064X	Home IV Therapy Services
065X	Hospice Services
066X	Respite Care
067X	Outpatient Special Residence Charges
068X	Trauma Response
069X	Not Assigned
070X	Cast Care
071X	Recovery Room
072X	Labor/Delivery
073X	EKG/ECG (Electrocardiogram)
074X	EEG (Electroencephalogram)
075X	Gastrointestinal Services
076X	Treatment or Observation Room
077X	Preventive Care Services
078X	Telemedicine
079X	Extra-Corporeal Shock Wave Therapy ESWT (formerly Lithotripsy)
080X	Inpatient Renal Dialysis
081X	Organ Acquisition
082X	Hemodialysis-Outpatient or Home
083X	Peritoneal Dialysis-Outpatient or Home
084X	Continuous Ambulatory Peritoneal Dialysis (CAPD) Outpatient or Home
085X	Continuous Cycling Peritoneal Dialysis (CCPD) Outpatient or Home
086X	Reserved for Dialysis (National Assignment)
087X	Reserved for Dialysis (National Assignment)
088X	Miscellaneous Dialysis
089X	Reserved for National Assignment
090X	Behavioral Health Treatments/Services (See also 091X)
091X	Behavioral Health Treatments/Services
092X	Other Diagnostic Services
093X	Medical Rehabilitation Day Program
094X	Other Therapeutic Services (See also 095X)
095X	Other Therapeutic Services (See also 094X)
096X	Professional Fees (See also 097X and 098X)
097X	Professional Fees (See also 096X and 098X)
098X	Professional Fees (See also 096X and 097X)
099X	Patient Convenience Items
100X	Behavioral Health Accommodations
210X	Alternative Therapy Service
310X	Adult Care

A complete listing of all current Revenue Codes is listed in the Appendix section of this book, beginning on page 269.

Let's try some more exercises for UB-04 billing. Please fill out the following UB-04 claim forms with the information provided in the attached HARs and Itemized Listings of Charges. Look carefully for all information necessary to complete the forms. It will all be located either on the HAR, the daily itemized listings, or the IL Summary Sheet. Remember, there will be multiple daily itemized charge sheets for each patient. Find the summary total page and carry those figures forward to the UB-04. Also, review all the itemized listings to see the totals for each revenue code category. Review all your answers against the completed forms at the end of the section.

UB-04 Exercises

Exercise #1

Hospital Admittance Request Form

Today's Date: 11/21/08

Name of Patient: Mary Smith

Patient Account number: 006-03462

Patient Social Security Number: V00-01-T001

Patient's address: 1698 Ivoryton Way, Sacramento, CA 95820

Patient's Phone Number (Home and Work): 916-916-9166

Patient's occupation: Bookkeeper

Sex: F

Marital Status: S

Primary Insurance Company

Name and Address: Healthnet, P.O. Box 100, Rancho Cordova, CA 96666

Primary Insurance company phone number: 800-832-3111

Employer: AM Sunrise Gas Station

Employer Address and Phone Number: 2340 Sunrise Ave., Sacramento, CA 95883, 916-331-1113

Subscriber/Relationship: Self

Subscriber ID#: 138742-006

Subscriber DOB: 12/1/1964

Secondary Insurance Company Name and Address: none

Secondary Insurance Company Phone Number:

Subscriber/Relationship:

Subscriber ID#:

Subscriber DOB:

Date patient is seen (Date of Service): 11/21/08

Chief Complaint: Back Pain

Condition on Admission: Ambulatory

Admitting Diagnosis: Back Pain 724.2; Dizziness 780.4

Time Presented at Hospital: 10:02 A.M.

Time Admitted to Room: 11:48 A.M.

Room Number Assigned: 1342

Name and ID# of Referring Physician: None

Hospitalization dates: 11/21/08 – 11/23/08

Outside lab: yes

Family Planning: no

EMG: no

COB: no

Prior Auth #: none

Disability Dates: 11/21/08–11/30/08

Date of First Injury, Illness, or Onset: 11/15/08

Place of service: IP Hospital

Type of service: Medical

Name and Address of Treating Physician: John Goody, M.D.

Name and Address Where Services Were Rendered: ABC Hospital, 1234 Main Street, Fairfield, CA 96341

Physician Lic. #: Z30184

NPI Number: 222222222

Tax ID #: 94-1111111

ITEMIZED LISTING

Patient Name: Mary Smith   Account Number: 006-03462
Admit Date: 11/21/08   Discharge Date: 11/23/08
Provider: ABC Hosp.   Service Date: 11/21/08

CPT Code	Rev Code	Service Date	Description	Category	Qty	Charge (ea unit)	Total Charge
88319	312	11/21/08	Enzyme cytochemistry	Lab	1	$27.50	$27.50
88313	312	11/21/08	Microorganism stain, Grp II	Lab	1	$38.00	$38.00
88311	312	11/21/08	Decalcification	Lab	1	$68.90	$68.90
Total:					3		$134.40

ITEMIZED LISTING

Patient Name: Mary Smith   Account Number: 006-03462
Admit Date: 11/21/08   Discharge Date: 11/23/08
Provider: ABC Hosp.   Service Date: 11/22/08

CPT Code	Rev Code	Service Date	Description	Category	Qty	Charge (ea unit)	Total Charge
84450	301	11/22/08	Aspartate amino	Lab	1	$28.00	$28.00
85025	305	11/22/08	Platelet count	Lab	1	$86.00	$86.00
85730	305	11/22/08	Thromboplastin time	Lab	1	$126.00	$126.00
Total:					3		$240.00

ITEMIZED LISTING:

Patient Name: Mary Smith
Admit Date: 11/21/08
Provider: ABC Hosp.

Account Number: 006-03462
Discharge Date: 11/23/08
Service Date: 11/23/08

CPT Code	Rev Code	Service Date	Description	Category	Qty	Charge (ea unit)	Total Charge
97001	424	11/23/08	Evaluation	Medicine	1	$238.50	$238.50
85610	305	11/23/08	Prothrombin time	Lab	1	$356.00	$356.00
99070	250	11/23/08	Motrin	Drugs	3	$80.00	$240.00
Total:					5		$834.50

ITEMIZED LISTING SUMMARY TOTALS

Patient Name: Mary Smith   Account Number: 006-03462
Admit Date: 11/21/08   Discharge Date: 11/23/08
Provider: ABC Hosp.   Service Date: 11/21/08

Date:	Total Charges
11/21/08	$134.40
11/22/08	$240.00
11/23/08	$834.50
Grand Totals:	**$1,208.90**

Rev Codes	Desc.	Units	Total Charges
312	Path and Lab	3	$134.40
301	Lab	1	$28.00
305	Lab	3	$568.00
424	Medicine	1	$238.50
250	IP Drugs	3	$240.00
Grand Total:		**11**	**$1,208.90**

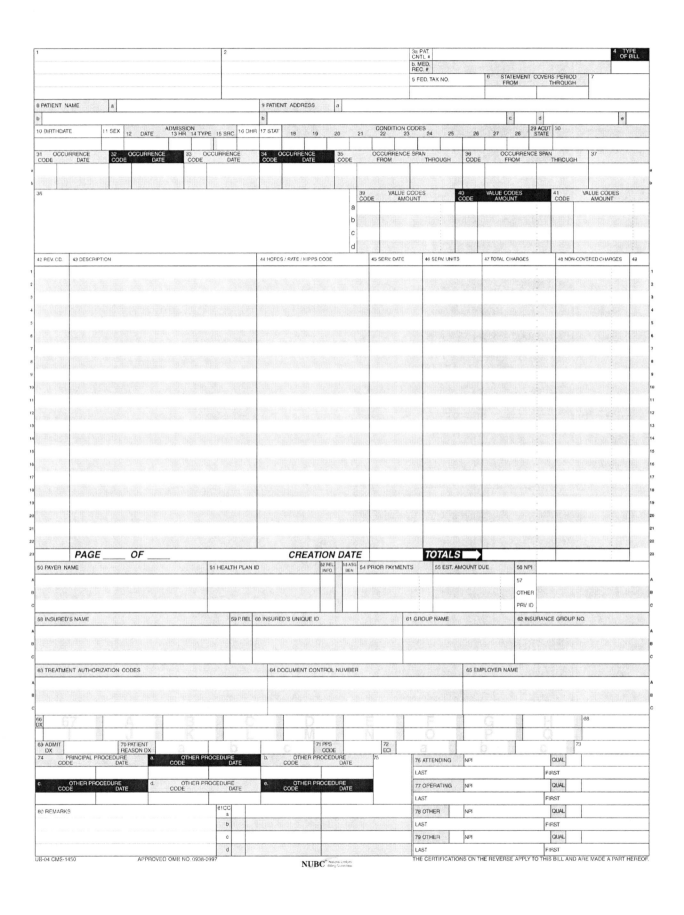

Exercise #2

Hospital Admittance Request Form

Today's date: 12/21/08

Name of Patient: Jean Bean III

Patient Account number: 348-164

Patient Social Security Number: 0P0-30-GH33

Patient's address: 1675 Drive Way, Oakville, NV 90528

Patient's phone number (home and work): 778-332-6489

Patient's occupation: Truck Driver

Sex: M

Marital Status: M

Primary Insurance company name and address: Trucker's Insurance, 118 Big Truck Way, Fallon, NV 38711

Primary Insurance company phone number: 888-888-1111

Employer: Safe Trucking

Employer address and phone number: 8342 Industrial Lane, Oakville, NV 89528

Subscriber/Relationship: Self

Subscriber ID#: 0387911622

Subscriber DOB: 7/18/1943

Secondary Insurance Company name and address: none

Secondary Insurance company phone number:

Subscriber/Relationship:

Subscriber ID#:

Subscriber DOB:

Date patient is seen (Date of Service): 12/21/08

Chief Complaint: leg pain, head pain

Condition on Admission: ambulatory

Admitting Diagnosis: concussion 850.9, fracture femur 821.0

Time Presented at Hospital: 6:42 P.M.

Time Admitted to Room: 8:41 P.M.

Room Number Assigned: 1261

Name and ID# of Referring Physician: John Smith, M.D. Z44113897

Hospitalization Dates: 12/21/08–12/23/08

Outside lab: yes

Family Planning: no

EMG: no

COB: no

Prior Auth #: none

Disability Dates: 12/21/08–1/30/09

Date of First Injury, Illness, or Onset: 12/21/08

Place of Service: IP Hospital

Type of Service: Medical

Name and Address of Treating Physician: Jerry James, M.D.

Name and Address Where Services Were Rendered: Main Hospital, 1241 O Street, Fresno, CA 32161

Physician Lic.#: Z34167

NPI Number: 333333333

Tax ID #: 94-22226

ITEMIZED LISTING

Patient Name: Jean Bean   Account Number: 348-164
Admit Date: 12/21/08   Discharge Date: 12/23/08
Provider: Main Hosp.   Service Date: 12/21/08

CPT Code	Rev Code	Service Date	Description	Category	Qty	Charge (ea unit)	Total Charge
73510	320	12/21/08	X-ray, hip 2 views	Radiology	1	$331.50	$331.50
73550	320	12/21/08	X-ray, femur 2 views	Radiology	1	$583.50	$583.50
73562	320	12/21/08	X-ray, femur 3 views	Radiology	1	$312.50	$312.50
Total					3		$1,227.50

ITEMIZED LISTING

Patient Name: Jean Bean   Account Number: 348-164
Admit Date: 12/21/08   Discharge Date: 12/23/08
Provider: Main Hosp.   Service Date: 12/22/08

CPT Code	Rev Code	Service Date	Description	Category	Qty	Charge (ea unit)	Total Charge
99070	250	12/22/08	Drugs	Drugs	18	$28.00	$504.00
Total:					18		$504.00

ITEMIZED LISTING

Patient Name: Jean Bean   Account Number: 348-164
Admit Date: 12/21/08   Discharge Date: 12/23/08
Provider: Main Hosp.   Service Date: 12/22/08

CPT Code	Rev Code	Service Date	Description	Category	Qty	Charge (ea unit)	Total Charge
93005	730	12/23/08	ECG Tracing	Medicine	2	$46.00	$92.00
99285	450	12/23/08	ER visit	ER	1	$3126.00	$3,126.00
70450	352	12/23/08	CT head	Radiology	1	$321.00	$321.00
Totals:					4		$3,539.00

ITEMIZED LISTING SUMMARY TOTALS

Patient Name: Jean Bean   Account Number: 348-164
Admit Date: 12/21/08   Discharge Date: 12/23/08
Provider: Main Hosp.   Service Date: 12/21/08

Date:	Total Charges
12/21/08	$1,227.50
12/22/08	$504.00
12/23/08	$3,539.00
Grand Total:	$5,270.50

Rev Codes	Desc.	Units	Total Charges
320	Radiology	3	$1,227.50
250	IP Drugs	18	$504.00
730	Medicine	2	$92.00
450	ER Visit	1	$3,126.00
351	Radiology	1	$321.00
Grand Total:		**25**	**$5,270.50**

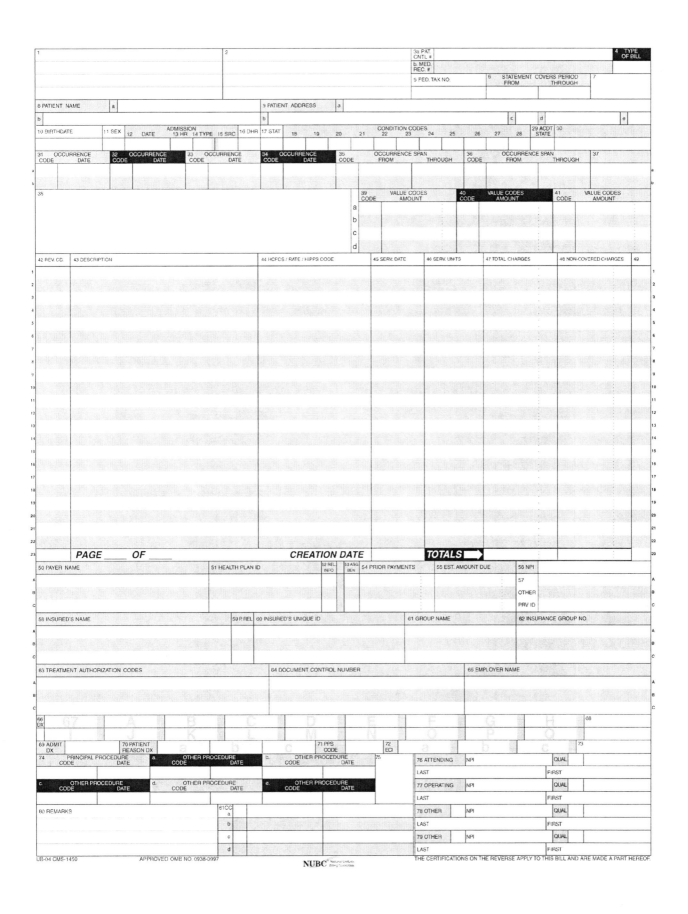

EXERCISE #3

Hospital Admittance Request Form

Today's date: 1/1/08

Name of Patient: Chris James

Patient Account Number: 63187-221

Patient Social Security Number: 0B1-01-U142

Patient's Address: 8901 Oakridge Street, Elk Grove, CA 83741

Patient's Phone Number (Home and Work): 913-728-1463

Patient's occupation: student

Sex: M

Marital Status: S

Primary Insurance Company Name and Address: Student Health Insurance, 1542 College Lane, Stockton, CA 97209

Primary Insurance Company Phone Number: 800-008-5551

Employer: Student

Employer Address and Phone Number: None

Subscriber/Relationship: Self

Subscriber ID#: 1111111

Subscriber DOB: 9/26/1968

Secondary Insurance Company Name and Address: None

Secondary Insurance Company Phone Number:

Subscriber/Relationship:

Subscriber ID#:

Subscriber DOB:

Date Patient Is Seen (Date of Service): 1/1/08

Chief Complaint: Lethargy, Disorientation

Condition on Admission: Ambulatory

Admitting Diagnosis: Drug Overdose 977.9

Time Presented at Hospital: 1:03 A.M.

Time Admitted to Room: 4:17 A.M.

Room Number Assigned: 1013

Name and ID# of Referring Physician: None-ER Visit

Hospitalization dates: 1/1/08–1/3/08

Outside lab: yes

Family Planning: no

EMG: yes

COB: no

Prior Auth #: 123874126AZ142

Disability dates: 1/1/08–1/15/08

Date of First Injury, Illness, or Onset: 1/1/08

Place of Service: IP Hospital

Type of Service: Medical

Name and Address of Treating Physician: Bethany Jones, M.D.

Name and Address Where Services Were Rendered: Main Street Hospital, 123 Main Street, Ontario, OR 97831

Physician Lic#: Z63891

NPI Number: 444444444

Tax ID #: 94-33334

Itemized Listing

Patient Name: Chris James   Account Number: 63187-221
Admit Date: 1/1/08   Discharge Date: 1/3/08
Provider: Main St. Hosp.   Service Date: 1/1/08

CPT Code	Rev Code	Service Date	Description	Category	Qty	Charge (ea unit)	Total Charge
99070	250	1/1/08	Aspirin	IP Drugs	6	$1.00	$6.00
99070	258	1/1/08	IV Drugs	IV Narc	3	$31.00	$93.00
99282	450	1/1/08	ER Visit	ER	1	$869.00	$869.00
Total:					10		$968.00

Itemized Listing

Patient Name: Chris James   Account Number: 63187-221
Admit Date: 1/1/08   Discharge Date: 1/3/08
Provider: Main St. Hosp.   Service Date: 1/2/08

CPT Code	Rev Code	Service Date	Description	Category	Qty	Charge (ea unit)	Total Charge
99273	424	1/2/08	Confirm Consult	Medicine	1	$198.00	$198.00
Total:					1		$198.00

ITEMIZED LISTING

Patient Name: Chris James   Account Number: 63187-221
Admit Date: 1/1/08   Discharge Date: 1/3/08
Provider: Main St. Hosp.   Service Date: 1/3/08

CPT Code	Rev Code	Service Date	Description	Category	Qty	Charge (ea unit)	Total Charge
80051	312	1/3/08	Electrolyte Panel	Path and Lab	1	$87.00	$87.00
80100	312	1/3/08	Drug Screening	Path and Lab	1	$96.00	$96.00
99201	510	1/3/08	Office Visit	Clinic	1	$115.00	$115.00
Total:					3		$298.00

Itemized Listing Summary Totals:

Patient Name:	Chris James		Account Number:	63187-221
Admit Date:	1/1/08		Discharge Date:	1/3/08
Provider:	Main St. Hosp.		Service Date:	1/1/08

Date:	Total Charges
1/1/08	$968.00
1/2/08	$198.00
1/3/08	$298.00
Grand Totals:	$1,464.00

Rev Codes	Desc.	Units	Total Charges
250	IP Drugs	6	$6.00
258	IP Narcotics	3	$93.00
450	ER Visit	1	$869.00
424	Medicine	1	$198.00
312	Path and Lab	2	$183.00
510	Clinic	1	$115.00
Grand Total:		14	$1,464.00

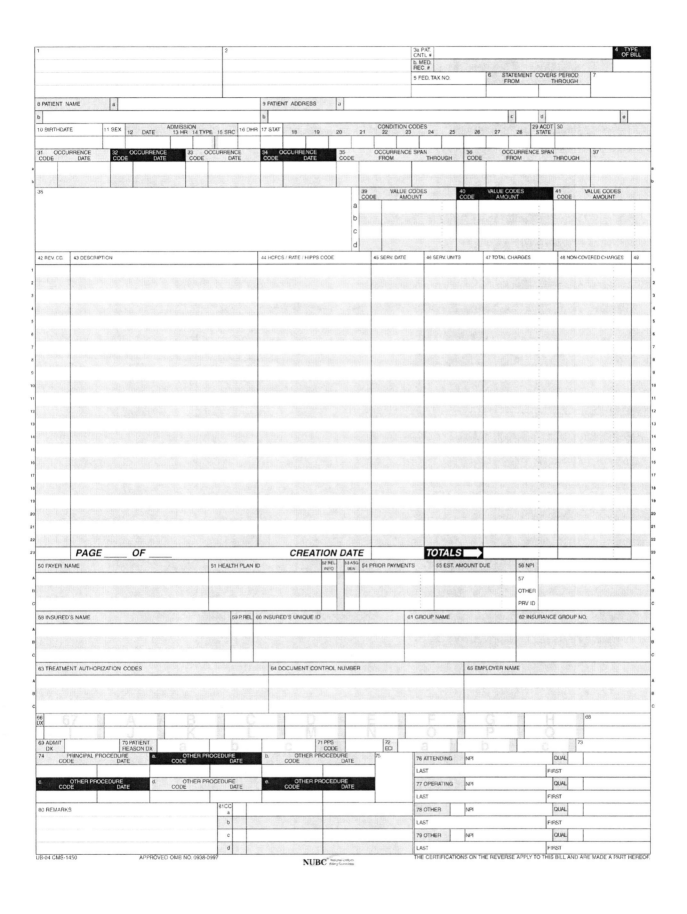

EXERCISE #4

Hospital Admittance Request Form

Today's date: 6/26/08

Name of Patient: Kelly Leejack

Patient Account Number: 626-4817

Patient Social Security Number: F00-X3-4448

Patient's Address: 4704 Chandler Lane, Wilton, OR 97032

Patient's Phone Number (Home and Work): (503) 305-5503

Patient's occupation: cook

Sex: F

Marital Status: S

Primary Insurance Company Name and Address: Food Service Employees Insurance, 28 Union Lane, San Francisco, CA 30341

Primary Insurance Company Phone Number: (888) 777-1241

Employer: A Big Hamburger Joint

Employer Address and Phone Number: 621 A Street, Bend, OR 83701

Subscriber/Relationship: Self

Subscriber ID#: 3334413689

Subscriber DOB: 1/26/1962

Secondary Insurance Company Name and Address: None

Secondary Insurance Company Phone Number:

Subscriber/Relationship:

Subscriber ID#:

Subscriber DOB:

Date patient is seen (Date of Service): 6/26/08

Chief Complaint: Leg Pain

Condition on Admission: Ambulatory

Admitting Diagnosis: Leg Pain 729.5

Time Presented at Hospital: 9:12 P.M.

Time Admitted to Room: 12:16 A.M.

Room Number Assigned: 621

Name and ID# of Referring Physician: Mary Tingler, M.D. Z1122334

Hospitalization dates: 6/26/08-6/28/08

Outside lab: yes

Family Planning: no

EMG: no

COB: no

Prior Auth #: none

Disability Dates: 1/10/08–7/15/08

Date of First Injury, Illness, or Onset: 1/10/08

Place of Service: IP Hospital

Type of Service: Medical

Name and Address of Treating Physician: John Deere, M.D.

Name and Address Where Services Were Rendered: St. Luke's Hospital, 924 Church Street, Roseville, CA 92121

Physician Lic.#: Z86241

NPI Number: 555555555

Tax ID #: 94-33368

ITEMIZED LISTING

Patient Name: Kelly Leejack   Account Number: 626-4817
Admit Date: 6/26/08   Discharge Date: 6/28/08
Provider: St. Luke's Hosp.   Service Date: 6/26/08

CPT Code	Rev Code	Service Date	Description	Category	Qty	Charge (ea unit)	Total Charge
99202	510	6/26/08	Office Visit	Office Visit	1	$87.00	$87.00
Total:					1		$87.00

ITEMIZED LISTING

Patient Name: Kelly Leejack   Account Number: 626-4817
Admit Date: 6/26/08   Discharge Date: 6/28/08
Provider: St. Luke's Hosp.   Service Date: 6/17/08

CPT Code	Rev Code	Service Date	Description	Category	Qty	Charge (ea unit)	Total Charge
	270	6/27/08	Leg Lifter	Supplies	1	$50.00	$50.00
	270	6/27/08	Sock Pull	Supplies	1	$69.00	$69.00
	270	6/27/08	Reacher	Supplies	1	$99.00	$99.00
99202	510	6/27/08	Office Visit	Medicine	1	$96.00	$96.00
Total:					4		$314.00

ITEMIZED LISTING

Patient Name:	Kelly Leejack			Account Number:	626-4817		
Admit Date:	6/26/08			Discharge Date:	6/28/08		
Provider:	St. Luke's Hosp.			Service Date:	6/28/08		

CPT Code	Rev Code	Service Date	Description	Category	Qty	Charge (ea unit)	Total Charge
97799	434	6/28/08	Consult	Eval and Mgmt	1	$562.00	$562.00
Total:					1		$562.00

ITEMIZED LISTING SUMMARY TOTALS

Patient Name:	Kelly Leejack	Account Number:	626-4817
Admit Date:	6/26/08	Discharge Date:	6/28/08
Provider:	St. Luke's Hosp.	Service Date:	6/26/08

Date:	Total Charges
6/26/08	$87.00
6/27/08	$314.00
6/28/08	$562.00
Grand Totals:	$963.00

Rev Codes	Desc.	Units	Total Charges
510	Medicine	2	$183.00
270	Supplies	3	$218.00
434	Eval and Mgmt	1	$562.00
Grand Total:		6	**$963.00**

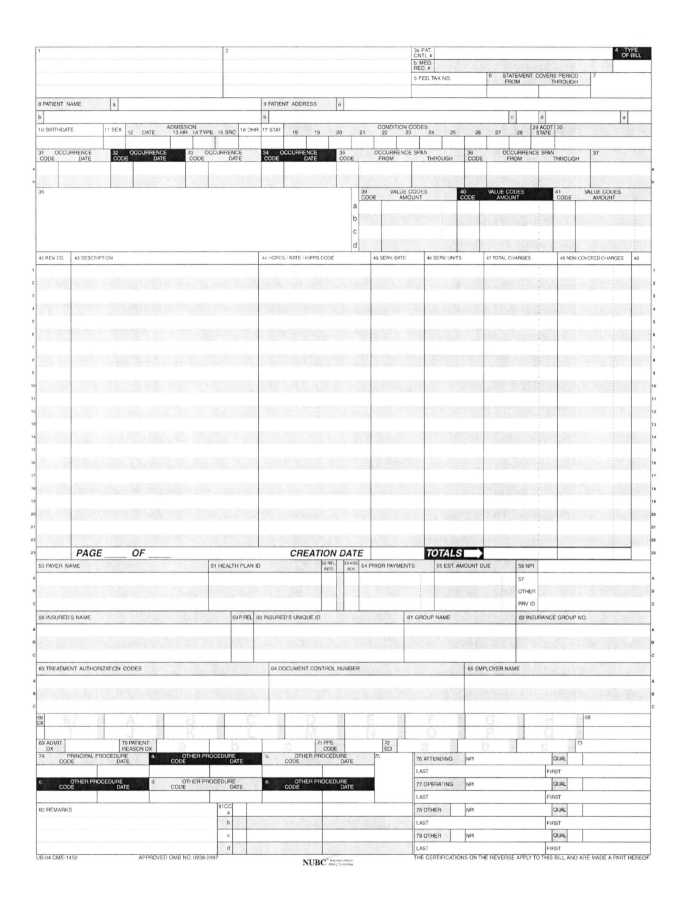

EXERCISE #5

Hospital Admittance Request Form

Today's date: 9/27/08

Name of Patient: Tim Hickory

Patient Account Number: 006-3489

Patient Social Security Number: AB6-06-060X

Patient's Address: 1439 Smith Drive, Davis, GA 30368

Patient's Phone Number (Home and Work): (308) 649-1879

Patient's Occupation: Janitor

Sex: M

Marital Status: M

Primary Insurance Company Name and Address: Blue Cross, P.O. Box 60090, Los Angeles, CA 91606

Primary Insurance Company Phone Number: (888) 379-1642

Employer: Mr. Clean-Up

Employer's Address and Phone Number: 8649 Janitor Drive, Los Angeles, CA 38901

Subscriber/Relationship: Self

Subscriber ID#: 87439621

Subscriber DOB: 9/1/1974

Secondary Insurance Company Name and Address: none

Secondary Insurance Company Phone Number:

Subscriber/Relationship:

Subscriber ID#:

Subscriber DOB:

Date Patient Is Seen (Date of Service): 9/27/08

Chief Complaint: Chest Pain

Condition on Admission: Ambulatory

Admitting Diagnosis: Kidney Failure 586; Chest Pain 786.50

Time Presented at Hospital: 10:12 P.M.

Time Admitted to Room: 1:39 A.M.

Room Number Assigned: 142

Name and ID# of Referring Physician: Mary Stoltz, M.D. Z4477589

Hospitalization Dates: 9/27/08–9/30/08

Outside Lab: yes

Family Planning: no

EMG: no

COB: no

Prior Auth #: none

Disability dates: 9/27/08–10/15/08

Date of first Injury, Illness, or Onset: 9/15/08

Place of Service: IP Hospital

Type of Service: Medical

Name and Address of Treating Physician: John Tyler, M.D.

Name and Address Where Services Were Rendered: Tyler Medical Center, 143 Tyler Road, Tyler, TX 78411

Physician Lic#: Z9876421

NPI Number: 666666666

Tax ID #: 94-883629

ITEMIZED LISTING

Patient Name: Tim Hickory   Account Number: 006-34892
Admit Date: 9/27/08   Discharge Date: 9/30/08
Provider: Tyler Med Center   Service Date: 9/27/08

CPT Code	Rev Code	Service Date	Description	Category	Qty	Charge (ea unit)	Total Charge
85730	305	9/27/08	Thromboplastin time	Lab	2	$268.00	$536.00
82565	301	9/27/08	Creatine, blood	Lab	18	$38.50	$693.00
85651	305	9/27/08	Sedimentationrate	Lab	6	$238.50	$1431.00
Total:					26		$2,660.00

ITEMIZED LISTING

Patient Name: Tim Hickory   Account Number: 006-34892
Admit Date: 9/27/08   Discharge Date: 9/30/08
Provider: Tyler Med Center   Service Date: 9/28/08

CPT Code	Rev Code	Service Date	Description	Category	Qty	Charge (ea unit)	Total Charge
82040	301	9/28/08	AlbuminSerum	Lab	1	$310.00	$310.00
85025	305	9/28/08	Platelet Count	Lab	1	$181.00	$181.00
94760	460	9/28/08	Pulseoximetry	Medicine	1	$64.50	$64.50
Total:					3		$555.50

ITEMIZED LISTING

Patient Name:	Tim Hickory	Account Number:	006-34892
Admit Date:	9/27/08	Discharge Date:	9/30/08
Provider:	Tyler Med Center	Service Date:	9/29/08

CPT Code	Rev Code	Service Date	Description	Category	Qty	Charge (ea unit)	Total Charge
99070	250	9/29/08	Drugs	Misc. Drugs	6	$28.00	$168.00
99070	258	9/29/08	IV Drugs	IV Drugs	16	$35.00	$560.00
71020	324	9/29/08	X-ray Chest 2 views	Radiology	4	$492.00	$1968.00
94640	410	9/29/08	Inhalation Treatment	Medicine	1	$62.50	$62.50
93005	730	9/29/08	ECG Tracing	Medicine	1	$146.00	$146.00
Total:					28		$2,904.50

ITEMIZED LISTING

Patient Name:	Tim Hickory	Account Number:	006-34892
Admit Date:	9/27/08	Discharge Date:	9/30/08
Provider:	Tyler Med Center	Service Date:	9/30/08

CPT Code	Rev Code	Service Date	Description	Category	Qty	Charge (ea unit)	Total Charge
C1733	272	9/30/08	Ocular Implant	Medicine	1	$1125.00	$1125.00
82374	301	9/30/08	Carbon Monoxide	Lab	1	$34.00	$34.00
82435	301	9/30/08	Chloride Blood	Lab	6	$35.00	$210.00
85027	305	9/30/08	Platelet Count	Lab	1	$147.00	$147.00
	710	9/30/08	Recovery Room	Medicine	12	$190.00	$2280.00
Total:					21		$3,796.00

Itemized Listing Summary Totals

Patient Name:	Tim Hickory	Account Number:	006-34892
Admit Date:	9/27/08	Discharge Date:	9/30/08
Provider:	Tyler Med Center	Service Date:	9/27/08

Date:	Total Charges
9/27/08	$2,660.00
9/28/08	$555.50
9/29/08	$2,904.50
9/30/08	$3,796.00
Grand Totals:	$9,916.00

Rev Codes	Desc.	Units	Total Charges
301	Lab	26	$1,247.00
305	Path and Lab	10	$2,295.00
460	Medicine	1	$64.50
250	IP Drugs	6	$168.00
258	IP Narcotics	16	$560.00
324	Radiology	4	$1,968.00
410	Medicine	1	$62.50
730	Medicine	1	$146.00
272	Medicine	1	$1,125.00
710	Medicine	12	$2,280.00
Grand Total:		78	$9,916.00

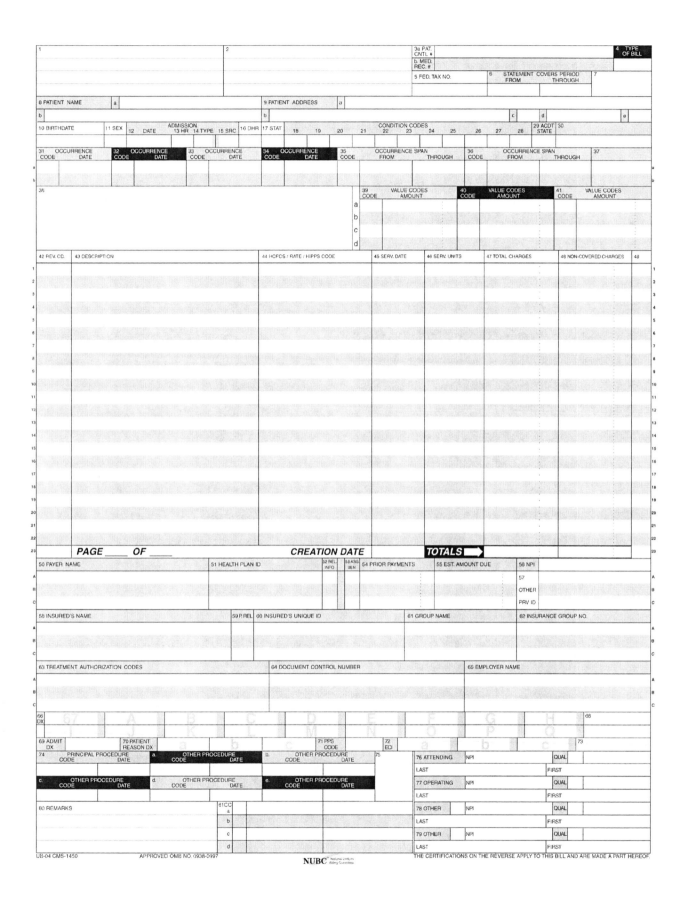

EXERCISE #6

Hospital Admittance Request Form

Today's date: 2/14/08

Name of Patient: Christine Nomad

Patient Account Number: 434

Patient Social Security Number: 345-D7-89G0

Patient's address: 142 Slolam Lane, Houston, LA 44309

Patient's Phone Number (Home and Work): (032) 143-6189

Patient's Occupation: Nurse

Sex: F

Marital Status: M

Primary Insurance Company Name and Address: Blue Shield, P.O. Box 439, Amhurst, LA 39841

Primary Insurance Company Phone Number: (800) 642-1689

Employer: ABC Healthcare

Employer Address and Phone Number: 389 Nurse Lane, Waco, TX 33333

Subscriber/Relationship: Self

Subscriber ID#: 4343434

Subscriber DOB: 1/12/1952

Secondary Insurance Company Name and Address: None

Secondary Insurance Company Phone Number:

Subscriber/Relationship:

Subscriber ID#:

Subscriber DOB:

Date Patient Is Seen (Date of Service): 2/14/08

Chief Complaint: Leg Pain

Condition on Admission: Non-ambulatory

Admitting Diagnosis: Phlebitis 451.2

Time Presented at Hospital: 9:03 A.M.

Time Admitted to Room: 2:57 P.M.

Room Number Assigned: 1216

Name and ID# of Referring Physician: Tyler Jake, M.D. Z0000321

Hospitalization Dates: 2/14/08-2/17/08

Outside Lab: yes

Family Planning: no

EMG: no

COB: no

Prior Auth #: 4389712K

Disability Dates: 2/14/08-2/17/08

Date of First Injury, Illness, or Onset: 2/12/08

Place of Service: IP Hospital

Type of Service: Medical

Name and Address of Treating Physician: John Jakinson, M.D.

Name and Address Where Services Were Rendered: Community Hospital, 423 Hospital Lane, Waco, TX 32143

Physician Lic.#: Z65132

NPI Number: 777777777

Tax ID #: 94-44493

ITEMIZED LISTING

Patient Name: Christine Nomad   Account Number: 434
Admit Date: 2/14/08   Discharge Date: 2/17/08
Provider: Community Hosp   Service Date: 2/14/08

CPT Code	Rev Code	Service Date	Description	Category	Qty	Charge (ea unit)	Total Charge
97116	420	2/14/08	Gait Training	Medicine	2	$468.00	$936.00
97530	420	2/14/08	Kinetic Activity	Medicine	1	$328.00	$328.00
Total:					3		$1,264.00

ITEMIZED LISTING

Patient Name: Christine Nomad   Account Number: 434
Admit Date: 2/14/08   Discharge Date: 2/17/08
Provider: Community Hosp.   Service Date: 2/15/08

CPT Code	Rev Code	Service Date	Description	Category	Qty	Charge (ea unit)	Total Charge
	121	2/15/08	Room Charge	Room and Board	1	$3997.00	$3997.00
99070	258	2/15/08	IV Drugs	IV Drugs	16	$48.00	$768.00
Total:					17		$4,765.00

ITEMIZED LISTING

Patient Name: Christine Nomad Account Number: 434
Admit Date: 2/14/08   Discharge Date: 2/17/08
Provider: Community Hosp.   Service Date: 2/16/08

CPT Code	Rev Code	Service Date	Description	Category	Qty	Charge (ea unit)	Total Charge
	121	2/16/08	Room Charge	Room and Board	1	$3997.00	$3997.00
99070	258	2/16/08	IV Drugs	IV Drugs	16	$48.00	$768.00
Total:					17		$4,765.00

ITEMIZED LISTING

Patient Name: Christine Nomad Account Number: 434
Admit Date: 2/14/08   Discharge Date: 2/17/08
Provider: Community Hosp.   Service Date: 2/17/08

CPT Code	Rev Code	Service Date	Description	Category	Qty	Charge (ea unit)	Total Charge
	121	2/17/08	Room Charge	Room and Board	1	$3997.00	$3997.00
99070	258	2/17/08	IV Drugs	IV Drugs	16	$48.00	$768.00
Total:					17		$4,765.00

ITEMIZED LISTING SUMMARY TOTALS

Patient Name:	Christine Nomad	Account Number:	434
Admit Date:	2/14/08	Discharge Date:	2/17/08
Provider:	Community Hosp	Service Date:	2/14/08

Date:	Total Charges
2/14/08	$1,264.00
2/15/08	$4,765.00
2/16/08	$4,765.00
2/17/08	$4,765.00
Grand Totals:	$15,559.00

Rev Codes	Desc.	Units	Total Charges
420	Physical Therapy	2	$1,264.00
121	Room and Board	3	$11,991.00
258	IV Solutions	48	$2,304.00
Grand Total:		53	$15,559.00

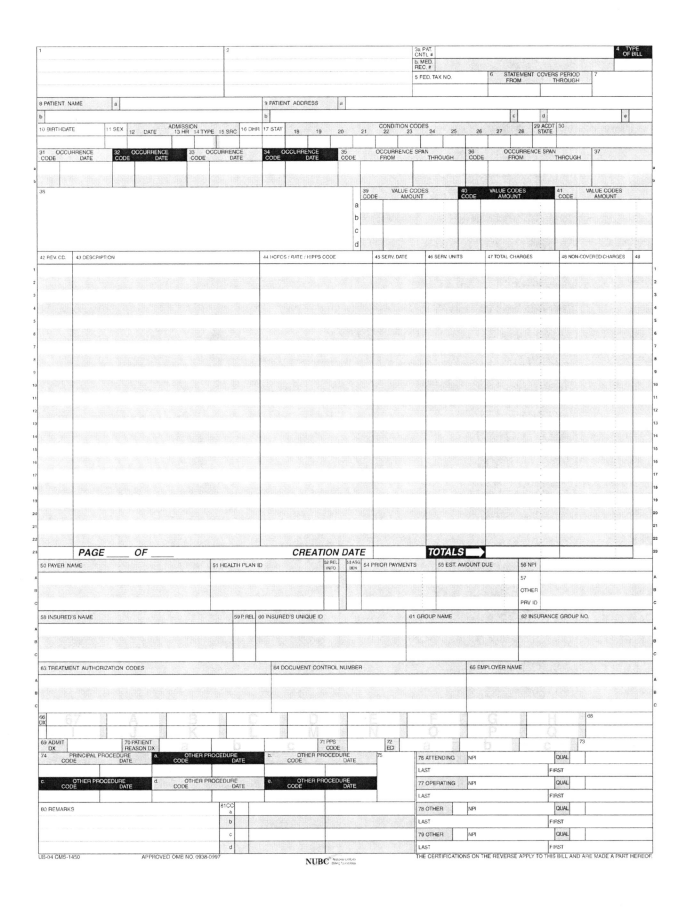

EXERCISE #7

Hospital Admittance Request Form

Today's date: 7/18/08

Name of Patient: Petunia Potter

Patient Account Number: 001-389

Patient Social Security Number: 00Q-33-V967

Patient's Address: 111 Flower Lane, Citrus Heights, CA 21039

Patient's Phone Number (Home and Work): (831) 318-8813

Patient's Occupation: Florist

Sex: F

Marital Status: S

Primary Insurance Company Name and Address: Gardner's Insurance, 12340 Flower Lane, Gladiola, NJ 20000

Primary Insurance Company Phone Number: (800) 877-7162

Employer: Rose Flowers

Employer's Address and Phone Number: 112 Garden Hwy, Waco, TX 20163

Subscriber/Relationship: Self

Subscriber ID#: 1389216

Subscriber DOB: 2/14/1943

Secondary Insurance Company Name and Address: None

Secondary Insurance Company Phone Number:

Subscriber/Relationship:

Subscriber ID#:

Subscriber DOB:

Date Patient Is Seen (Date of Service): 7/18/08

Chief Complaint: Asthma

Condition on Admission: Ambulatory

Admitting Diagnosis: Asthma with Acute Exacerbation 493.92

Time Presented at Hospital: 8:41 P.M.

Time Admitted to Room: 8:59 P.M.

Room Number Assigned: 1439

Name and ID# of Referring Physician: Mary Jo Jeans, M.D. Z8888690

Hospitalization Dates: 7/18/08–7/21/08

Outside Lab: yes

Family Planning: no

EMG: no

COB: no

Prior Auth #: 421

Disability Dates: 7/18/08–7/25/08

Date of First Injury, Illness, or Onset: 7/18/08

Place of Service: IP Hospital

Type of Service: Medical

Name and Address of Treating Physician: David Stockholm, M.D.

Name and Address Where Services Were Rendered: Our Lady of Love Hospital, 13892 Catholic Lane, Citrus Heights, CA 98341

Physician Lic#: Z31187902

NPI Number: 888888888

Tax ID #: 94-7776321

ITEMIZED LISTING

Patient Name: Petunia Potter   Account Number: 001-389
Admit Date: 7/18/08   Discharge Date: 7/21/08
Provider: Our Lady of Love   Service Date: 7/18/08

CPT Code	Rev Code	Service Date	Description	Category	Qty	Charge (ea unit)	Total Charge
	206	7/18/08	Room Charge	Room and Board	1	$5900.00	$5900.00
99070	250	7/18/08	Drugs	Drugs	16	$16.00	$256.00
99070	258	7/18/08	IV Drugs	IV Drugs	3	$158.00	$474.00
Total:					20		$6,630.00

ITEMIZED LISTING

Patient Name: Petunia Potter   Account Number: 001-389
Admit Date: 7/18/08   Discharge Date: 7/21/08
Provider: Our Lady of Love   Service Date: 7/19/08

CPT Code	Rev Code	Service Date	Description	Category	Qty	Charge (ea unit)	Total Charge
	206	7/19/08	Room Charge	Room and Board	1	$5900.00	$5900.00
99070	258	7/19/08	IV Drugs	IV Drugs	3	$158.00	$158.00
Total:					4		$6,374.00

ITEMIZED LISTING

Patient Name: Petunia Potter   Account Number: 001-389
Admit Date: 7/18/08   Discharge Date: 7/21/08
Provider: Our Lady of Love   Service Date: 7/20/08

CPT Code	Rev Code	Service Date	Description	Category	Qty	Charge (ea unit)	Total Charge
	206	7/20/08	Room Charge	Room and Board	1	$5900.00	$5900.00
99070	258	7/20/08	IV Drugs	IV Drugs	3	$158.00	$158.00
Total:					4		$6,374.00

ITEMIZED LISTING

Patient Name: Petunia Potter   Account Number: 001-389
Admit Date: 7/18/08   Discharge Date: 7/21/08
Provider: Our Lady of Love   Service Date: 7/21/08

CPT Code	Rev Code	Service Date	Description	Category	Qty	Charge (ea unit)	Total Charge
	206	7/21/08	Room Charge	Room and Board	1	$5900.00	$5900.00
99070	258	7/21/08	IV Drugs	IV Drugs	3	$158.00	$474.00
Total:					4		$6,374.00

Itemized Listing Summary Totals

Patient Name:	Petunia Potter	Account Number:	001-389
Admit Date:	7/18/08	Discharge Date:	7/21/08
Provider:	Our Lady of Love	Service Date:	7/21/08

Date:	Total Charges
7/18/08	$6,630.00
7/19/08	$6,374.00
7/20/08	$6,374.00
7/21/08	$6,374.00
Grand Totals:	**$25,752.00**

Rev Codes	Desc.	Units	Total Charges
206	Intermediate ICU Room	4	$23,600.00
250	Pharmacy	16	$256.00
258	IV Solutions	12	$1,896.00
Grand Total:		32	$25,752.00

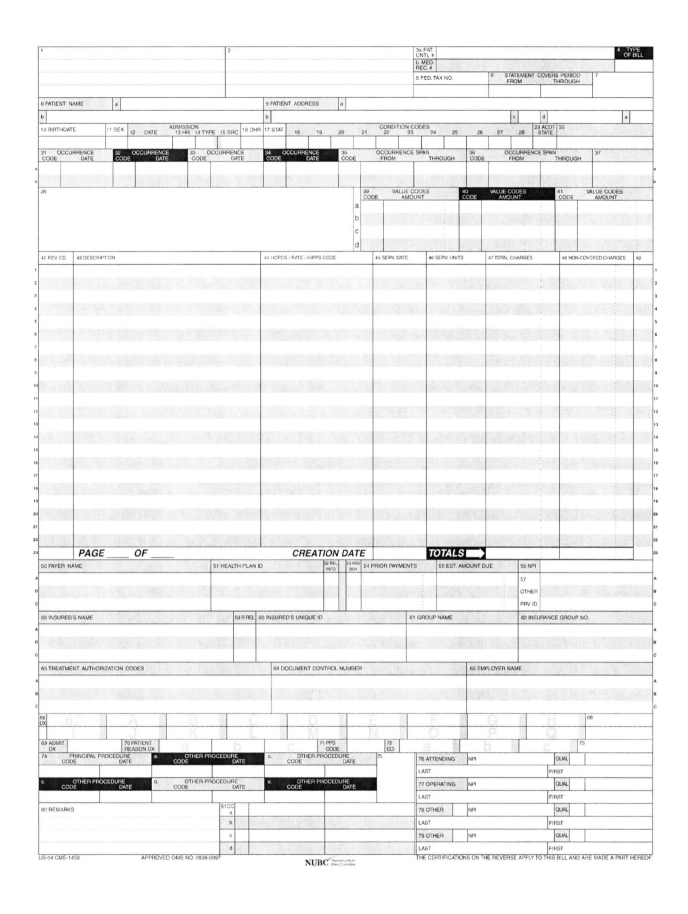

1 ABC Hospital 1234 Main Street Fairfield, CA 96341	2 ABC Hospital 1234 Main Street Fairfield, CA 96341	3a PAT. CNTL # 006-03462 4 TYPE OF BILL 111 b. MED. REC. # 5 FED. TAX NO. 94-1111111 6 STATEMENT COVERS PERIOD FROM 11/21/08 THROUGH 11/21/08 7

8 PATIENT NAME Smith, Mary   9 PATIENT ADDRESS 1698 Ivoryton Way, Sac., CA 95820

10 BIRTHDATE 12/01/64 11 SEX F 12 DATE 11/21/08 13 HR 22 14 TYPE 01

38 Healthnet
P.O. Box 100
Rancho Cordova, CA 96666

42 REV. CD.	43 DESCRIPTION	44 HCPCS/RATE/HIPPS CODE	45 SERV. DATE	46 SERV. UNITS	47 TOTAL CHARGES	48 NON-COVERED CHARGES
312	Pathology and Lab			003	134.40	
301	Lab			001	28.00	
305	Lab			003	568.00	
424	Medicine			001	238.50	
250	IP Drugs			003	240.00	

PAGE 1 OF 1   CREATION DATE 12/31/08   TOTALS 1208.90

50 PAYER NAME	51 HEALTH PLAN ID	52 REL INFO	53 ASG BEN	54 PRIOR PAYMENTS	55 EST AMOUNT DUE	56 NPI
Healthnet			Y	00.00	1208.90	57 OTHER PRV ID

58 INSURED'S NAME Mary Smith 59 P.REL 01 60 INSURED'S UNIQUE ID 138742-006 61 GROUP NAME Sunrise AM Gas 62 INSURANCE GROUP NO

63 TREATMENT AUTHORIZATION CODES   64 DOCUMENT CONTROL NUMBER   65 EMPLOYER NAME Sunrise AM Gas

66 DX 724.2 780.4   68

69 ADMIT DX 724.2 70 PATIENT REASON DX 71 PPS CODE 72 ECI 73

76 ATTENDING NPI 123333344 QUAL CAZ30184 LAST Goody FIRST John

80 REMARKS Itemized Listing Attached

UB-04 CMS-1450   OMB APPROVAL PENDING   NUBC   © 2005 NUBC

F245-367-000

1 Main Hospital 1241 O Street Fresno, CA 92161	2 Main Hospital 1241 O Street Fresno, CA 32161		3a PAT CNTL # 348-164 b MED REC #		4 TYPE OF BILL 111
			5 FED. TAX NO. 94-2222226	6 STATEMENT COVERS PERIOD FROM 12/21/08 THROUGH 12/21/08	

8 PATIENT NAME a Bean, Jean II	9 PATIENT ADDRESS a 1675 Drive Way, Oakville, NV 89528

| 10 BIRTHDATE 07/18/1943 | 11 SEX M | 12 DATE 12/21/08 | 13 HR 06 | 14 TYPE 01 | CONDITION CODES | 29 ACDT STATE | 30 |

| 31 OCCURRENCE | 32 OCCURRENCE | 33 OCCURRENCE | 34 OCCURRENCE | 35 OCCURRENCE SPAN | 36 OCCURRENCE SPAN | 37 |

| 38 Truckers Insurance
118 Big Truck Way
Fallon, NV 38711 | 39 VALUE CODES | 40 VALUE CODES | 41 VALUE CODES |

42 REV. CD	43 DESCRIPTION	44 HCPCS / RATE / HIPPS CODE	45 SERV. DATE	46 SERV. UNITS	47 TOTAL CHARGES	48 NON-COVERED CHARGES
320	Radiology			003	1227.50	
250	IP Drugs			018	504.00	
730	Medicine			002	92.00	
450	ER Visit			001	3126.00	
351	Radiology			001	321.00	

PAGE 1 OF 1   CREATION DATE 12/31/08   TOTALS ➡ 5270.50

50 PAYER NAME	51 HEALTH PLAN ID	52	53	54 PRIOR PAYMENTS	55 EST. AMOUNT DUE	56 NPI 333333333
Truckers Insurance			Y	00.00	5270.50	57 OTHER PRV ID

| 58 INSURED'S NAME Jean Bean II | 59 P.REL 01 | 60 INSURED'S UNIQUE ID 0387911622 | 61 GROUP NAME Safe Trucking | 62 INSURANCE GROUP NO |

| 63 TREATMENT AUTHORIZATION CODES | 64 DOCUMENT CONTROL NUMBER | 65 EMPLOYER NAME Safe Trucking |

| 66 DX 850.9 | 821.0 | 68 |

| 69 ADMIT DX 850.9 | 70 PATIENT REASON DX | 71 PPS CODE | 72 ECI | 73 |

74 PRINCIPAL PROCEDURE	OTHER PROCEDURE	OTHER PROCEDURE	75	76 ATTENDING NPI 112233445	QUAL CAZ34167
				LAST James FIRST Jerry	
OTHER PROCEDURE	OTHER PROCEDURE	OTHER PROCEDURE		77 OPERATING NPI	QUAL
				LAST FIRST	

| 80 REMARKS
Itemized Listing attached
ER Report attached | 81CC a / b / c / d | 78 OTHER NPI LAST FIRST |
| | | 79 OTHER NPI LAST FIRST |

UB-04 CMS-1450 © 2005 NUBC   OMB APPROVAL PENDING   NUBC LIC9213257   THE CERTIFICATIONS ON THE REVERSE APPLY TO THIS BILL AND ARE MADE A PART HEREOF

F245-367-000

Main Street Hospital 123 Main Street Ontario, OR 97831	Main Street Hospital 123 Main Street Ontario, OR 97831	3a PAT. CNTL # 63187-221	4 TYPE OF BILL
		b. MED. REC. #	111
		5 FED. TAX NO. 94-3333334	6 STATEMENT COVERS PERIOD FROM 01/01/08 THROUGH 01/01/08	7

8 PATIENT NAME	a	James, Chris	9 PATIENT ADDRESS	a	8901 Oak Ridge Street, Elk Grove, CA 83741
b			b		

10 BIRTHDATE	11 SEX	12 DATE	ADMISSION 13 HR	14 TYPE	15 SRC	16 DHR	17 STAT	18	19	20	21	CONDITION CODES 22 23 24 25 26 27 28	29 ACDT STATE	30
09/26/86	M	01/01/08		04	01									

31 OCCURRENCE CODE DATE	32 OCCURRENCE CODE DATE	33 OCCURRENCE CODE DATE	34 OCCURRENCE CODE DATE	35 OCCURRENCE SPAN CODE FROM THROUGH	36 OCCURRENCE SPAN CODE FROM THROUGH	37

38	39 VALUE CODES CODE AMOUNT	40 VALUE CODES CODE AMOUNT	41 VALUE CODES CODE AMOUNT
Student Health Insurance 1642 College Lane Stockton, CA 97209	a b c d		

42 REV. CD.	43 DESCRIPTION	44 HCPCS / RATE / HIPPS CODE	45 SERV. DATE	46 SERV. UNITS	47 TOTAL CHARGES	48 NON-COVERED CHARGES	49
250	IP Drugs			006	6.00		
258	IP Narcotics			003	93.00		
450	ER Visit			001	869.00		
424	Medicine			001	198.00		
312	Pathology and Lab			002	183.00		
510	Clinic Visit			001	115.00		

PAGE 1 OF 1   CREATION DATE 12/31/08   TOTALS ⟹   1464.00

50 PAYER NAME	51 HEALTH PLAN ID	52 REL INFO	53 ASG BEN	54 PRIOR PAYMENTS	55 EST. AMOUNT DUE	56 NPI 444444444
Student Health Insurance			Y	0.00	1464.00	57 OTHER PRV ID

58 INSURED'S NAME	59 P.REL	60 INSURED'S UNIQUE ID	61 GROUP NAME	62 INSURANCE GROUP NO.
James, Chris	01	1111111		

63 TREATMENT AUTHORIZATION CODES	64 DOCUMENT CONTROL NUMBER	65 EMPLOYER NAME
43874126AZ142		

66 DX 977.9						68

69 ADMIT DX 977.9	70 PATIENT REASON DX	71 PPS CODE	72 ECI	73

74 PRINCIPAL PROCEDURE CODE DATE	a. OTHER PROCEDURE CODE DATE	b. OTHER PROCEDURE CODE DATE	75	76 ATTENDING NPI 888776666	QUAL CAZ63891
				LAST Jones	FIRST Bethany
c. OTHER PROCEDURE CODE DATE	d. OTHER PROCEDURE CODE DATE	e. OTHER PROCEDURE CODE DATE		77 OPERATING NPI	QUAL
				LAST	FIRST

80 REMARKS	81CC a	78 OTHER NPI	QUAL
Itemized Listing Attached ER Report Attached	b c d	LAST 79 OTHER NPI LAST	FIRST QUAL FIRST

UB-04 CMS-1450
© 2005 NUBC   OMB APPROVAL PENDING   NUBC   LIC9210257   THE CERTIFICATIONS ON THE REVERSE APPLY TO THIS BILL AND ARE MADE A PART HEREOF.

F245-367-000

1 St. Luke's Hospital 924 Church Street Roseville, CA 92121	2 St. Luke's Hospital 924 Church Street Roseville, CA 92121		3a PAT CNTL # 626-4817 b MED. REC. #		4 TYPE OF BILL 131
		5 FED. TAX NO. 94-3333368	6 STATEMENT COVERS PERIOD FROM 06/26/08 THROUGH 06/26/08		7

8 PATIENT NAME a Leejack, Kelly	9 PATIENT ADDRESS a 4704 Chandler Ln, Wilton, OR97032				
b	b		c	d	e

| 10 BIRTHDATE 01/26/62 | 11 SEX F | 12 DATE 06/26/08 | ADMISSION 13 HR 09 14 TYPE 01 15 SRC | 16 DHR 17 STAT | 18 19 20 21 CONDITION CODES 22 23 24 25 26 27 28 | 29 ACDT STATE | 30 |

31 OCCURRENCE CODE DATE	32 OCCURRENCE CODE DATE	33 OCCURRENCE CODE DATE	34 OCCURRENCE CODE DATE	35 OCCURRENCE CODE	OCCURRENCE SPAN FROM THROUGH	36 CODE	OCCURRENCE SPAN FROM THROUGH	37
a								
b								

38 Food Service Employees Insurance 28 Union Lane San Francisco, CA 30341		39 CODE VALUE CODES AMOUNT	40 CODE VALUE CODES AMOUNT	41 CODE VALUE CODES AMOUNT
	a			
	b			
	c			
	d			

42 REV. CD.	43 DESCRIPTION	44 HCPCS / RATE / HIPPS CODE	45 SERV. DATE	46 SERV. UNITS	47 TOTAL CHARGES	48 NON-COVERED CHARGES	49
510	Medicine	99202	06/26/08	001	87.00		1
270	Supplies		06/26/08	003	218.00		2
510	Medicine	99202	06/26/08	001	96.00		3
434	Medicine	97799	06/26/08	001	562.00		4

PAGE 1 OF 1	CREATION DATE 12/31/08	TOTALS ➡	963.00	23

50 PAYER NAME	51 HEALTH PLAN ID	52 REL INFO	53 ASG BEN	54 PRIOR PAYMENTS	55 EST. AMOUNT DUE	56 NPI 555555555	
A Food Svc Emp Insurance			Y	00.00	963.00	57 OTHER PRV ID	A
B							B
C							C

58 INSURED'S NAME	59 P.REL	60 INSURED'S UNIQUE ID	61 GROUP NAME	62 INSURANCE GROUP NO	
A Kelly Leejack	01	3334413689	A Big Hamb Joint		A
B					B
C					C

63 TREATMENT AUTHORIZATION CODES	64 DOCUMENT CONTROL NUMBER	65 EMPLOYER NAME	
A		A Big Hamb Joint	A
B			B
C			C

66 DX 729.5						68

69 ADMIT DX 729.5	70 PATIENT REASON DX			71 PPS CODE	72 ECI		73

74 PRINCIPAL PROCEDURE CODE DATE	a. OTHER PROCEDURE CODE DATE	b. OTHER PROCEDURE CODE DATE	75	76 ATTENDING NPI 993311111	QUAL CAZ86241
c. OTHER PROCEDURE CODE DATE	d. OTHER PROCEDURE CODE DATE	e. OTHER PROCEDURE CODE DATE		LAST Deere	FIRST John
				77 OPERATING NPI	QUAL
				LAST	FIRST

80 REMARKS Itemized Listing Attached	81CC a		78 OTHER NPI	QUAL
	b		LAST	FIRST
	c		79 OTHER NPI	QUAL
	d		LAST	FIRST

UB-04 CMS-1450   © 2006 NUBC   OMB APPROVAL PENDING   NUBC™ National Uniform Billing Committee LIC9213257   THE CERTIFICATIONS ON THE REVERSE APPLY TO THIS BILL AND ARE MADE A PART HEREOF.

F245-367-000

Tyler Medical Center 143 Tyler Road Tyler, TX 78411	Tyler Medical Center 143 Tyler Road Tyler, TX 78411		3a PAT CNTL # 006-34892 b. MED REC # 5 FED. TAX NO. 94-883629	4 TYPE OF BILL 111 6 STATEMENT COVERS PERIOD FROM 09/27/08 THROUGH 09/27/08

8 PATIENT NAME a Hickory, Timothy	9 PATIENT ADDRESS a 1439 Smith Dr., Davis, CA 30368

10 BIRTHDATE 09/01/74	11 SEX M	12 DATE 09/27/08	ADMISSION 13 HR 10 14 TYPE 01 15 SRC	16 DHR	17 STAT	18 19 20 21	CONDITION CODES 22 23 24 25 26 27 28	29 ACCT STATE	30

31 OCCURRENCE CODE DATE	32 OCCURRENCE CODE DATE	33 OCCURRENCE CODE DATE	34 OCCURRENCE CODE DATE	35 OCCURRENCE SPAN CODE FROM THROUGH	36 OCCURRENCE SPAN CODE FROM THROUGH	37

38 Blue Cross P.O. Box 60090 Los Angeles, CA 91606	39 CODE VALUE CODES AMOUNT	40 CODE VALUE CODES AMOUNT	41 CODE VALUE CODES AMOUNT

	42 REV. CD.	43 DESCRIPTION	44 HCPCS / RATE / HIPPS CODE	45 SERV. DATE	46 SERV. UNITS	47 TOTAL CHARGES	48 NON-COVERED CHARGES	49
1	301	Lab			026	1247.00		
2	305	Pathology and Lab			010	2295.00		
3	460	Medicine			001	64.50		
4	250	IP Drugs			006	168.00		
5	258	IP Narcotics			016	560.00		
6	324	Radiology			004	1968.00		
7	410	Medicine			001	62.50		
8	730	Medicine			001	146.00		
9	272	Medicine			001	1125.00		
10	710	Medicine			012	2280.00		

PAGE 1 OF 1	CREATION DATE 12/31/08	TOTALS ⇒	9916.00

50 PAYER NAME	51 HEALTH PLAN ID	52 REL INFO	53 ASG BEN	54 PRIOR PAYMENTS	55 EST AMOUNT DUE	56 NPI 666666666
A Blue Cross			Y	00.00	9916.00	57 OTHER PRV ID
B						
C						

58 INSURED'S NAME	59 P.REL	60 INSURED'S UNIQUE ID	61 GROUP NAME	62 INSURANCE GROUP NO
A Timothy Hickory	01	87439621	Mr. Clean-Up	

63 TREATMENT AUTHORIZATION CODES	64 DOCUMENT CONTROL NUMBER	65 EMPLOYER NAME
		Mr. Clean-Up

66 DX 586	786.50							68

69 ADMIT DX 586	70 PATIENT REASON DX	71 PPS CODE	72 ECI	73

74 PRINCIPAL PROCEDURE CODE DATE	a. OTHER PROCEDURE CODE DATE	b. OTHER PROCEDURE CODE DATE	75	76 ATTENDING NPI 121212121 QUAL CAZ9876421
c. OTHER PROCEDURE CODE DATE	d. OTHER PROCEDURE CODE DATE	e. OTHER PROCEDURE CODE DATE		LAST Tyler FIRST John
				77 OPERATING NPI QUAL
				LAST FIRST

80 REMARKS	81CC a	78 OTHER NPI QUAL
Itemized Listing Attached	b	LAST FIRST
	c	79 OTHER NPI QUAL
	d	LAST FIRST

UB-04 CMS-1450
© 2005 NUBC   OMB APPROVAL PENDING   NUBC National Uniform Billing Committee LIC9213257   THE CERTIFICATIONS ON THE REVERSE APPLY TO THIS BILL AND ARE MADE A PART HEREOF

F245-367-000

				3a PAT CNTL # 434		4 TYPE OF BILL
1 Community Hospital 423 Hospital Lane Waco, TX 32143	2 Community Hospital 423 Hospital Lane Waco, TX 32143			b. MED. REC. #		111
				5 FED. TAX NO. 94-4444493	6 STATEMENT COVERS PERIOD FROM 02/14/08 THROUGH 02/14/08	7

8 PATIENT NAME	a	Nomad, Christine	9 PATIENT ADDRESS	a 142 Slolam Lane, Houston, TX 44309		c	d	e
b			b					

10 BIRTHDATE	11 SEX	12 DATE	ADMISSION 13 HR	14 TYPE	15 SRC	16 DHR	17 STAT	18	19	20	21	CONDITION CODES 22	23	24	25	26	27	28	29 ACDT STATE	30
01/12/52	F	02/14/08	09	01																

31 OCCURRENCE CODE DATE	32 OCCURRENCE CODE DATE	33 OCCURRENCE CODE DATE	34 OCCURRENCE CODE DATE	35 OCCURRENCE SPAN CODE FROM THROUGH	36 OCCURRENCE SPAN CODE FROM THROUGH	37
a						
b						

38	39 VALUE CODES CODE AMOUNT	40 VALUE CODES CODE AMOUNT	41 VALUE CODES CODE AMOUNT
Blue Shield P.O. Box 439 Amhurst, LA 39841	a		
	b		
	c		
	d		

42 REV. CD.	43 DESCRIPTION	44 HCPCS / RATE / HIPPS CODE	45 SERV. DATE	46 SERV. UNITS	47 TOTAL CHARGES	48 NON-COVERED CHARGES	49
1 420	Medicine			002	1264.00		1
2 121	Room and Board			003	11991.00		2
3 258	IP Narcotics			048	2304.00		3
4							4
5							5
6							6
7							7
8							8
9							9
10							10
11							11
12							12
13							13
14							14
15							15
16							16
17							17
18							18
19							19
20							20
21							21
22	PAGE 1 OF 1	CREATION DATE 12/31/08	TOTALS ➡		15559.00		23

50 PAYER NAME	51 HEALTH PLAN ID	52 REL INFO	53 ASG BEN	54 PRIOR PAYMENTS	55 EST. AMOUNT DUE	56 NPI 777777777	
A Blue Shield			Y			57 OTHER PRV ID	A
B							B
C							C

58 INSURED'S NAME	59 P.REL	60 INSURED'S UNIQUE ID	61 GROUP NAME	62 INSURANCE GROUP NO.	
A Christine Nomad	01	4343434	ABC Healthcare		A
B					B
C					C

63 TREATMENT AUTHORIZATION CODES	64 DOCUMENT CONTROL NUMBER	65 EMPLOYER NAME	
A 4389712K		ABC Healthcare	A
B			B

66 DX	451.2								67

69 ADMIT DX 451.2	70 PATIENT REASON DX			71 PPS CODE	72 ECI		73
74 PRINCIPAL PROCEDURE CODE DATE	a. OTHER PROCEDURE CODE DATE	b. OTHER PROCEDURE CODE DATE	75	76 ATTENDING NPI 444552222		QUAL CAZ65132
c. OTHER PROCEDURE CODE DATE	d. OTHER PROCEDURE CODE DATE	e. OTHER PROCEDURE CODE DATE		LAST Jakinson FIRST John		
				77 OPERATING NPI	QUAL	
				LAST FIRST		

80 REMARKS	81CC a		78 OTHER NPI	QUAL
Itemized Listing Attached	b		LAST FIRST	
	c		79 OTHER NPI	QUAL
	d		LAST FIRST	

UB-04 CMS-1450
© 2005 NUBC

OMB APPROVAL PENDING

NUBC™ LIC9213257

THE CERTIFICATIONS ON THE REVERSE APPLY TO THIS BILL AND ARE MADE A PART HEREOF.

F245-367-000

1 Our Lady of Love Hospital 13892 Catholic Lane Citrus Heights, CA 98341	2 Our Lady of Love Hospital 13892 Catholic Lane Citrus Heights, Ca 98341		3a PAT CNTL # 001-389			4 TYPE OF BILL
			b MED REC. #			111
			5 FED. TAX NO. 94-7776321	6 STATEMENT COVERS PERIOD FROM 07/18/08 THROUGH 07/18/08		7

8 PATIENT NAME a Potter, Petunia	9 PATIENT ADDRESS a 111 Flower Lane, Citrus Heights, CA 21036			c	d	e
b	b					

10 BIRTHDATE	11 SEX	12 DATE	ADMISSION 13 HR	14 TYPE	15 SRC	16 DHR	17 STAT	18	19	20	21	CONDITION CODES 22 23 24 25 26 27 28	29 ACDT STATE	30
02/14/43	F	07/18/08	08	01										

31 OCCURRENCE CODE DATE	32 OCCURRENCE CODE DATE	33 OCCURRENCE CODE DATE	34 OCCURRENCE CODE DATE	35 OCCURRENCE SPAN CODE FROM THROUGH	36 OCCURRENCE SPAN CODE FROM THROUGH	37

38 Gardner's Insurance 12340 Flower Lane Gladiola, NJ 20000		39 VALUE CODES CODE AMOUNT	40 VALUE CODES CODE AMOUNT	41 VALUE CODES CODE AMOUNT
	a			
	b			
	c			
	d			

42 REV. CD.	43 DESCRIPTION	44 HCPCS / RATE / HIPPS CODE	45 SERV. DATE	46 SERV. UNITS	47 TOTAL CHARGES	48 NON-COVERED CHARGES	49
1 206	Room and Board			004	23600.00		
2 250	IP Drugs			016	256.00		
3 258	IP Narcotics			012	1896.00		

PAGE 1 OF 1   CREATION DATE 12/31/08   TOTALS ➡   22752.00

50 PAYER NAME	51 HEALTH PLAN ID	52 REL INFO	53 ASG BEN	54 PRIOR PAYMENTS	55 EST. AMOUNT DUE	56 NPI 888888888
A Gardner's Insurance			Y	0.00	25752.00	57 OTHER PRV ID
B						
C						

58 INSURED'S NAME	59 P.REL	60 INSURED'S UNIQUE ID	61 GROUP NAME	62 INSURANCE GROUP NO.
A Petunia Potter	01	13892106	Rose Flowers	
B				
C				

63 TREATMENT AUTHORIZATION CODES	64 DOCUMENT CONTROL NUMBER	65 EMPLOYER NAME
A 421		Rose Flowers
B		

66 DX 493.92								68

69 ADMIT DX 493.92	70 PATIENT REASON DX			71 PPS CODE	72 ECI		75

74 PRINCIPAL PROCEDURE CODE DATE	a. OTHER PROCEDURE CODE DATE	b. OTHER PROCEDURE CODE DATE	75	76 ATTENDING NPI 654321111	QUAL CAZ31187902
c. OTHER PROCEDURE CODE DATE	d. OTHER PROCEDURE CODE DATE	e. OTHER PROCEDURE CODE DATE		LAST Stockholm FIRST David	
				77 OPERATING NPI LAST FIRST	QUAL
80 REMARKS Itemized Listing Attached	81CC a b c d			78 OTHER NPI LAST FIRST	QUAL
				79 OTHER NPI LAST FIRST	QUAL

UB-04 CMS-1450   OMB APPROVAL PENDING   NUBC   THE CERTIFICATIONS ON THE REVERSE APPLY TO THIS BILL AND ARE MADE A PART HEREOF
© 2005 NUBC   LIC9213257

F245-367-000

REVIEW

Let's take a brief review of which forms would be appropriate to use under what circumstances.

1. You work for a single physician's office. A patient comes in for an office visit and you are billing for professional services.

    Will you use a UB-04 or HCFA-1500?

2. You work for an independent lab. A sample is sent to you from an independent physician's office for processing. You are billing for the physician on staff at the lab to diagnose from the test results as a consult. You are billing for professional services.

    Will you use a UB-04 or HCFA-1500?

3. You work for a skilled nursing facility. You are billing for long-term room and board care for the residents. There are no professional fees involved. You are billing for facility charges involved in running the home.

    Will you use a UB-04 or HCFA-1500?

4. You work for an outpatient clinic owned and operated by a major hospital. You are billing for clinic fees for the use of the facility. There are no professional fees involved.

    Will you use a UB-04 or HCFA-1500?

5. You work for a multi-physician group. You work in a private office and bill for physician's professional services within the office.

    Will you use a UB-04 or HCFA-1500?

6. You work for a radiology group. You bill for professional fees for the radiologist on staff to read the results of the X-rays and report back to the primary care physician.

    Will you use a UB-04 or HCFA-1500?

(See answers in Section V)

For additional exercises, please see the Medical Billing, Coding, and Reimbursement Supplemental Workbook.

RUNNING YOUR OWN HOME MEDICAL BILLING SERVICE

Setting Up an Office

In setting up an office, very little equipment is required, beyond a few basics. One of the most frequent questions that I receive is, "What equipment do I need to start?" The answer is simple.

To begin your home office, the basics are these:

1. A computer. Make sure that it is not an antiquated dinosaur that was handed down to you from Aunt Mildred when she bought a new one for Christmas last year. Since it will be your primary piece of equipment and the one that will hold all the essential information for you and your clients, it needs to be an up-to-date and reliable piece of equipment. It also needs to be able to meet the technical requirements of the software you will purchase. A sufficient amount of memory and hard drive space are crucial to the direct success of your business, so don't skimp here. You are certainly able to take an older computer and upgrade it if you need to. Simply bring your computer in to any reputable computer shop with a list of the technical requirements of your software package and let them upgrade the system for you. This is usually a minimal cost and well worth the investment.

2. Your software package will be your biggest initial investment. Investigation and some good shopping skills will be required here, in order to determine which software package is best for you and how much you will pay. Just like in any other retail business, different retailers can sell the same product for different prices, depending on mark-up. After determining what your specific needs are and shopping around for the best price, your software company should be able to send you a demonstration program along with complete system requirement information. This can help you determine not only how much you will spend on the billing package but how much you will need to put into your own computer for these applications to run appropriately.

In addition to the computer, the software package will probably recommend a specific form of information back-up. This is absolutely mandatory. Your information must be protected from all possible damage of any kind. Daily back-ups are absolutely required in order to protect your income as well as your clients. Make sure you purchase something that is recommended by your manufacturer. The program that I used came with a recommendation for a specific type of external tape drive back-up. When I asked why this more expensive back-up program was needed, they explained that if anything were to go wrong with my program I could simply overnight express a back-up tape to them. They would fix it and overnight it back. That way my business was guaranteed not to be down for more than two days. When this scenario actually came about, I was glad I had purchased the required equipment. It saved me a lot of headaches and money down the road.

Also, while we are all normally protected from break-ins and fires, we need to think about computer protection as well. If you have an Internet connection of any kind, you are subject to hackers. Firewall protection (keeping others out of your computer), anti-spyware, and virus protection are all necessary, as well as surge protectors for your electrical outlets. More computers are damaged by power surges and computer viruses than any other kinds of damage. Also, if there are others in the household, password protection is essential to keep others from accidentally deleting or damaging your files while you're not around.

Additionally, you will need some forms and documents that will not be covered by your billing software. These will primarily be local authority forms such as workers' compensation forms needed for local court filings within your own jurisdictional region. These forms can usually be purchased or even generated yourself on your own computer. A good word processing program and a few extra hours can yield these forms at an insignificant cost to you. A good word processing program will also be required for your correspondence and personal documents. These can be purchased through a discount software retailer at a significantly reduced rate. They generally come without the manuals and fancy packaging, but if you are able to install software yourself by finding the setup.exe file you can save a huge amount of money. Software manuals generally aren't needed, since each program will come with an online tutorial you can access and learn from.

3. Next, you will need a good printer. Again, it is essential that you check with the software company and see what type of printer you need. Certain software packages can only use one style of printer for their forms (for example a dot matrix, or impact printer, for pin-fed forms). Make sure you know what you are looking for and what your exact needs will be before you buy. Also, it may be advisable for you to invest in more than one printer. You can use your impact printer for your billing forms, and then use either an ink jet printer or bubble jet printer for your correspondence to look more professional. A color printer is nice for advertisements, although this is certainly not required to start. This purchase can come later when there is more money coming in to the business. A laser printer is required for all medical-legal documents and court filings. If any of your clients will be issuing any court-ordered findings, a laser printer will be an up-front requirement for your office. Laser printed documents will stand up to time and environment. An ink jet or bubble jet printer will use ink that will run if gotten wet, and will smear to the touch. A laser printer will not do this.

4. You will need a telephone with an answering machine. There will be times you will be out of the office, especially when you are out trying to enlist your first clients. You will need a way of professionally letting your callers know that while you are temporarily out, you will return their call as soon as you return. An older phone, or perhaps even one you already have, will be good for this. Answering machines are pretty standard, so as long as you can record a professional message and have reliable messages when you return, then use it.

5. A fax machine is pretty much essential anymore. While there are certainly some offices that function without them, it can be a hardship for your clients to work without. They can save you literally time and money when you consider the time and gas you would spend running around picking up documents that you could just as easily fax instead. They are economical and convenient, most costing less than fifty dollars now for a basic model. I would highly recommend a fax machine as soon as you can afford to purchase one.

A fax modem can be purchased for your computer at a ridiculously cheap rate these days. The problem with a fax modem is that you need to be there to turn it on. The convenience factor is almost completely eliminated with this choice. Your clients will need to contact you and ask you to turn it on. After receiving your fax, you will need to remember to turn it off or your computer will continue to answer the phone until you tell it not to. Other business phone calls will not be able to get through during this time. Also, you are unable to fax out unless your information happens to be a document on your computer. If it is a document not associated with your computer, then you must either type it all in as a document, scan it (if you have purchased a scanner), or drive somewhere with a fax machine and send it from there. With a free-standing fax machine, the equipment will only pick up the call if it is a fax; if it is a regular phone call, the fax machine will allow the phone to ring, filtering out only other fax calls. If another caller tries to call in while the fax is in use, they will simply get a busy signal and will try back in a few minutes. In my professional opinion, your own independent free-standing fax machine will work best for this situation. An older hand-me-down fax will be fine, as the technology for them has not changed drastically in recent years.

6. A few reference manuals are required for this business. They are an ICD-9 book (International Classification of Diseases), a CPT manual (Current Procedural Terminology), a HCPCS manual (Hospital Current Procedural Coding System), and a good medical dictionary. The ICD-9 manual is a listing of all diagnoses for diseases and injuries that are recognized by the AMA ™ (American Medical Association ™). The CPT and HCPCS are lists of current procedure codes also recognized by both the U.S. Department of Health and Human Services and the AMA ™. These code books are required for all medical billing, and are updated yearly by the AMA ™. They can be purchased on the Internet, through the AMA ™, or at any medical center bookstore. In addition to these, there are also specialty word books for each medical specialty and sub-specialty. So, for instance, if you are contracted with a podiatrist, you could pick up a specialty word book for podiatry and become familiar with all the terminology for that particular field. This will also be a leg-up on the competition who choose not to do their homework before the client is signed.

7. Finally, your office furniture and general office supplies will finish up this list. A desk with a good chair and good light that are comfortable and fit you will be necessary. These need not be new; in fact, I recommend they be either ones you already have or have bought used. Save the brand new big oak desk and filing cabinet for when you have income to sustain those kinds of bills. For now, just get something you can work on. Remember, you will be sitting in your chair for a good part of the day, so make sure it is one you can stand.

You will also need a filing cabinet for your documents. If you cannot find one, or cannot afford one, invest in some filing boxes for now. They fold so they make drawers on the front and can stack up just like a filing cabinet. These are both economical and practical.

Pencils, paper, stapler, staples, rulers, paper clips, tape, Post-It notes, etc., will round out your list of required equipment. Purchase a date stamp from the office supply store and use it on everything that comes into your office. This will come in handy with everything from superbills to correspondence to reports. If there are any discrepancies as to how long it took you to get to something, the date stamp on the document will instantly clear that up. It is for your own protection. Anything else, as far as equipment or large supplies, can wait until you have an actual need for that particular item. Since each office is run differently, it is hard to say what else you will need to have, versus what you just want to have. Only you can make this determination. Just remember to ask yourself, "Is this item required for me to do my job, or is it a convenience?" After consulting your checkbook, make your determination from there.

When looking for office equipment, make sure to consult your local office supply store. A lot of times they will have either returned or repossessed equipment at extremely reasonable costs. Also many local government agencies will have warehouse sales for the equipment they replace through the normal course of business. These are great places to find perfectly good stuff at dirt cheap rates. There are also online auctions and other Internet sources. Shop around for the best deal. Remember, you will be the only one seeing these items for a long while. Make sure this is a field that you like and plan on staying in before you make any major investments.

One simple thing you can do to protect very expensive equipment is to buy and use surge protectors on all your electrical outlets. They are cheap and very effective. In an electrical storm or power outage, they could save you thousands of dollars.

Another thing to consider when you do buy larger end equipment like printers, fax machines, and copy machines is whether to purchase a service contract on that equipment. This is an added expense on start-up, but the extra warranty on the equipment is good peace of mind in case anything goes wrong with your equipment. When you can afford them, these contracts can save you trouble, expense, and peace of mind later.

Let's say you've done everything listed above and your office is ready to go. You land your first client and begin working away. The problem is that things just aren't working out from your home. Things are too confusing and you can't keep your business life separate from your personal life. You need an office. There are some options there as well. If you can't afford to rent an entire office by yourself, and you probably can't if you're just starting out, try to see if you can just rent some cubicle space or perhaps one room in someone else's existing office. This is something that many struggling businesses are open to. You wouldn't necessarily need an office five days a week to start. If you could rent some desk space a couple of days a week to start, that may be enough to get you by until you begin making enough money to move up. When I needed to meet with clients or attorneys for business meetings, I would simply rent a conference room from one of my clients. That way the person I was meeting with did not know that I was working from my home. I got the use of a well-kept business office and professional staff, and they benefited from the barter by an increase in services provided to them. It was a win-win situation all the way around.

Wherever you decide to set up your office and work, make sure it is a comfortable space. This is a room you will be spending a significant amount of time in. It will be the room in which you will earn your living, and with any luck, put your children and grandchildren through college in. Make sure it is a comfy space, secure and apart from the rest of the household. A room that you can feel at ease in and be relaxed enough to work extended hours in, if needed.

HOME PHONE VS. BUSINESS PHONE

It is more professional, and will simplify you keeping your business and personal affairs separate, to have an additional phone line installed within your home for use strictly as a business phone. Check with your local phone company regarding regulations of having a business phone in your home in your particular area. Many phone companies have a separate fee schedule for businesses as opposed to simply adding an additional line in your home for your personal use. Do you need to have a separate business line right away? No. It is entirely possible to function as a small business from your home using your personal phone number. Here are a few tips that will help to make this transition easier.

Set certain business hours for your office and stick to them. This business is a job just like any other. Your clients will need to know when they can get hold of you for business matters. On your away message for your voice mail, you may actually want to state your business hours for their convenience. During these hours, always consider yourself to be working, whether there is actually work to do or not.

One thing that still surprises me about being self employed is the attitude of friends and family. They often feel that because you are self employed, that means you magically have more free time to spend either lunching or shopping than you did before. While it is true you will have more control over your schedule than at any traditional employment situation, your time is still just as precious as it was before. You will need to be firm in your business hours and setting, making it clear that an occasional lunch or mid-day meeting is okay, however it cannot become a habit, because you still have a great deal of work to do. Work should be an even greater priority for you now because your business literally hinges on whether or not you can land enough clients to make your office float. Using up your precious business hours and opportunities for social activities will not make this work. One thing that will, however, save you time is the lack of freeway commute. There are some extra minutes, or even hours, in your day because of the lack of drive to your office in the morning and evening rush hour traffic times. My husband and I used to joke that rush hour was when we both hit the hallway at the same time. There are definitely some timesavers here and there, but make sure to watch them and not overcompensate too much. You could end up going too far the other way, making things once again stressful due to the lack of hours in the day.

If you have a cell phone or a pager, use it. You can either advertise your cell phone number and pager number to your clients as a way of getting in touch with you, or simply turn on your "call forwarding" option when you are away from your home office. This gives your phone line complete coverage whether you are actually in your office or out. Remember, when you initially start your business, you will be spending a great deal of time out in the workplace. You will either be working another steady job until this one takes off and begins generating income, or you will be out soliciting new clients. Either way you can have all of your calls immediately attended to by keeping a cell phone or a pager with you at all times.

Also caution young children about answering your business phone and fax lines. You want to show the appearance of being in an independent office. Ideally, the person at the other end of the phone should not know that this is your house. If your children are older and are competent message takers, then instruct them how you want your phones answered. If they are not, tell them they can answer the phones after your office closes. Set a specific time for this so everyone is clear when the phones are for the family again.

You can also initially hook up your fax machine and your modem to your home phone line as well. After your business takes off and you become busier, you will have conflict over a single line. At that point you may want to consider two additional lines. Use one as a business voice phone and another line strictly for your computer and your fax machine. The computer will need a separate line to be able to transmit all your electronic billings. Additional phone features like "call forwarding" and "call waiting" will interfere with your electronic transmissions, so it is best to have a line with no additional features on it. It is perfectly acceptable for the computer and fax to share the same phone line. They rarely conflict with one another, unless your office is so busy that it needs both the computer and the fax to be available at all times. If this is the case, you can afford another phone line.

Always answer your business phone. Don't depend on an answering machine to do your marketing for you. I have known some prospective clients who will not do business with your company if there is not a live person to answer the phone when it rings. You don't want anyone to assume that you being out of the office is a regular thing. One chiropractor that I signed told me that when he had fired his current biller he picked up the yellow pages and kept calling billing services until a real person answered the phone. Since I was there and answered, I got the client. Answering machines are convenient and cheap, but they do not take the place of a real person.

The actual necessity for unlimited access to you is more psychological than business related. Anyone who has young children in school knows that they just feel better knowing that the school can get in touch with them no matter where they are. Doctors' offices are the same way. Occasionally, emergencies will come up, although bookkeeping emergencies are rare. Primarily, medical offices just need to know that you are there and available for them when they need you. It may seem a bit trivial at first, but remember, when you are billing for a physician you are literally in charge of his income. This is a very important position and not one to be taken lightly. When doctors want an answer to their questions, they want it now. This is a simple customer service thing that you can do to put your clients' minds at ease and show them that they are important to you and your business. Surely there will be times when this is not an option, but whenever possible, always keep yourself available.

When you do get messages of one kind or another, call all messages back immediately. Check your message machines and other sources regularly and be prompt in your response. Don't wait. This is another way to lose a prospective client. You may feel that their questions are silly or trivial, but they do not. If they took the time to pick up the phone and call you to ask something, then they deserve the time to get an answer. If it is important enough to ask, it is important enough to respond.

PURCHASING SOFTWARE

When you sell your services to a potential client, you are selling yourself, not your software. Your software is a tool to assist you in your business, but it will not make or break the business itself. One of the most important keys to success is to know and understand exactly what your software can and cannot do. With that in mind, there are several points that need to be considered before you make a major purchase like this.

1. What kind of practice do I want to have?
2. What types of specialty physicians do I intend to have as clients?
3. What are the special needs of those physicians?
4. Do those needs have to be programmed into the billing software, or can I manufacture them myself at a cheaper rate?

These questions are important in determining what type of software you will need. Medical, dental, chiropractic, and veterinary software are all different. Each specialty uses specialized codes and the software that is available is designed specifically for these specialties. Knowing what kind of market you would like to go after in your business is vital before beginning your software search.

After these questions are answered, then you can begin questioning different suppliers. Call as many different suppliers as you can. You can generally get a good listing of software programmers or suppliers from the Internet. Some yellow pages will list medical billing suppliers, or the business opportunity section of your local paper may list some as well. If none of these options pan out, you can contact the major insurance companies in your area and ask for a list of suppliers that they are compatible with. Many companies will have what they call a "vendors list." This is a list of programs compatible with their system. After you have a list of software suppliers, you are ready for the next step.

Have a list of questions ready that you need to know, including: program cost, system requirements, hidden additional costs, and equipment necessary in addition to the basic computer. Is there a continuing monthly cost (lease program), or do I own the program outright? What special features does your system have? What is the advantage of your system as compared to other programs? Is there a guarantee? What happens when I have programming problems? Is the system able to be upgraded at a later time? How much does that cost? Is a clearing house required? Have all of these questions answered by as many different software suppliers as you can, and then use the answers to narrow down your choice and make a decision.

When purchasing software, the lease option vs. outright purchase must be carefully considered. If you lease a program and equipment from a company, you will be forever tied to that company through your contract. While this may be cheaper than a direct purchase, you need to take into account the long-term cost as well. How long do you plan on being in business? A lease for a year or so, until you are well established might be a good idea. After that, a purchase plan would be more economical if you plan on staying around for some time. Also, the financial stability of the company you are leasing from needs to be taken into account. If that company fails, for whatever reason, you will lose your software and information in the closure. The software you begin with does not necessarily need to be the software you continue with. Let's say you begin with a lease to see how you like the business. A year or so into self-employment, you know this is the field for you and are ready to stay through retirement. You can purchase the same software at that point, if that is an option, or purchase a different program. Some programs out there are compatible, and others are not. Consult a computer expert to see if your information can be transferred (imported) into your new program. If not, you may have some data entry costs entering everything into the new system, but this might be worth the cost for the upgraded and more secure program. With a program that you own, you can make changes to it anytime you want, in any manner you want. With a lease option, this is not the case. The leasing company actually still owns the software and you are bound to what they choose to do with it. If the company you have outright purchased software from fails, simply hire a programming expert to take over and continue on as though nothing happened.

Make sure that the system you choose can generate paper claims as well as file electronically. Do not get stuck with a system that can only bill via your modem. Some things *must* be billed on paper. Any court filing will require a hard copy billing attached for the court's records. Also, workers compensation evaluations filings are required to be hard copy, as well as any procedure that requires an attached report, also known as by-report procedures. This will consist mainly of surgeries, chiropractic claims, and new or experimental procedures.

Your program should also be able to print reports that split information many different ways: by diagnosis, date of service, charge amount, procedure code, and type of insurance, just to name a few. This information will be extremely valuable down the road when collections are large and when the doctor needs to renegotiate his contracts with the insurance companies involved.

I got a call one day from a client who needed to know right then how many pregnant patients he had. I ran a report using the ICD-9 code for pregnancy (V22.2) and came up with a number of four. I returned the information with the names of the patients. He thanked me and hung up. Confused, I asked the office manager later that day what the commotion was for. She explained that the doctor had gotten a call from his malpractice insurance carrier. Since he was a family practice doctor, the limitations on his policy prevented him from treating more than five pregnant females at any given time. With that information he was able to prevent an expensive rate increase in his policy. With this information at my fingertips, I was able to help resolve what could have been a frustrating situation by simply printing out one report. It was a quick, simple, and painless. These options are inexpensive to purchase and valuable in the long run.

In addition to purchasing a billing software package, you should subscribe to an Internet service provider and get on the "net." This will also give you an e-mail address. Check this everyday, just like a phone answering machine. If you get e-mail, make sure to answer it promptly. In addition, you will appear more "high-tech" as compared to the competition who do not subscribe to this option. There are still a great number of people, including business people, who do not feel that the Internet is of any particular value to them as a service. Learning how to incorporate this valuable tool into your office will keep you more in touch than those who do not. Also check the electronic bulletin boards for information. These are either public bulletin boards or corporate bulletin boards from your insurance carriers.

You will also need a good word processing program. During the course of your follow-up, you will need to write many letters and send out other general correspondence, as well as your advertising and your personal documents. You should be familiar with this program and how to use it quickly and easily. A one-day class at your local computer store will generally serve this purpose, or take some time to read the manual thoroughly. There are also courses offered at a very cheap rate at your local community college. These will take longer to get through than a private course or learning from the manual. Make your business documents and advertisements look as professional as possible. If necessary, have them printed at a professional printer for a few more dollars. This will be worth it in the long run. If your advertisements look cheap and homemade, it will reflect poorly on you as a business professional. Take the time to learn your programs, or let the professionals do it for you.

There are also some very valuable medical programs available. These can include anatomy programs, drug programs, and tutorials in medical, dental, and business operations. Depending on your level of knowledge at the beginning, you may find some of these programs helpful. Spend some time at your local computer store and browse the software section. The prices for these programs are very reasonable and they can give you a great amount of knowledge if you have the time to spend learning from them. I would not recommend buying them if you don't have time to use them. It would be just a waste of money. Only buy what is in your initial set-up budget and what you will have time to use.

ORGANIZING WORK FLOW

Now that you have purchased all your furniture and equipment, it's time to get organized. This should actually be done before you get any clients; this way your office and software system will be set up and ready when you land your first client. You can get to work as soon as you receive information from the office and don't have to waste valuable time organizing yourself later. Remember, billing left sitting around is money sitting around. The more you collect and the faster you collect, the more money and business you will get. The quicker the bills go out, the faster the money comes in, the happier the doctor is, the more business you get. It's a good cycle to get into.

First, sit down at your desk and pretend you already have your first client. How will you get the work? How will you get your requests and reports back to the doctor? Will you pick up and deliver? Or will you use a courier? What days and times will delivery be? How many times a week? When you go in for your first interview with a prospective client be prepared to state a day and time that is convenient for you, because the doctor will probably ask you this. So, if you know that you have children to pick up from school at 3:30 every day, make sure to note that as a bad time for you. Try, as much as you can, to work with the doctor and his staff to make things convenient for them. If you simply cannot connect with them during the times that they want their work picked up, then invest in a courier. It is a cheap and efficient way of guaranteeing that your client will be happy.

Now that you have the work in your office, what will you do? Does it need to be coded (ICD-9 or CPT), or will the doctor's office code it before it gets to you? Will you do the data entry, or will someone else do it for you? After you enter it and process the claims (either electronic or paper), how will you store your paperwork? How will you follow it up? What happens to the claims that you enter and never get paid? These are all things that need to be worked out ahead of time.

Ideally, you want the doctor's office to do all coding for you whenever possible. This will cut down on billing errors later on. Physicians' handwriting is notoriously horrid. I believe this comes from so many years of taking endless notes in medical school. Whatever the cause, if you are to decipher it, make sure you can read it. Errors will result otherwise. Insurance companies generally don't get too upset over an occasional error here and there; however, if large amounts of errors are being made, or the same error is made over and over again, they may choose to look at it as fraud. Any precautions to avoid this should be taken, including proper training and continuing education. The physician's office is usually happy to code claims and superbills for you, but if they are too busy, they need to provide you with a very specific and detailed diagnosis and description of the services provided. If, when you are coding, you have any questions whatsoever regarding either of these two points, questions should be immediately referred to the physician's office—as should any patient questions later on. If you have sent a patient a bill for services rendered and they question the services provided, refer them to the doctor. Billing, collection, and co-pay questions are your field of expertise. Anything medically related should be handled by the office staff directly, unless they have previously briefed you on what to say.

One example of this is a lady that I worked for my first year in business. She was a physical medicine and rehabilitation doctor that worked on-call for consultations at a local hospital. She was called in to consult on patients that were diagnosed with heart attack and stroke. Since a large number of these patients were either unconscious or comatose when she examined them, they had no memory of her being there. My staff was instructed to tell patients when they called that the doctor saw them on an emergency consultation basis while they were unconscious. Most of them at that point would say okay, and send a check since they remembered being in the hospital and remembered being told they were unconscious for an extended period of time. Those patients that chose to push the issue further were then referred to the office staff. If you have a special situation like this that can be worked out ahead of time, then do so just to be prepared. There will always be other situations that come up. Those you will have to deal with as best you can and on a one-by-one basis.

Data entry and billing will most likely be a one-person job at the start. Try setting up a practice directory in your computer with made-up names and charges for these pretend patients. We called ours the practice file for Doctor Jekyl. Here, you will learn how to use your software. Enter in the names of pretend patients. Make up addresses, phone numbers, insurance identification numbers, charges, and diagnoses. Enter them in as though they were brand new patients. Follow the system through and actually print up claims. Then pretend that you have sent them out (you should shred the originals) and pretend to file the copies. Then pretend that insurance checks have come in for them, post the payments to your dummy directory, and file the check stubs (EOBs) for your records. Doing this will ensure that when you do land that big client, you will be completely ready for them to come on board.

One way to assure the doctor that you are ready for his business is to have your software loaded onto a laptop computer, to bring with you to the doctor's office. You don't have to load an actually directory onto the computer, but rather a working sample. Your practice directory would work nicely, because then you could turn it on and show him how it works rather than tell him. Most people are visual. They respond better and remember more if they can see how something works right in front of them. This is a good tool that is portable and convenient. If you cannot afford one right at the start, then simply print out copies of as many reports and sample billings that you can and use these instead. It is still a good visual and will give them a hands-on item to study up close. A laptop (even a used one) can be purchased at a later date when you have some income generated.

What about the claims that you file and never get paid? This is pretty common. While probably 80–90 percent of claims will be paid without problem, there is always that small percentage that either will not be paid or will be paid at the wrong rate. These will require what is commonly called "follow-up." That simply means that you will need to contact the insurance by whatever means (either a phone call, letter, or re-billed claim) and inquire why the claim has not yet been paid. Your software should be able to print what is commonly called an ageing report. This will be a report split by the age of the claim. It generally splits claims by 30-day, 60-day, 90-day, 120-day, and over 120-day categories. This way you can work claims from the oldest to the newest, calling the insurance companies and finding out what is tying up payment on them. With this report, you will be able to review every claim in your system quickly and easily.

Another suggestion is to use your computer's calendar, or diary, function. When you speak to an insurance company and they tell you the claim should be paid within two weeks, skip two weeks ahead on your calendar and enter a note: Call Blue Shield for Mary Smith, DOS 11/12/04. With this system, two weeks to the day, you can again follow-up with the same patient, rather than waiting for the ageing report to print again. With some systems this is feasible, and with others it is not, depending entirely on the number of patients you are seeing and how often they require follow-up. In higher volume offices this might be more of a hindrance than anything else because it would interfere with your monthly review of client balances. In this case, more help might be in order. Whichever follow-up system you use, accounts should be reviewed at least monthly for appropriate action.

Denied claims and requests for more information will also need follow-up. A phone call, or re-billed claim will generally handle these problems without incident. If they are still denied or unpaid after that, an appeal letter will be in order. An appeal letter simply states: 1) who you are and why you are writing, 2) detailed explanation of the problem with all attached documentation, and 3) what your contractual solution is. Make sure and back up your proposed solution with documentation as well. For instance, if your contract states that a specific service is to be paid at 80 percent, and the EOB shows that it was only paid at 65 percent, attach a highlighted copy of the contract for them to review. Insurance companies will have all of your physician's specific information loaded into a computer database that they pay claims from. Occasionally, information gets typed into the file wrong. They just need to be made aware of the problem so it can be corrected. This is a simple task, once they are aware that there is a problem. Finding and correcting problems like this is also a good selling point for your business and a good customer service point also.

Now that you have all the bugs worked out of your set-up, sit back and imagine anything that could possibly go wrong and account for it. Planning is the key. If your computer system goes down, how will you function? Where are your manual files? How will you get the computer back up and running again? What if your courier doesn't show up with your work? How will you trace it down? What if one of your children gets sick at school and you can't work today? When will the work get done? What if stuff arrives that has not been coded? Try to imagine all the possible scenarios for trouble and plan for them. If you have thought these things through ahead of time, they will not seem so much of a problem when they actually occur. They will be more like speed bumps than mountains in your path.

One of the difficult things in running a home medical billing service is arranging for vacation and sick leave coverage. This is generally not a problem for most offices. In fact, most small physician's offices usually employ only one biller and do not hire replacement coverage when that employee goes on vacation or is out ill. When a medical claim is sent in to an insurance company, it generally takes between six to eight weeks to receive payment for a paper claim and ten days to two weeks for an electronic claim. So, the money that is coming in today is actually for work that was done an average of two months ago. If an office balks at the fact that you will not be working for a week or so, make sure and point out that money will not cease coming in because you are not on the job. Their income will remain consistent during the time you are gone. If you plan taking off more than a week or two, it would be advisable to arrange for vacation coverage to make sure that there is no interruption in work flow. This can be someone that you trust, such as a family member or trusted friend, who can come into your home and bill the pending claims for you. If there are no family members or friends who are trained in this area, work out a coverage situation with another billing service. You can cover their vacation if they will cover yours. If you choose not to have any coverage, just ensure the client that you will complete all backed-up billing as soon as you return. Everyone is entitled to a vacation, or an occasional day off. This will keep your attitude good, your mind clear, and the stress level down.

When I first started my business, I was determined. I wanted this business to succeed more than anything else in my life at that time. I worked seven days a week, sometimes until late into the evening to get everything done and to keep my clients happy. It worked. The clients were incredibly happy, but I was a wreck. I never got a day off and I never took a vacation. About four years into being self employed, my family and I decided to take a trip to the Grand Canyon. I would be gone for a period of thirteen days, including two weekends and one holiday. This meant only missing eight working days. My clients had an absolute fit. They were so stressed and convinced that if I took that much time off that they would lose their businesses and go into bankruptcy. It took quite a bit of talking and convincing on my part to assure them that would not be the case, but because I had been so dedicated and hard-working at the beginning, it was hard to break free from that mold. Over the next two years I took only one other vacation and ran into the same situation again.

If your clients insist on constant coverage, then that needs to be taken into account. I am certainly not suggesting that you forego any vacation time that you can muster. I truly believe that each person should take what is reasonably theirs. But, your clients are, in fact, your paycheck. If they feel very uncomfortable with you being gone, then try to make the best arrangements that you can. Compromise on what you can, and satisfy them whenever possible. While their fears are probably unfounded and unwarranted, they are the customer, and the number one rule in business is: "The customer is always right."

SETTING UP A FILING SYSTEM

Setting up a filing system depends primarily on whether most of your billing will be done on paper or electronically. If your claims are generated electronically, there will be a minimal amount of paperwork to store. You can probably get away with an A–Z file folder system. Since all claims would then be stored on the computer, an actual file for each claim will not be necessary. Any information that would have to be referenced would be done on the computer. Extra precautions would have to be made to make sure that your system was backed up each and every time you entered any information. Filing in this instance would be only for correspondence and the EOBs that come in attached to the payments.

If your claims have to be generated on paper, either workers' compensation reports or by report procedures, then you will probably have to go to an individual file folder for each patient. This is where a fair amount of filing space will be necessary. A file should be kept handy at all times (until the claim is paid) so that it can be referenced quickly and easily. Insurance companies will need more information on a by-report procedure than they would for a simple office procedure. You will likely be asked to send additional copies of the report and multiple copies of the billings to several different agencies. Keeping this at your fingertips (within your office) is advisable. A general rule of thumb is to send files out to storage after a period of six months with no activity. After this reasonable time period, they can be sent to an off-site storage facility or even out into your garage to make more filing room in your own office files.

You will occasionally run into an old manual bookkeeping system, known as a peg board system. This is a system where each person has a ledger card and their accounts are kept on the ledger system. When that patient comes in or makes a payment, the ledger card is pulled and placed under a piece of carbon paper. The cover sheet will be the day sheet, showing all of the transactions for that day, and the carbon underneath will be on each individual patient's charges and payments. This will be your only record of a patient's account, so if you run across this system, do not destroy these ledger cards. They must be kept and stored safely with all your other records, even after conversion into your computer system. Store them in a cool, dry place, and keep them accessible for quick reference when you need them.

You will also have certain computer files that need to be stored for an extended period of time. These will be in the form of either computer printouts, or disks or back-up tapes. Tax records on computer disk, medical transcription, and your professional invoices to your clients are examples of other documents that need to be protected. Make sure that these are safely stored somewhere easily accessible and protected from the weather.

Whatever filing system you have, make sure it is an organized and clear system, particularly if someone else will be using it (a spouse or other employee). It needs to make sense to others at a glance, or directions need to be given to those who may fill in for you when you are ill or on vacation.

STORAGE OF OLD RECORDS

Something that must be discussed between you and your client is who will be legal "custodian of records." This is a very important point to be decided between your two offices up front. Medical records, including billing records, are legal documents, admissible in a court of law when necessary. Don't think that just because your client is a small town family practice physician, you won't get into legal issues like that. Most people at some point in their lives will get into a car accident or get some minor injury at work. Insurance claims to auto carriers or work comp carriers are lawsuits filed against the insurer, which will require documentation. This is where you will come in. It must be clearly decided who will keep the original records and who will keep the copies. If you are the custodian of records for the provider's office, you cannot destroy anything with patient information on it. These all must be stored for the legally prescribed period of time. This can vary from state to state and may also involve IRS tax regulations. Make sure you understand exactly what the documents are that you are dealing with and check with the appropriate agencies before destroying anything.

If you no longer work for a specific client and you have their records, forward them back to the office for them to decide what action to take with them. If, for some unknown reason, they refuse to take them or you are unable to get an answer from them, send a certified letter. Inform them of the reason that you are no longer able to keep the position of custodian of records (i.e. no longer work for them, etc.) and that if you do not hear from them by a specific date, you will have the records destroyed. Give them plenty of time to respond (several weeks at the least, up to thirty days at most) and then have the documents shredded. Keep a copy of the letter that you sent to the client, and the post office receipt verifying delivery. Try every avenue to return the documents to them first. As provider, the ultimate responsibility for these records lies with them. Make that clear in all communications with them regarding these documents, both verbal and written.

When you do decide to get rid of documents, you cannot simply throw them away in the trash. Federal regulations require that anything with any identifying patient information needs to be destroyed. You can have a professional document management company do this for you, or invest in your own personal shredder. They can also be burned, or torn up by hand, but they cannot be thrown away whole into the trash where anyone else can pick them up and utilize the information found on them. The law defines identifying patient information as anything that can be used to breach the confidentiality of a specific individual. This includes patient's name, date of birth, address, phone number, social security number, insurance identification number, spouse, next of kin, medical record number, credit card numbers, banking information, or anything else that can reveal the identity of a specific individual. Anything containing such information must be destroyed.

Besides patient confidentiality, remember professional confidentiality. Never talk to one doctor about billing issues or problems with another doctor's office. This is a clear breach of professional ethics. Always get a physician's permission to discuss his personal business matters with another office first. If you do not wish to do this, or don't get permission for some reason, then speak in general terms otherwise: "I have another client...." Never mention any names or any other identifying features such as "a tall cardiologist on the third floor of this very building...." Finances are very personal matters for businesspeople and should not be discussed with strangers. Even though someone might not be a stranger to you, they are a stranger to the client, so respect that aspect of your business as well.

As far as your personal documents, store everything. Don't throw anything away; you never know when you may need it. Remember, these are your tax documents. They also must be kept for a mandated time by law. Figure out a storage or filing system that makes sense to you and store them away in your home office or garage. If you get audited, you'll be glad you have them.

Another thing to keep handy are old "day sheets" or "posting logs." These will be documents that your computer will generate every time you enter a transaction. Primarily, you will use them to balance your daily accounts. For instance, you open today's mail and find $1,500 worth of insurance checks in there. You look up who the patients are, and post them to the accounts. At the end of the day your computer will generate a posting log for that day. It should show payments posted to the various patient accounts in the amount of $1,500. If your computer day sheet is off, then you need to go back and recheck to make sure that all of your payments are posted correctly. This could be simply a typo or posting error, but these day sheets will help you to find errors in your billing. They will also generate categories for total amount of charges and adjustments that should be balanced as well.

In addition to balancing your daily transactions, day sheets are also handy for reconstructing your computer if it crashes and there are no recent back-ups. You should always back up your computer system every single day. Computer crashes happen all the time and for the strangest reasons. It could be something as simple as a power surge or as complicated as equipment failure, but they do happen. A back-up will guarantee that within hours, you can be backing-up and running on possibly a new computer without the loss of any data. Occasionally, you will work for several hours in the morning and then your computer will crash. A posting log will help you reconstruct the work done in the few hours since your last back up, ensuring that you have not lost any work. They are extremely valuable. Just take an empty copy paper box or computer paper box, and place it in the corner of your office next to your printer. When the forms are generated, and after you balance your transactions, just throw them into the box, newest forms on top. When the box gets full, take the top few pages from the top and keep them. Shred the rest and start a new box. You only need to keep the logs since your last back-up; however, I have had back-up disks fail and had to go back to a previous back up for restoration of information. It is best to be prepared for anything.

Most banks and financial institutions will advise you to have a written business plan, complete with profit and loss statements, income statements, tax records, bank statements, and balance sheets. Keep these stored with your tax records as well. These will be useful if you ever try to go get a business loan or federal grant. Most community colleges or small business development centers have classes or workshops to teach you how to draw these up. Contact your local branch of the Better Business Bureau with any questions or to get a referral. Small business information is also available at your local bank. Go in and speak directly to the loan officer or new accounts person and ask what services they have available for new or small businesses or home businesses. Keep your eyes open. Home-based business information springs up all over the place. For loans and general banking purposes, financial institutions will require income and expenses documented over a period of time, usually six months to a year. You will also need to be able to document income and expenses if you ever get to the point of selling your business. You will need to prove these numbers for the company financing the purchase. Since you never know what the future will bring, it is much easier to be prepared for any situation.

When I was in the sixth year of business and going strong, my family was hit with a series of tragedies. We lost four family members to cancer in a short period of time. I was no longer able to give my clients the attention they needed and deserved, due to the personal draws on my time and attention. At that point I decided to sell the business and concentrate on what my family needed. You may indeed love your business and be quite successful at it, but sometimes life has other plans. Other career options, children, mid-life crises, and divorce can all take their tolls on successful businesses. Try to be as prepared as you can for anything. With proper and complete documentation at your fingertips, the quick sale of your business, if necessary, will be a much easier process.

HOW TO GET AND KEEP CLIENTS

P&P: Patience and persistence is the key. It is highly unlikely that you will land the very first client you go after, although it does occasionally happen. The more comfortable and knowledgeable you feel going into the interview, the better your chances of doing business with that client. Here are a few tips.

To the greatest extent possible, spoil your clients. Make sure they understand they are a priority for you, no matter how much or little they may pay you. Simple ways of doing this are always being available during business hours. Return phone calls promptly and keep in touch often. Remembering their birthdays and holidays with cards is a simple gesture that will make an impression, as will a thank you card when it is appropriate. People will remember these simple acts of kindness that you have taken time out of your day for.

Dress professionally. Always look your best. You never know when or where you will run into a client. First impressions are the most important. You are a business professional so look the part. One thing to be aware of in the medical field, particularly if you are in a hospital or office with traumatic injuries, is to be very careful with your choice of wardrobe coloring. There is one color that is an absolute taboo in this field, and that is the color red. It reminds patients of blood. If you walk into a hospital and look around, red is the one color you will never see, or if so, only in very small limited quantities. This applies to red nail color and bright red lipstick. Also, be aware of your vocabulary within earshot of patients as well. Don't make comments like "deader than a doornail," "I killed that pen" when it runs out of ink, or "I buried it" when you throw something away. While most people recognize and know that this is slang, it may not set well with a patient in a fragile emotional state. Always be aware of who you are around and what you say.

Don't be late! Punctuality is a deal-breaker. If a doctor, or anyone else for that matter, has to sit around and wait for you, it will show him that you don't respect his time or business. A medical office runs on the appointment basis. If you are late, they will simply move on to the next appointment, thinking you have forgotten or don't care. If they have reserved a time block for you to be there, you need to make it on time in order not to throw their whole day off. Unless you have a good excuse, like a flat tire, this will be something that will be incredibly difficult for you to overcome. Try not to make it an issue from the start.

Always be prepared. While you are networking and going out into the business world, you will meet all kinds of people from all professions. Referrals are a great way to get your foot in the door. While you may not necessarily meet with a doctor at the corner café having lunch, you might run into an office manager who is looking to hire someone. Keep business cards with you at all times and be ready to hand them out.

Don't wait for business to come to you; go out and get it. No one is sitting around the corner waiting to hand you anything. Nothing in life is free. You will have to work for everything you get. Contrary to some opinions, home businesses are not get-rich-quick schemes. They are a job just like any other. You will get up in the morning and go to work just like at any other job. Make it count.

My first year in business, I decided to take a day off. I had been working hard and making decent money and decided that I needed an afternoon just for myself. So, after dropping the kids off at school and arranging for some office coverage from my spouse, I headed to the mall to do a little shopping. The first person I ran into was the wife of a chiropractor. She informed me that his biller had just quit and he was very stressed about it. I gave her a business card and asked her to have him call me. I felt very good about this chance meeting. I was prepared, and it had turned out to be a productive afternoon after all. After about an hour or so at the mall, I went on to take in a movie. While standing in line at the popcorn stand I struck up a conversation with the lady in front of me. She was the office manager for a large family practice office near my home and had decided to play hooky from work that day because she had been working so hard lately. You see, they were understaffed and she needed to hire another biller for their office. I handed her a business card and asked her to call me. Again, I felt good about the day and my decision to take time off. After the movie, that evening I went to my first workshop through the small business development center to learn how to write a business plan. I walked in and sat down next to a friendly looking lady and we struck up a conversation. She told me that she was getting ready to graduate from chiropractic school and was learning how to set her own business up. Another opportunity through my daily walk. I tell you this story so you will see that business opportunities are everywhere. You never know who that person standing in line next to you at the grocery store is, or that person who parked next to you at the mall. Take advantage of every opportunity and be prepared for whatever life may decide to throw at you. The more business cards and advertisements you have out there floating around, the more likely you are to be called. Place them in drawings and contests, post them in bulletin boards, use them as bookmarks, and pass them out with reminder notes to your friends. You never know when a potential referral will come through.

The very first client I landed as an independent business person was a doctor that I made an average of thirty-five dollars a month on for the life of the contract. Many other billing services had already turned her away because she was too small for them to deal with. I was excited about the $35, since at that time I had no income at all, but in the long run she gave me something much more valuable than money. She gave me the referrals that landed every single other client I had. So, in essence, she alone was responsible for the over $100,000 a year I was making a short time later. I never let her forget it either. She always knew the appreciation I felt for her and the boost to my business. She took care of me, and I took care of her. Business is a two way street.

The next tip is to keep a briefcase in your car that is packed and ready for an interview at all times. In there should be copies of your forms and other visual aids to show the client, paper and pens for taking notes, business cards, clips, Post-It ™ notes, resumes, references, fliers, and anything else you can think of that will be useful. If you use a laptop for your visual presentations, try to keep it with you as much as you can, while still keeping it in a safe and secure location.

When you are first starting out, and before your business has built up a reputation, you will probably be asked for a resume. This is a good idea to keep on hand, along with a list of references. Think of each meeting with a client just like a job interview. They don't know who you are. They will need to be convinced as to why they should allow you to be in charge of their collections. Make sure to clear all your references ahead of time and know what they will tell prospective clients.

When you walk into a meeting, be self-assured. Have a sales pitch prepared before you arrive, and practice it before you get there. Make an outline or use index cards to work from if you can't remember what you want to say. Practice this speech every chance you get so it is smooth and natural. List all the major selling points for your business. Be prepared to explain each of them, if asked. Use your index cards to refer to during the interview if you need to. What a provider wants to know is why you are more qualified than anyone else to do this job. Why should they hire you over anyone else?

What should you expect when you walk into an interview? There are basically two scenarios. One is where the physician takes charge and runs the meeting just like a traditional job interview. They will ask you questions, and you should answer until they are satisfied. The other scenario is when the provider will sit back and allow you to make a sales pitch and convince them that you are the best candidate for the job. They will generally ask a few questions and let you go through your sales pitch. One thing I have learned is that you have to be prepared for either scenario. If you only have your sales pitch to work from and try to keep going back to that when you are being asked a direct question, you will offend the interviewer. You must be confident enough to stray from your sales pitch and answer direct questions. This also goes to your type of personality and how well you function under pressure. A medical office is a very busy place. There are people coming and going all day long, and every one is there because they have a problem. It is the responsibility of their office and staff to take care of that problem. Sometimes it takes a quick-thinking person who is not rattled by stress to accomplish this. It is entirely reasonable for a prospective employer to ask questions and test your ability to think on your feet.

Generally at the close of the interview, the doctor will ask if you have any questions for them. Always take this opportunity. It shows interest in them and their business. You will need a thorough understanding of how the office runs. Good questions to ask are 1) how many patients do you see a day? 2) What is your average charge? 3) What insurance company contracts do you have? 4) What is your average turnaround time for payment on claims?, etc. Don't ask their specialty because you should already know this before you arrive. Try to do as much homework on the client as you can before you walk in the door so you know whom you are dealing with. It will impress the client and you will stand a much greater chance of landing their account.

The last thing you should do is have a written agreement prepared ahead of time, in case the office decides to hire you on the spot. (Yes, that does happen.) It can be an empty, fill-in-the-blanks contract, with another more professional one being typed up and delivered at a later date. Make all your presentations look as professional as possible, even if they are just temporary documents. Place your letterhead and phone number on everything. The contract should state exactly what services you are to provide for the doctor and under what terms. It should spell out who will code, how work will be delivered and on what days, and how much you will charge for these services. It should also cover payment expectations; at what point do you consider the payment delinquent and what will happen if that occurs. Late fees and penalties should be spelled out as well. Finally, the term of the contract should be agreed upon and listed. I would recommend an initial period of at least six months, since it will take you several months to get a good turnaround on your billing, and you will probably not make any money during that time period anyway. This gives both parties a fair chance to get to know each other. There are sure to be a few little bumps in the beginning; there always are in any new employment situation. But, after the initial six-month period, those should all be worked out for the better and the work should be rolling in. After your initial trial period, you can set whatever terms you want, either month-to-month or a yearly contract. That is entirely between you and your client. Determine what is in everyone's best interest and stick with that.

One question that has been asked of me is whether you need to have a lawyer draft your contract, or can you simply write the agreement out yourself. This is a good question. The answer is not as simple as you would think.

I always wrote out my own agreements. They were simple and concise. I didn't call them "contracts" simply business agreements. Through my years of business I ran into several situations where the agreements were challenged or questioned. After consulting with an attorney, I found out that the law will take into account who actually wrote the agreement, their intentions behind the agreement, and the legal background of the writer when determining the validity of the agreement. So, in other words, had a lawyer written the agreement, both signing parties would be held to the full extent of the law regarding its contents and limitations. However, since I had written the agreement myself, with no legal background or training, and for the sole purposes of having no misunderstandings in the normal everyday course of business, the law took into account my intentions and education level and did not allow others to use legal technicalities against me when trying to get out of payment of my bills. Agreements such as these still must follow the law. If you write into your agreement something that is not legal, for instance an exorbitant late fee, the law will not allow you to collect on that, even though both parties agreed in writing. You will still be held to the extent of the law; however, the law will back you up from others trying to use legal maneuvering to get out of what you are entitled to for the work that you have performed and agreed to in advance.

When you begin billing for a new client, you will not make any money for probably thirty to sixty days. The reason for this is it takes that long for insurance checks to be processed and sent back to the client. There are supplies to be purchased as well. Each time you set up a new client on your electronic claims system, there is an initial testing period that takes time as well. There are also contracts that need to be signed and paperwork processed before you will be allowed to bill for them. You need to be prepared to last this time period without making any money. The exception to this will be if you take over the accounts receivable that someone else has already billed. You will have instant income in this circumstance, but you will also have an additional expense of transferring all of those accounts over to your system. You will either be doing a lot of data entry yourself or will need to invest in a temporary employee to do this for you. The other option would be to purchase the software that the other biller used and transfer the files through the help of the software consultants on a data-import basis. Again, a timesaver but at a potentially huge cost. You will need to weigh the individual situation and see what is best for everyone involved.

Some established businesses will charge a set-up fee. This is an upfront fee that is paid by the physician for you to convert their existing files into your system. It can be anywhere from $100 into the thousands, depending on the size of the client and the amount of outstanding accounts receivable they have. A set-up fee ensures that you will make money and be paid for your work, but it could potentially scare off a client. If the client will not agree to the initial six-month trial period, then I think that a set-up fee is a good idea. That way you will not lose money on the deal. However, if the client will agree to the six-month period, you may want to consider foregoing the set-up fee. Your money will be made in the long run and you will be in better standing with the client than someone who demands money up front. Again, each situation needs to be weighed on an individual basis.

I would recommend having blank copies of the electronic billing contracts and agreements with you from all major insurers in the area, ready for the doctors to sign. The faster you can get them on electronic billing, the faster their turnaround time will be for money coming in. Getting these contracts signed and sent out as soon as possible will show that you indeed do know what you are doing, and will speed up not only their income, but yours as well.

On the same note, when you become busy enough to hire employees or to make use of subcontractors, write out everything. Have a prearranged agreement between yourself and your subcontractors. For employees, write out a detailed job description and have regular reviews. It will save a lot of time and money later on down the road. Hire clericals for menial tasks. Keep good records. Certain states have very strict hiring and firing laws. In order to terminate an employee who is not properly doing their job, very meticulous records must be kept. This is in everyone's best interests. The more clearly an employee understands what you want of them, the more likely they are to come through. If directions are fuzzy and vague, no one will be happy and work will not be performed efficiently. For everyone's best interests, detail it all out.

Here is a sample agreement that might be used between two agreeing parties. It must be altered to meet the exact needs of the two individuals involved.

SAMPLE SERVICE AGREEMENT

ABC Billing Company
11111 Somewhere Drive
Anytown, CA 99494
(555) 686-3938 office
(555) 686-9595 fax

SERVICE AGREEMENT

This document is a service agreement between ABC Billing Company and ___My Big Client, M.D.___, for the purpose of outlining services and payment between the two parties.

ABC Billing agrees to the following:

1. Pick up and delivery of billing and correspondence on the following days and times (detail out here) for the purpose of billing and collections.
2. Billing and processing of all such documents to be done within forty-eight hours (or mutually agreed upon time frame) from the time of pick up.
3. To have, for the client and at their request, copies of any billings or documents from the insurance company regarding any billing or collection matters.
4. To provide for the client monthly reports and print outs showing complete accounts receivable information and detailing out any other information that the client wishes (numbers of patients seen, time elapsed from billing to payment of claims, diagnoses of patients, services provided most often, etc.).
5. To provide bank depositing services (optional) at the client's request.
6. To provide monthly statements for services rendered.
7. To provide customer service between the client and insurance companies to attempt to resolve any billing issue that may arise for any reason.

My Big Client, M.D. agrees to the following:

1. To have all documents copied, coded, and ready for pick up on the appointed day and time.
2. To be available for questions and problems regarding any coding issues and medical questions or problems with the claims process and to help with letters of justification or medical necessity for the payment of claims.
3. To pay ABC Billing Service within ten days of receipt of invoice for services rendered to my office.

Payment to be as follows:

- Six percent of all monies collected for patient accounts.
- $25.00 an hour for additional services, agreed upon in advance.
- Reimbursement of postage costs for billings generated.
- A late fee of no more than 18 percent per year, or 1 ½ percent per month (the maximum legal limit) will be incurred for any billings over thirty days.
- Both parties agree to an initial six-month trial period.
- Either party has the right to terminate this agreement with a thirty-day notice after the initial trial period, for any reason. If the agreement is terminated by either party,   My Big Client, M.D.   agrees to pay ABC Billing Company for any work that has already been performed but has not yet been paid in accordance with all federal, state, and local labor laws. Such services will be paid at the usual and customary rate mutually agreed upon by both parties.

Signatures:

ABC Billing Company representative: Date:

    My Big Client   representative: Date:

NETWORKING AND ADVERTISING

Advertising should always be a priority. Even if you think you have enough clientele to keep you busy. Clients move. They quit groups, join other groups, move to hospital-based settings, get married, get divorced, and move around in life just like everyone else does. No matter how much you like each other and how well things are going, things change. You should always be ready for this.

Also, beware of the putting-all-your-eggs-into-one-basket syndrome. If you have only one large client and that client more than pays your bills, you will be forever tied to what that client wants and does. If they close up shop for whatever reason, so do you. Always try to guard against this, if at all possible. Sometimes it can't be helped, and so we accept the risks and work on. Just be aware of what the possibilities are in this situation.

By making advertising a priority in your business, you will guarantee that your business will not become stagnant. The more new clients and new types of billing (specialties and sub-specialties) that come through your office, the greater the education and income opportunities are. Even if these are small clients, your opportunity to learn will be worth more than the money you will make. This is an ever-changing field, and the more you learn, the better service you can provide to your existing clients.

Create your own personal marketing strategy, something that is unique to only you. Research what the other billing services in your area do and come up with something even greater. This can be either a marketing technique that they have not thought of or perhaps a service that they do not provide. You need to have something to corner the market with; something that will make the general public say, "No one else does that."

One of the most important pieces of advice that I can give you is to check everything for accuracy, both with punctuation and grammar, but most importantly spelling. A misspelled word will stick out of your advertisements like a sore thumb. When other errors are less noticeable and even forgivable, a gross misspelling will convey a lack of attention and accuracy, or sometimes intelligence. People will not only notice this, but they will remember it for a long time. A simple thing like this can have a negative connotation to that all-important business reputation you are trying to build up. Make sure and get things right.

People like stuff that is free, and doctors are no different. Anything with your name on it will make them remember you. Calendars, pens, pencils, and note pads with your name and logo on it are good ways of getting your name out there. These are things that people will keep and use, even if you don't initially land them as clients. Then, perhaps later on when they are looking for someone to hire, your name and phone number are right in front of them. Another good method is refrigerator magnets. Guess what? They're not just for refrigerators anymore. Nearly every office has filing cabinets or other metal fixtures they can stick to. You can buy business card sized peel-and-stick magnets at your local office supply store for a very inexpensive rate, then simply apply your own business cards to them. These can be handed out to each office you visit as well.

On every item that leaves your office, make sure your name and address are on it. Every envelope and every patient file. Get some 1x3 inch address labels from the office supply store and put your company name and address on them. Print them by the hundreds and then go sticker happy. Slap them on everything that another person might see. This is simple, cheap, and still very effective.

Try to offer some service that is worthwhile to your clients as well. Some suggestions are: vacation relief for their office staff (temp services), clerical or transcription services, or running errands for them. Whatever you decide to do, market this as your personal touch. Another effective tool is to offer to take their worst billing problems and resolve them. You can take any accounts receivable over ninety days and collect on them for a higher percentage than your normal billing. You can take over all of the appeals they have, or any other job that they find difficult or just don't have time to do. This, then will become your niche. There are recovery agencies and collection services that will perform this job function for anywhere between 25–40 percent. This can be a very profitable corner of the market.

Most billing services advertise in the local phone book, both the yellow pages and the white pages. There are also some local trade journals that some people will buy advertising space in (i.e. your local medical society or trade journals). These can be expensive, and it is hard to say whether they are effective or not. Other forms of advertising are:

- Direct mail
- Web page
- Newspaper
- Magazines
- TV/radio
- Golf courses
- Cold calling (walking in to an office without an appointment)
- Blanket fliers (in a particular neighborhood)
- Billboards/signs
- Bus benches

Which method is most effective? The most effective method of advertising is the one that will get you directly to the most amount of potential customers. This may vary for each of you. Determine where your business is going to be situated and what the customer potential is for your individual area, then capitalize on it. Also remember, you are not tied to any particular geographic area for your business. With electronic billing, overnight mail, e-mail, fax machines, and web pages, you are connected to literally anywhere in the world. You can bill for anyone, anywhere, as long as you have a plan in place for transfer of information back and forth. Interviews and face-to-face meetings will require planning as well, but it certainly can be done.

The least effective form of advertising is going to be the one that will gain you the least amount of contact with potential customers. This would have to be, in my opinion, cold calling. Cold calling is simply walking into an office, unannounced, and asking to speak to the person in charge. Using this method you will rarely be able to get past the front office staff and talk directly to the physician. Physicians' practices are based on patient appointments. Chances are, when you walk into the office, the doctor already has prior scheduled appointments. You also want to make the most effective use of your time and funds available. Spending all day walking into doctors' offices and being told that the doctor is busy is very frustrating and most times futile.

So what is the best answer? In my professional opinion it is a combination of several methods. I think every business should advertise in the phone book. A white pages listing generally comes free with your phone number. A one-line ad in the yellow pages is generally very economical. The larger-sized ads (business-card size, quarter-page, half-page, and full-page) can be very pricey, so watch out for them and determine your actual need before placing a large ad.

I found the most effective method to be a combination of direct mail and web page. Target specific physicians that you want to bill for. These can be either in your general area or a certain specialty. Send them a postcard or flier at bulk postage rate, and on it cue them in to your web page with more detailed information. This will be of minimal cost to you and give them the most amount of information at their fingertips. You will also not waste valuable time and gas driving around town trying to see doctors but rarely being successful.

And just where do you find the doctors to mail these fliers to? Simple. Start with the phone book. All of your local physicians will be listed. From there, go to your local newspaper and look in the help-wanted section. These are offices that are already in need of help and are looking for it. This is a great way to get your foot in the door quickly and easily. After you try these two sources, you can branch out to your local medical society. They will have a list of all physicians licensed to practice medicine in your local area (probably the entire county or multiple-county area you live in). You can check with your state licensing bureau as well. Many hospitals will also have directories of all physicians they contract with to work there, and your nearest teaching hospital is about to graduate a new class of brand new physicians and other healthcare providers that will need to get their billing set up as soon as possible. If none of these work, we always have golf courses, gyms, and country clubs. Don't laugh. Doctors do still join these.

Networking with other like-business professionals is an incredibly valuable tool. By getting to know other billers, both independent and traditionally employed, you will be able to share information, services, and connections that you would not be able to share otherwise. This can be a great way to keep up on industry trends and to know who is looking for help and who is not. It is also a source of referrals and references that can lead to more clients and more work for you. If you don't have a local medical billing association, then start one. Meet at the local café for an early breakfast once a month or even once a quarter. Spend some time getting to know one another and what specific needs you all have, then try to work together to resolve those needs. You'll not only make business contacts, you'll also make friends.

Medical
Billing
Service

A Full Service Medical Billing Company

Offering:

Direct Electronic Claim Submission for Medicare,
Medi-Cal, FHP, Blue Cross and Blue Shield;

Access to the NEIC computer network system;

Computer generated insurance forms for
all other carriers and by-report procedures;

Monthly patient statements;

Full A/R management with optional
banking services;

Medical Transcription;

Customized fee schedule.

Monthly reports available by:
Patient Name (Alphabetical), New Patients,
Insurance Type, Referring Doctor,
Aging Report (30,60,90 days, etc.),
Procedure Code, Diagnostic Code,
Adjustment, Insurance Write-Off,
Credit Balance, Account Balance,
Collection Report, Date of Last Payment,
Charges Report (by Date of Service),
and Business Report (for Accounting)

Experienced in a large number of specialties
Specializing in Workers' Compensation
Med-Legal (QME, AME, IME) filings

WHAT SHOULD I CHARGE?

How much you should charge depends entirely on what kind of office set-up you have and what services you perform. There are several different options for this.

The first, and most popular option, is to be paid by percentage. This is the most advantageous to all parties involved. It has a built-in guarantee to the physician. If you don't know what you're doing, you won't get paid. The down side is that neither will he. The market will tend to fluctuate a bit during tough economic times, but for the past decade, the industry standard has been between 6 percent and 8 percent of the amount collected. I have seen billing as low as 4 percent, and as high as 12 percent. This is completely negotiable and between you and your client. You should not charge more than what the market will bear. If your prices are too high, it is almost certain that another service will come in and try to undercut you, as you should do if the situation is reversed. Try to contact as many other billing services as you can and see what they charge. Try to keep your rates comparable. One marketing trick you can utilize is to undercut the average rate for the first several months. Call it a special rate or signing bonus for your clients. This period can be any amount of time you are willing to set. Half price for the first three months, or the first months free, are good advertising tools to use.

The second pricing method is to charge by the hour. This will generally be used when you are working a temporary job or doing some task that is out of the ordinary for your business. Again, this is completely negotiable and entirely between you and your client. Try not to charge a rate that is too high, keeping in mind that while you are self-employed, your taxes and insurance are your sole responsibility. A good rule of thumb is the 150 percent rule. Let's say you need to make ten dollars per hour to make your business work. One hundred-fifty percent of that would be fifteen dollars per hour. That way, after self-employment taxes and other expenses (supplies, insurance, gas, etc.), you end up with ten dollars per hour in your pocket, just like you would at traditional employment.

The third option is to be paid per piece of work. For instance, if a doctor gives you twenty claims to bill, and you decide to charge him one dollar per claim, you have just made twenty dollars. Traditionally, with this type of billing, no follow-up or appeals are involved. This is a flat fee to file the claim alone. If further services are required, they are then negotiated at one of the rates above. With this option, you will need to sit down at your computer with your practice directory and determine how long it will take you to enter your claims in. If you can enter and post one single claim in five minutes, and you charge five dollars a claim, that would have you making sixty dollars per hour; a little steep for the market. If you charge $2.50 per claim, you would then make thirty dollars per hour—closer to what the market will bear. Also, keep in mind that while you may be making thirty dollars per hour when you work, you will not be getting paid for forty hours either. This needs to be calculated into your quote as well.

I did run across one billing service that was paid on a salary basis. The amount of money that the service was paid remained the same every month regardless of how much work was done or how much was collected. This is certainly an option for you, but it is rare, and would put you back into the category of an employee rather than self-employed. Part of the appeal for this business is the potential for income if you work hard and produce great results. The financial gains can be great and are directly tied to how hard you work. If you place yourself on a salaried option, you limit these income potentials for yourself.

As far as the percentage option goes, one thing you will need to find out from your client before you quote a price is what their average charge is. If you have an allergist who charges ten dollars per allergy shot, and you quote him 6 percent for billing, then you have just made sixty cents per claim. If, on the other hand, you have a brain surgeon whose average charge is one hundred thousand dollars per claim, and you again quote a fee of 6 percent, you have just made six thousand dollars for the same amount of work. Either contract would be a bad one. The allergist would have you working yourself right into bankruptcy and the brain surgeon would be seriously taken advantage of by you. Neither situation is a good one. Before quoting a blanket fee, make sure to ask questions of the potential client, and weigh all the payment options before quoting a price. There are no set rules or regulations here. Charge what works best for both you and your client.

Here is a sample invoice to bill your clients.

ABC Medical Billing Service
12340 Boxer Lane
Anytown, MI 67899
(163) 555-0394
TIN#: 94-0505050

Invoice Date:	Service Description:	Total Amount Collected:	Total Amount Charged:	Billed Total:
12/9/08	6% fee on chgs collected for Nov	$100,000.00	$6,000.00	$6,000.00
12/9/08	$5.00 per claim for Nov. bills	120 claims billed	$600.00	$600.00
12/9/08	Postage reimb.		$120.95	$120.95
12/9/08	$25.00 per hr for Nov. billings	6 hours services	$150.00	$150.00
Total:			$6,870.95	$6,870.95

All invoices are due and payable upon receipt. For questions regarding this invoice, please call (163) 555-0394.

Please remit. Thank you for your business.

Always make sure and enclose a self-addressed (possibly stamped) envelope for them to return your check in. You can also make arrangements to pick up the check. If you use a courier, have them place your payment in the courier bag or leave it at their office and you can pick it up at your convenience.

CUSTOMER SERVICE AND PROFESSIONALISM

There is a lot to learn, in any business, to understand the working dynamic between all the parties involved in the day-to-day operations of the organization. This business is no different. In addition to the client you work for, you will be involved with their office staff, salespeople, other physicians' offices (referrals), multiple insurance companies, attorneys, possibly the court system, software vendors, and other computer experts, all of whom are there to keep your business running at peak efficiency. Try not to be intimidated by these other professionals. Just remember that each person is there to do a specific job and that your job is unique and different from any of these other persons. Make every attempt to work with them and provide them with the information they need to the best of your ability, while still staying within the confines of the law.

The best way to efficiently work with these other individuals is to know and understand completely what your job is. Get a clear definition from your client as to exactly what your job duties are. Be self-assured and confident in your abilities. You don't need to know everything, but you do need to know where to find it. Don't be afraid to tell someone, "I don't know," but always follow that up with, "but I will find out." Follow-through is essential. Don't promise what you can't (or won't) deliver. People might not remember every little thing you have ever done for them, but they will never forget when you have let them down. There are so many insurance company rules and regulations that it is impossible for one person to remember them all. Attorneys do not memorize every law that has ever been passed, but they do know where to go and find what they are looking for. Your experience should be the same way. You need not memorize every single ICD-9 or CPT code that has ever been written, but you do need to know where to go to find them, even if coding is not your primary job function. Remember, this industry can be fast-paced and ever-changing. It is essential that you keep up on the latest in all legislation regulating what is required for all billing situations.

Keep in regular, personal contact with your clients. This is extremely important. When you are placed in charge of someone's accounts receivable, you are essentially in charge of their checkbook. You have just been placed in charge of their income. All clients, no matter what field they are in, will feel more at ease knowing that you are around and they can get in touch with you at a moment's notice. Make appointments to see them at least once a week and call in between. Drop by, if that works for your office, just to see if they have any questions or problems. Make your face be seen and known. Let them know that they are important enough for you to drive across town just to check on them. Spoil them with your attention. This will not only earn their trust and respect, but it will also earn you the all-valuable referrals that will build your business and reputation.

If your client's office is having some problems in specific areas, take the initiative to try to correct them. If their paperwork process is confusing, help them streamline it. If their forms are outdated and unclear, design new ones for them. If they are having issues with specific insurance companies, arrange meetings for them with the provider representatives from those insurance companies to try and resolve those issues. Take the initiative in these matters. Make suggestions. Voice your ideas. They have hired you for a reason. If something is not working smoothly within an office setting, chances are the office staff already know about it. They will appreciate your help and attempts to make things more efficient for them all. After all, the ultimate goal is to improve efficiency and productivity for everyone. The greater the income for the office, the happier everyone will be. Raises will be more likely for everyone and the client will be happier.

Back at your own office make sure your client's information is easily accessible. Keep it available and at your fingertips, either on the computer or in files that are close by. When they call—and they will—they will need to get things from you at a moment's notice. Patient charts get lost, invoices are misplaced. They will need you to be a backup for them when they are unable to locate certain information.

Double, triple, and quadruple check your work for accuracy. Don't ever send anything (especially billing) out without double checking it first (especially if someone else is doing it). You alone are responsible for explaining things (i.e. reports, etc.). As the owner of the business, you are ultimately responsible for everything your employees and subcontractors do. As Harry Truman put it, "The buck stops here." Check everything for errors.

Document everything. Follow-up important phone calls with a letter reiterating what was said. Log all phone calls, especially patient calls, for your own reference and protection. Keep good records of who you spoke to and for what purpose. When you have several thousand accounts to collect on, it is impossible to keep straight what happened more than a few days ago. By keeping a log, either on the computer or in a patient file, you will be able to do your collections more accurately and keep records straight. Memories fade with time. A good vacation can make you completely forget all the issues and problems that plague you before you leave. Upon your return, you will need to recall all those little details that make your business so successful. Logs will ensure that you can do this.

Be prepared for audits and investigations; they are inevitable. If you are in this business long enough you will run into this. Audits, in and of themselves, are not bad things; more of an inconvenience than anything else. Consider them to be more of a training process than anything else. They are designed to catch errors and correct them so that everyone's job can be done more efficiently. This is a good thing. Just because you are selected for an audit doesn't mean that you have done anything wrong. While certainly you will be audited if the insurance company has reason to believe you are not being honest with your billing, the vast majority of them are random. Make sure that the person conducting the audit has the authority to do so. They must be an employee or contracted entity of the insurance company. Keep clear and organized records and be able to explain thoroughly how your system works and why. The majority of audits that I have seen (both my own offices and others) end up with minor offenses or no offenses at all.

Know what a subpoena is and how to respond to it. There are very limited situations in which patient information can be released. One is with a subpoena, the second is with a written release of information signed by the patient, and the third is by direct court order. If someone calls your office and states they are calling on behalf of the patient, while they may mean well, they are not legally entitled to that information. Neither is a third-party collection agency hired by any other agency. Refer them to the insurance company or to whomever hired them. Their information must come directly from that entity.

The newest subspecialty in the insurance billing field is known as "recovery agencies." These are independent companies, hired by insurers, to review their books as well as their contracts with providers and determine whether providers have been overpaid, according to their contracts. It is a cost-saving measure for the insurance company that has become a very successful new field. These companies are paid on a percentage of what they recover for the insurance company. There is no disagreement that this is a necessary step in the insurance process, and these companies are very, very good at their jobs, but as third-party entities with no connection to the patient, they are not legally entitled to confidential patient information. Many of these companies will sport a letter of reference from the company stating that they are working for XYZ Insurance Corporation. The legalities of these letters of reference are still being hashed out in the courts. The bottom line is that if they were hired by the insurance company, then their information must come directly from the insurance company. Don't release anything to anyone without proper documentation.

Follow the letter of the law regarding billing regulations. Don't do something you don't feel comfortable with. Don't use second hand information (from other billing services or unrelated offices). Go directly to the source. Call the insurance company or entity with which you are dealing directly. Don't bill incorrectly because an office tells you "Its okay, we do this all the time." If you're not sure about something, check it out. Listen to your initial gut reaction and follow your instincts. What you have to sell is your knowledge and reputation. Make sure it is accurate.

Always make backups of your system. This includes not only your billing information but also your own personal information as well. At least two sets are standard; one on site at your office for easy reference and one off site for safety. Remember, your backups will do you no good if they burn down when your house burns down. You need to have another set in a safe setting (outside office, safe deposit box, etc.) that you can get to when and if you need to. Always prepare for the worst. Hopefully, you will never have to face that situation, but you can rest assured knowing that you are ready for it.

LAWS OF CONFIDENTIALITY

Your patients' confidentiality is guaranteed by federal law. As the Custodian of Records, you are required, under that same law, to take all reasonable and necessary actions in order to keep those records safe and confidential. Currently, medical records can be released under minimal circumstances: 1) with a written authorization and release of information signed by the patient, and 2) by subpoena, and 3) by direct court order. You can usually get around this by referring the requesting party directly to the medical office. If what they are after is billing records, then clear their release with the doctor's office first. If medical records are being looked at for any reason, your client will want to know both when and why. If there is any type of court case involved, it is entirely possible that the doctor will be called as a witness. They need to be prepared for this by knowing exactly what is going on with their patients. Make sure and keep them up to date on all legal matters involving their office dealings.

There are two major pieces of legislation regulating the healthcare industry. One is HIPAA (Health Insurance Portability and Accountability Act) and the other is the Patient Bill of Rights.

PATIENT'S BILL OF RIGHTS

This is a lengthy document governing all aspects of patient care. It can be found in its entirety on the Internet. For our purposes, we will cover only those areas relevant to billing and collections. Bookkeeping-wise, the patient has two major rights. They are:

1. The right to know and understand exactly what they are being charged for. You must know and be able to explain what services were performed and why. If there are any questions regarding the latter (why), then have the name of someone you can refer them to for that information, possibly an office manager or nurse within the office or clinic. The doctor should do this at the time of service, but sometimes the patient's medical condition prevents them from making important decisions and family is asked instead. Patients also forget, especially if they have undergone any type of anesthesia. It is common to have people call the office and ask again what procedure they had done and why. If you are not prepared to answer these questions, you need to refer them on.
2. The patient has the right to a complete accounting and penny-by-penny explanation of what their charges are. "Previous balance" or "balance forward" billing is unacceptable, unless the patient has previously gotten an itemization of charges. Even so, if they call the office and ask for another complete accounting of their charges, you need to provide this to them. It is a courtesy for them and to your client as well. People are more apt to pay bills that they understand than ones that they do not.

HIPAA REGULATIONS

The HIPAA regulations are the newest legislation regarding healthcare. This law protects a person's privacy and personal health information. Again, this is a lengthy document, available on the Internet, so we will address only the portions relevant to billing. HIPAA regulations provide for electronic and physical security of protected health information (PHI) including, but not limited to: name, address, phone number, insurance identification number, social security number, group insurance number, account number, medical record number, procedures, diagnoses, or any other information that can identify you as a patient, who your insurance company is, and what you were seen for. HIPAA regulations allow for the transfer of information (portability) *only* between providers and insurance carriers for the sole and expressed purpose of filing and payment of claims. Your personal information cannot be sold, advertised, or transferred in any other way or for any other purpose without your expressed written consent first. This law mandates that providers inform you as a patient on your first visit, and in writing, what their privacy practices are, and that they are, as an office, HIPAA compliant. Violations are subject to stiff fines and possible loss of business, as well as criminal charges if applicable. These are tough laws designed to protect patients from the ever-increasing problem of identity theft. By holding anyone with access to a person's PHI accountable, the government is setting up a tracking system to be able to better protect and prosecute those who abuse the privileged position they are in. This information needs to be guarded with the same diligence that a cash deposit would. Identity theft is a serious problem that can ruin lives. It costs consumers and taxpayers figures well into the billions every year.

HIPAA regulations require that all PHI you are responsible for is protected to the greatest extent of your ability under the circumstances. This means receiving information, filing of claims, storage of records, DDE transmissions, e-mail and fax transmissions, phone calls, and Internet access. All must be reasonably locked down and secure according to all federal regulations. If you use a courier service, particularly one that does not specialize in transporting medical documents and information, it is essential that you make them understand the importance of confidentiality. You should have courier bags that can be closed and locked. Canvas book bags work well. They are cheap and can hold a large number of documents. They can be locked with either a luggage lock or simply a nylon zip tie (they can be found at any hardware store) only to be removed by you or the physician's office. It must also be clearly understood that if the office or your home is closed for whatever reason, the documents are never to be left unattended at the door, as delivery companies sometimes do. This is an unacceptable delivery location, and the driver must either wait or return when someone is there. Sometimes a locking delivery box with keys given to both you and the delivery driver will work, as long as the box is secure and out of the weather.

Another thing to consider in this field is the VIPs (Very Important People) that will come through. There are many big name celebrities, musicians, sports figures, and politicians out there today. These are people for whom the press would pay a high price for information that would sell magazines and newspapers. Often times they will check into the hospital as John Doe or Jane Doe. Their true identity is shielded from the press and often from mainstream hospital workers for just this reason. If you are to run across any documents revealing the identity of any of these patients, it is your solemn responsibility to keep those documents protected, as you would any other PHI (Protected Health Information). These persons are trusting your office with their confidentiality, as are other lesser known patients. This is a responsibility not to be taken lightly. It is also punishable by law.

FRAUD

It's unfortunate, but fraud is rife within this field. Rest assured that there are investigations and audits set in place to uncover these situations, but also be aware that it is out there, so you should be prepared for it. If you are in this field long enough, you will more than likely run into it in one degree or another. Every person I have ever known, or known of, that has crossed this line has been caught and punished. The attitude to keep is that nothing is worth not only the loss of your business and your reputation but also possibly your freedom, house, and family. If the problem is serious enough, legal charges and jail time will result.

Personally, I have been approached to commit fraud on three separate occasions. These situations range from patients trying to make a fast buck at the insurance company's expense, to a massive fraud operation involving several corrupt attorneys and physicians, ending in an elaborate FBI investigation and criminal charges being filed. Everywhere there are people who don't think that the rules apply to them, and they can bypass the system for whatever they want. Beware of these people and steer clear of them and their business dealings as often as you can.

My advice to you is to follow the letter of the law as closely as you can and keep as many records of your transactions as you can. If you have a clean paper trail, that any auditor can follow, you will generally not have any problems as far as cash flow is concerned. If your physician's office is doing all of your coding for you, procedures and diagnoses, you will have a trail to follow there. If an error occurs, or series of errors, simply explain to the auditor that you were using the wrong code in error, and you will make the situation right. This will probably require corrected billings and possibly refunds of overpaid amounts. If you acknowledge the error and work with the auditor to correct the problem, there will generally be no repercussions. While they are looking for mistakes, they are hunting for fraud. If you are earnestly trying to do your job and are willing to work with others to grow and learn, you will do fine. If you try to cover things up and refuse to cooperate with official entities for reporting purposes, you are setting yourself up for trouble. Try whenever possible, with proper paperwork in place, to work with auditors as much as possible. There is absolutely nothing wrong with the statement "I'm sorry, I've made a mistake. How can I fix it?"

Many providers and facilities, in their contracts, are actually given a percentage of errors that they are allowed to make. For example, one local hospital that I deal with has an error rate of 8 percent. Up to 8 percent of the billings can contain errors and have no legal issues resulting from it, so long as the errors are corrected when found. If the facility crossed the 8 percent mark, whether intentional or not, it was deemed fraud and a fine would ensue. There needn't be any actual fraud involved. The problems could still be reasonably considered human error, but due to the level of the error rate, the auditing entity would then consider it a fraud investigation. Make sure and review all contracts for any fraud or error language of this kind. If you find any errors, do whatever it takes to correct them as soon as you can. It will benefit everyone in the long run.

There is an insurance product that can be purchased now called Errors and Omissions Insurance (E and O insurance). This is an insurance policy safeguarding against problems resulting from billing errors or omissions on your part. When these types of policies first came out, they were very expensive, although they are coming down in price now. It is entirely up to you whether this is something you wish to invest in. For a beginner, it could potentially save you money if you're not entirely sure how the extended system works. For a more experienced biller, it may seem like overkill. Carrying this insurance will have both risks and benefits. The risk would be the possibly high cost, the limitations of what would and would not be covered, and the circumstances under which payment would be made. The benefits would be the saving should a problem actually occur. The choice to carry this product would have to be an individual one, weighed against your own personal situation and comfort level.

WHAT HAPPENS
IF MY CLIENTS DON'T PAY ME?

Hopefully this will be an issue you will never have to deal with, but like the fraud issue, sooner or later it will probably become an issue on one level or another.

First, I would try to have an understanding between you and your client, so they understand this is your paycheck. Also, if you have employees, this is their paycheck also. Nonpayment of bills is unacceptable. The money you are billing for is for services that have already been rendered. The cash has already been deposited into their bank account and ready for them to spend it. Payment due on receipt of the bill is not unreasonable. A clause should be written right into your contract agreement regarding exactly when you expect to be paid and what consequences there will be for non-payment. On the flip side, a clause should also be written in there about the services you are to provide and what the consequences would be for non-delivery of services. A truly fair contract will work both ways. Services are provided as well as payment rendered. Both sides should be protected in any good business situation.

Should the situation ever arise where you are not paid, I would first go and talk to the client. Make sure that this occurs after the bill has been received and after the payment period has elapsed with no check forthcoming. My first inclination would be to ask how things are going and if there are any problems that are preventing the payment of your bill. See what the response is. Generally it will be a good one. Offer another grace period and ask if there is anything that you can do to help financial matters along—after all, that is your job. If there is a negative cash flow situation, you need to know about it.

If there is enough cash coming in to cover expenses, including yours, and you are still not getting paid, then it is time for another step. It sounds harsh, but you can't let someone else's cash problems become your cash problems. We all would like a new car and a new house and sometimes even an entire new life. These things cost money—big money. If your bill is not being paid due to a new item that has been purchased, this is unacceptable. Make another meeting, or write a letter and state what your problem is. You feel you should be paid because . . . You feel it is unacceptable that you have not been paid because . . . If payment is not received, the consequences will be . . . Lay your case out in black and white. Have it delivered to the doctor and allow another grace period. If no payment is forthcoming, suspend all future billings, give formal notice of termination of the contract for non-payment, and file a suit in small claims court. It should be no problem getting a judgment with all your documentation in order. Detail out the work that was done with no payment. Show the invoices, the contract that you both signed, and the demand letters sent. Courts are extremely pro-employee these days. If you did the work, you should be paid. If an argument comes up that perhaps your work is not up to par (some people will try anything to get out of paying a claim), simply point out that the monies you are billing for is for payments already received by the client. This will generally shut them down with no possible response. The work can't be shoddy if the claims have already been paid. The claims that haven't been paid aren't being billed for. I had one doctor even claim that he never hired me. After producing the contract that he signed, I received payment in full, plus damages. Again, keep good records in good order and you should have no problems in the long run.

Occasionally a client will declare bankruptcy. While this may be nothing personal toward you, it will have a significant impact on your business. Things that will need to be addressed at that point are: 1) What is my working relationship with this client like? 2) Do I wish to continue and start with a fresh slate? or 3) Will I cut my ties and find a new client? If this is a hard-working client that you like and have worked well with but just needs a fresh start for whatever reason, you may want to consider keeping him. The business loss may be more beneficial for you at tax time than the loss of a good client. If, however, the client is one that you were at odds with for other reasons, this may be a good time and reason to get out of the contract and look elsewhere for new business. Make sure you are served with all proper bankruptcy paperwork for your tax records and possibly even show up at the bankruptcy hearing, as is your right. Personal experience has taught me that once a person actually files for bankruptcy, there aren't a lot of choices left for you to make. You will more than likely never see that money. Thankfully, these situations are rare. Most business situations are beneficial for everyone involved, as they should be.

Working with Spouses— Is This a Good Idea?

Many people when they enter into business will make their spouse their partner. I have been asked if this is actually a good idea. I don't really have a good answer for that. Like most things, I think this will be an individual choice. I think it depends entirely on the type of relationship that exists between the two individuals and exactly what job functions each will have. There are spousal partnerships that have worked out well and have lasted for years, and there are those that have not. I don't know that there are any statistics on this, but there are some common sense steps that can be taken to avoid blow-ups later on.

First, talk about it beforehand and not just in the sense of how great it will be and how life will be perfect after you are self-employed. Believe me, that doesn't happen. Talk realistically about how the day-to-day operations will happen. When something breaks, who will be responsible for fixing it? If overtime is required, who will stay and work it? If the kids need something, who will go and get them? You need to know who will perform which job functions, and will each of you be happy with that? Overall, you need to know who will be the main decision-maker. There needs to be one. You can split this up if need be: one can make financial decisions and the other can make business decisions. Whatever the case, both parties need to respect the decisions of the other party.

Second, when disagreements come up, ask yourself: Is this worth a huge battle? If your partner is simply trying to save money on paper clips and buys a cheaper brand, gauge your reaction and keep things appropriate. As in most arguments, it is easy to begin with something small and insignificant when the problem is genuinely much bigger and harder to handle. Keep communication open. Don't let things build up, and don't take them home with you. Try to leave the office in the office, even if it is only twelve feet down the hall. Remember, this is the partner you have pledged the rest of your life to. Cheap paper clips aren't worth ruining that. If there is something deeper wrong, don't waste valuable time arguing over paper clips or anything else that doesn't really matter. Get to the heart of the matter. Seek professional help, if necessary, and know when to quit. If your business partnership isn't working, and both parties realize it, sit down and figure out what to do. One partner can get out and return to traditional employment and let the other partner run the business, if that is mutually agreed upon. The main key here is: Talk it out.

ELECTRONIC BILLING VS. PAPER CLAIMS

Can you run a billing service without doing electronic billing? Certainly you can. It will be less costly initially to set up but will also be less efficient. There are, however, certain types of billing that cannot be done electronically. Anything that requires a copy of a written report, also known as a by-report procedure, must be billed on paper. If you can, and if the types of clients you are going after will be interested in electronic billing, I highly recommend it. It will increase revenue faster for both you and your clients.

There are certain advantages and disadvantages to both electronic and paper billing. Some of these can be used as selling tools for your company and others are simply things that you need to be aware of.

Advantages to Electronic

Electronic claims require less work to process. Since there is no paper, there is no additional cost for buying forms. There are both decreased manpower in filing and storage costs, and less postage costs to incur.

Disadvantages to Electronic

If you use a clearing house, you lose some control of the filing process. You must follow these accounts up more often to insure that nothing falls through the cracks. Sometimes, through an initial set-up and testing phase, you must still bill on paper as well as electronically.

Advantages to Paper

Certain claims are only billable on paper. They can hold required attachments where electronic claims cannot. Paper claims can be used for tracers and inquiries on unpaid claims, where electronic claims cannot.

Many secondary insurances can only be billed on paper since the primary EOB must be attached.

A lot of the claims that can only be billed on paper are the higher paying procedures, as in work comp and major surgical procedures. You will make more money on these accounts, so they are a very appealing portion of the potential workload.

Disadvantages to Paper

The claims take longer to process, so payment will be tied up a little bit longer than electronic claims. There is more paperwork to print and file. There is an increased cost to purchase the forms, as well as increased postage costs, particularly if larger envelopes with report attachments and backup documentation are being sent.

WHAT IS A CLEARINGHOUSE?

A clearinghouse is an independent third party able to submit claims to many different insurance companies and entities. They pay for, and maintain a computer system that meets the technical requirements to many different insurance companies, saving you money since you only have to meet the technical requirements of one: theirs. Many independent agencies (billing services and small doctors' offices) will submit their claims to the clearinghouse electronically. The clearinghouse will then re-bundle the claims and send them on to the appropriate insurance company in a larger group. So, for instance, the group of claims that goes out to Medicare may have your claims, as well as the claims from several other offices, and the same for Blue Cross, Blue Shield, Aetna, and so on.

Advantages are that the majority of all claims can be sent electronically, quickly and efficiently. The doctor has a quicker return on his money, and you have less paper to process.

Disadvantages are that the clearinghouse will charge you per claim on submissions. Every time a claim goes through their system, there is a charge. So, if you have to bill the claim four times before it gets paid, you have to pay for that claim four times. You also lose control of the claim as soon as it leaves your computer system. If the clearinghouse does not re-bundle and forward your claims on to the appropriate entity in a timely manner, both you and your doctor will lose money. There will be an agreement between you and the clearinghouse on this to ensure that this should not happen.

There are also additional ways to follow up on these claims. The clearinghouse will have a built-in system edit program to tell you if your claims are incomplete or rejected. There will also be e-mailed reports that verify the number of claims that they have received from you and the number of claims that they have forwarded on. These reports must be checked for accuracy every time you submit a batch. If a claim falls through the cracks, it must be investigated and corrected immediately. Many insurance companies have a billing deadline of sixty days. If a claim is not received within that initial sixty-day period from the date of service, it will not be paid. If you miss the sixty-day deadline because of your own negligence, your company will be responsible. All claims sent through a clearinghouse must be followed and verified as received by the insurance company as soon as possible from the date of billing.

I had a girlfriend who decided that she wanted to start a medical insurance billing business. She knew absolutely nothing about billing and had never even seen an insurance claim before. She landed a large client (by undercutting the market and offering an incredibly cheap introductory rate) who did a large number of billing with a local insurer. After setting him up on an electronic system, she sent months and months worth of claims to the insurer through a clearinghouse without ever checking to make sure that the claims were received. The problem is that the claims were all rejected because her system had been set up incorrectly. Since no follow-up was done, hundreds of claims were rendered not payable because they had missed the billing deadline. The doctor was forced into early retirement, and she lost her business opportunity—all because she did not check her electronic e-mail until it was too late.

There are system edits and precautions in place to avoid this very situation. Make sure you know what they are and how to use them.

OFFICE MANAGER: FRIEND OR FOE?

Is the office manager someone to be revered or feared? While marketing you will discover that actually getting in to see the doctor is a very difficult thing. A physician's entire day is based on the appointment system. If he doesn't have appointments, he's probably not there. One thing you need to determine early on is who are the actual decision makers in that office.

Some physicians prefer to run their offices and tend to all details themselves. These are the offices you will have more difficulty getting in to. Other offices are run almost exclusively by the office manager, and the physician only shows up to see patients. In this instance, the office manager is the person you want to talk to. In either case, try not to alienate anyone in the office, including the front office or any managers.

A good deal of resistance you will run into is from the office staff. They mistakenly feel that you are there to take their jobs. This is not the case. An office cannot run entirely on the efforts of a billing service alone. Office staff is still necessary to greet and register patients, answer phones, make appointments, collect information, order supplies, tend to the doctor's needs, and generally keep things in the office in order. Try to make it clear that you are there to assist them or to enhance what they already do. There is no need to take anyone's job; and in fact, this rarely happens. You are there to make the office staff's job easier, not to replace them entirely.

In your sales pitch you can offer more than one level of service. Rather than the more time-consuming (and job-consuming) full A/R management services, offer a more minimal service, claims-submission-only service. This will be more attractive to the offices in fear of losing their jobs, and is a way of getting your foot in the door. After you have begun working at a minimal level, then try to increase your job duties later on.

Never criticize any member of the office, until you are completely aware of who all the players are and how that office works. It is not at all uncommon to have the office manager or head nurse be the wife of the head doctor in the practice. You don't want to put your foot in your mouth right from the start. When you start off on the wrong foot, it can be very difficult to get back on the right one. It is much better just to try to keep all personal comments to a minimum to start with.

When you do get an appointment, make sure to follow up with a thank you card in the mail. Acknowledging how very busy the office staff is and how much you appreciate them taking their valuable time to meet with you will impress them. If the office manager had any sway in getting you in the office, make a special note just for them. The more friends (both in high places and low ones), the easier time you will have in your marketing and your daily work.

Gratuities also work really well. I once worked for an office that would, on the first Wednesday of every month, bring cookies to all their clients. It didn't necessarily need to be a holiday or special occasion, just a way of letting them know that they were appreciated. It became such a habit that on the rare occasion when it wasn't possible to get the cookies there on Wednesday, the office staff became distressed that there were no cookies. Little things like this mean a lot to the people that we encounter all day. Our jobs can be stressful ones, and if a $1.99 box of cookies once a month will lift someone's spirits, I think it is money well spent.

The last thing that I would encourage you to do is to treat everyone as you yourself would like to be treated. In this country, we have a great deal of cultural diversity. This diversity must be embraced and cherished if we are all to live in a peaceful world. There are a great number of ethnic differences, socio-economic differences, geographic differences, educational differences, and religious differences to be dealt with on a daily basis. If we can all try to overlook those things that are different from us and treat one another with the respect and dignity that we all deserve, then our business will take off and fly to heights unknown. If, however, there is a situation that you are unable to handle for whatever reason, politely excuse yourself and refer that client to another service. Do not allow yourself into a situation that you are unable to handle emotionally. It would be far better for everyone involved to just get out.

The same line of thinking goes for a very large office. Don't promise something that you can't deliver. Don't enter into a contract bid to work for a large fifteen hundred physician hospital when you are a single office with no employees. Logic would dictate that you would be unable to take on that large amount of work. It would be better to take the job on in smaller stages or turn it down outright, than to promise something that you can't deliver. It only takes one large mistake to ruin a reputation in the medical community. Try not to make that mistake up front and deter your chances of ever having a successful business in the first place.

TAXES

Don't be so busy taking care of your client's figures that you neglect your own bookkeeping needs. Make arrangements for the keeping of your own books. Remember that most of what you do in connection with your business now is considered a tax issue (either taxable income or write-offs.) The write-offs for a home office are substantial; however, you must keep clear and accurate records. All the equipment and supplies that you buy, and your mileage and auto expenses, are now just a few things that need to be accounted for. I would actually recommend making an appointment with an accountant for a one-time consultation. They can help you to get your books set up and prepared correctly from the start. They can tell you the things you need to watch out for and what would be the best way to guard against problems. A one-time consultation will cost a minimal amount and will end up saving you money in the long run. The fee, of course, is tax deductible.

You must provide your clients with either your social security number or your federal tax ID number. This should go right on your invoices. A tax ID number is free and available from the IRS. With all of the trouble with identity theft and protection of social security numbers as confidential information, it would be advisable to obtain a tax ID number at the start of your business.

Keep good records. Save all receipts and billing stubs. Also, keep a mileage log in all cars and log everything you do (going to the office supply store, going on interviews, appointments, weekly courier routes, etc.). If you ever do get audited by the IRS, they will insist on seeing these documents. Get in the habit of writing everything down whether you think you will need it or not.

LICENSES AND REGULATIONS

In many counties, to operate a home-based business you must have a business license. This license restricts the numbers of clients and times of day that customers can visit you at your home office. It also will either limit or entirely prohibit the employment of on-site employees. You should keep this in mind when you become busy enough to begin subcontracting out some of your work.

When you do hire employees, in whatever capacity, workers compensation insurance is required by law. Also, if you are to have people coming to your home, a blanket liability policy is a good idea. They are very cheap, generally several hundred dollars for the year, and will protect you from simple little accidents that can turn into large headaches later on. People can manage to hurt themselves almost anywhere on almost anything. Most homeowner's insurance policies have a clause written in there releasing themselves of any liability when an on-site business is being operated. A special rider is often required for the policy to cover anyone working within your home, including housekeepers and gardeners. Make sure to read your policy and understand what you are covered for and what you are not. Be prepared and be insured. It can save you headaches and money later on. It may even save your home.

The business licenses for rented or leased offices will vary depending on the type of business. Some businesses are more highly regulated than others (i.e. toxic waste, businesses prone to high injury rates, etc.). It is also the law in many states that you must carry workers' compensation insurance for all employees upon the first date of employment. If you do not have insurance in place when the employee is hired, you can be subject to a fine from the state. Again, check it out and be prepared.

Experience Level Necessary to Begin

While it is not required that you have, in the past, been employed in the medical billing field in order to start this business, it is definitely a plus. There are, however, other ways around that, so don't be discouraged. If you can take the time to learn the basics and understand what you are looking at, you can have a successful business as well.

In order to begin a successful medical billing service, you need to know and completely understand what the CPT codes and the ICD-9 codes are and how to use them. Taking the time to become thoroughly acquainted with the reference manuals will be essential, even if you do not code the work that is received from the medical office. Questions will inevitably come up from time to time and you will need to know how to resolve them or how to intelligently relay the problem to the medical office so they can advise you as to what to do.

You must also have a basic understanding of the human body. You don't need to know the names of all 206 bones in the human body, but you do need to know the major ones. You need to know the difference between the different major systems and how they relate to the different specialties that you are billing for. Most importantly, you need to know where to go to look questions up when you have them. The Internet or online encyclopedia is a good source. There are also computer tutorials of the human body that can be very useful for things like this. These can be accessed and studied in your own leisure time and on your own schedule. That alone will be worth the price you will pay for them.

You must be able to read and understand sometimes complicated medical procedures or know where to go to find out what they are and how to explain them to the patients. This is a patient's basic right—to be able to understand what service was performed and exactly how much they are being charged for it. If you cannot reasonably explain this to the patient, then refer them to the doctor's office so they can make the answer clear. If you need to, take some time and ask the doctor how to best explain their services, in layman's terms, to the patients that ask. The physician will tell you how he wants you to handle the situation or whether to refer them directly to him.

You must know and understand how the insurance system in this country works, and you must continually keep up with the ever-changing insurance regulations and laws governing healthcare. This is where continuing education comes in. Most major insurance companies will offer periodic (either quarterly or semi-annually) training for office staff of their clientele. There is generally a small charge for this service (again, a tax deduction), but the information gleaned from this session will be invaluable in your service. These training sessions are well worth the time and the minimal cost you incur to attend them. Even if you've been to them before and most of the information is repeated for you, there will usually be something new or something that you had not picked up before.

While it is possible to gain all the information listed above from reading and speaking to others within the field, it is generally recommended that you have some actual prior billing experience to start with. Anything you can list on your resume that is in a related field will always be helpful. But how do you get experience when you have not been employed in this field before? One easy way is to volunteer. Contact several offices in your area and speak to the person in charge of hiring. Explain to them that you are beginning your own business and need some hands-on experience for your resume. Ask them if it would be possible to exchange some office hours on your part to do filing or miscellaneous work for some knowledge and experience in working in their highly respected office. If you have only a few hours to spend, then make the most out of them. Work as much as you can for several months. Then, on your resume, simply list the time span that you worked for that office. List January–June 2008 as having worked, and always use them as a reference if you can. You don't need to state that this was volunteer work or that you only worked six hours a week. Certainly don't lie, and always answer questions honestly when asked, but on the other hand, don't volunteer any information that wasn't specifically asked. You may need to volunteer several places before you feel confident enough to strike out on your own. Remember, this is a self-confidence game. When you feel you are confident enough to run your own business, then you are already there. Attitude is everything.

CONTINUING EDUCATION

Read everything. Be as informed and educated as you can. There are many trade journals and industry publications that can be subscribed to. Major hospitals will have newsletters and patient information available. Get on as many mailing lists as you can. The more you know, the farther you can go.

Every insurance company will have a billing manual for sale or to obtain. Get copies of all of the major billing manuals for your area and keep up on updates. Don't just get them and file them, but read them, even if they don't seem to apply. You never know when a little bit of information will come in handy.

Go to as many training seminars as you can, whether paid or free. Insurance companies will give you this information either for free or at a very minimal cost. It is in their best interests to keep you as educated and informed as they can. It cuts down on billing issues and problems later on. There are independent companies that will give you the same information but at a higher cost. Remember, independent companies are out to make money. While I don't begrudge anyone making a living, just be aware that there are other sources for the same information at a lesser cost. Convenience is one thing that we pay extra for. After attending these training seminars, often you will get a certificate of completion. Save these for your marketing. You can show them to the doctor or frame them and hang them on the wall of your office. They show your accomplishments.

Read current events in the newspapers, medical journals, and financial journals. Information is easily accessible if you take the time to hunt it up. Keep up as often as possible on new trends and new industry changes. It will help you immensely.

Take brush-up classes at the local community colleges. These are cost effective and incredibly helpful.

Search the Internet for interesting health/money-related issues. Register for automatic e-mail alerts from the major news sources for any information related to medical or health issues and also business information. This will be delivered straight to your e-mail box, ready for you to read when you have time. What could be easier than that?

Finally, keep up with the competition. Find out what everyone else is doing and how much they are charging. Network with as many people and associations as you have time for. Keep up on the specifics in your own local area. Be ready to spring on a business opportunity that you hear about through the grapevine. Keep your attitude good, your mind clear, and your heart ready. Good things come to those who wait. This can be a very rewarding and profitable field for those who are ready for a challenge. Work hard, be honest, and keep looking forward.

THE WAVE OF THE FUTURE

This business is quickly becoming one of the most scrutinized and regulated industries in the country, and rightly so. There have been very little and extremely lax regulations up to this point, allowing fraud to run rampant and unchecked. This is quickly changing. With the introduction of certified billers and coders, and fraud investigators, the industry is more closely examined in an effort to keep healthcare costs down. It is estimated that in less than five years all billing will be required to be electronically billed, going through a system of edits and check that will help ensure accuracy. What this means for billers and entrepreneurs is that there are tremendous ground level opportunities right now for the person ready and willing to begin a new business.

So what does the future hold for this profession? I believe it is more automated and electronic procedures each and every day. The time will come when paper claims are a thing of the past. Companies are already developing software and marketing contracts to major insurance companies for fully automated claims review and electronic funds transfer payment system. These will come with automatic review by an independent third-party auditor for accuracy in pricing and remittance. The more automated the system, the more efficient the process is and the quicker the claims submission and payment turnaround will be. I envision more and more third-party review agencies springing up and contracting with the insurance companies to audit their books and recover overpayments on their behalf.

What does this mean for the average home billing service? It means that you need to stay on top of the technological advancements in your profession. Know and understand all the new options and how to incorporate them into your business.

Does this advance in technology mean the end of the small businessperson in this industry? Absolutely not. It does, however, mean that you will not be able to use the billing software that your predecessor bought back in 1974 any longer. If you are already in business and using an outdated program that still "gets by," you will need to upgrade to something more efficient. Education and understanding of the field are an absolute must in order to stay current. Perhaps a slight adjustment of your business to make the insurance company your client rather than the doctor is a possibility. Offer your services as a consultant or an auditor if you feel comfortable with that. No matter what the claims process is, physicians and facilities will still need to find a way to get the information from their office into the insurance company computers the easiest way possible. This is where you come in. Research and develop the best way for that to happen with the possibilities on the market today and be prepared to walk into a new client's office and clearly explain the procedure as though it were as simple as taking out the trash. The possibilities are as endless as the ideas that will spring to mind as you learn more and more about this exciting field. It can be both very rewarding and extremely profitable and above all fun. Just stay on top of new advancements, keep educated, work hard, and have fun.

DON'T QUIT YOUR DAY JOB

Probably the most valuable piece of advice I will ever be able to give you is don't quit your day job too soon. This is a major mistake that many people make when starting a new business. If affects entrepreneurs across the board, not just billing services.

This field fluctuates. Your income from month to month will not be consistent. Don't fall into the trap of thinking that just because you have two or three good months in a row, every month will be like that from then on. It won't. The market fluctuates like any other. There will be good times and bad times. You need to be prepared to weather both. When you have a good month, stash some aside for a rainy day. When you have a bad month, don't panic, but draw from your storehouse until business picks up again.

There are three general guidelines to follow before leaving your steady source of income and benefits:

1. have a documented, sustained income for at least six months to a year;
2. have a secure client base; and
3. have sufficient savings to cover the hard times.

Without these three things, quitting your full time job will be an emotional and frustrating time for you. You will have greater feelings of failure if you have to turn around and get another day job, and you will have a tendency to give up on your dream and walk away.

Don't be a quitter. Don't walk away from your dream. You can do this, just be smart about it and plan for the future. With a little job security in the bank, you won't need to run for the unemployment office at the first sign of trouble. Most financial advisers will inform you that you need to have a minimum of six months' salary in the bank at all times for immediate use should an emergency come up. This is a good idea considering the fact that you are investing a huge amount of time, talent, and treasure into this new venture. Plan for the best and be prepared for the worst. This is one more way to ensure success in your new business.

ANSWERS

ANSWERS

1. A new patient presents for an office visit. He is an adult male and requires a comprehensive history and exam, followed by medical decision making of a highly complex nature. What code would you use? 99205
2. A new patient presents for an office visit. He is an adult male and requires a focused history taking and exam with medical decision making of a straightforward nature. What code would you use? 99202
3. An established patient presents for an office visit. She is a middle-aged female and requires an expanded history taking and exam with medical decision making of a low complexity. What code would you use? 99213
4. Your physician is called for a hospital visit. He has never seen this patient before. The patient is an older female. This visit will be for initial observation, with a detailed history and exam, with medical decision making of a low complexity. What code would you use? 99218
5. Your physician is called back to the hospital for subsequent hospital care for this same patient. She now requires a more focused history and exam but still has medical decision making of a low complexity. What code would you use? 99231
6. Can you have a subsequent hospital care visit for a new patient? No. Subsequent visit means that you have seen the patient before.
7. Your physician is called to the hospital for observation of an established patient. The history-taking and exam is of a comprehensive nature and decision making is moderately complex. What code would you use? 99235
8. Can you use an observation care code for a new patient? No. New patient would be an initial consultation code.
9. You have a patient being discharged from the hospital and you are called for a discharge service evaluation. This evaluation will be less than thirty minutes in length and the patient is a middle-aged male. What code would you use? 99238
10. You have a new patient that comes to your office for a consultation. This is an outpatient service at your office. It requires a detailed history and examination with medical decision making of a low complexity. What code would you use? 99243
11. Your physician has an initial inpatient new-patient consult hospital visit with an elderly gentleman. It requires a focused history and exam with straightforward decision making. What code would you use? 99251
12. This same gentleman has a follow-up inpatient consultation. He is an established patient with a detailed history and exam and decision making of a high complexity. What code would you use? 99263
13. Can you have a follow-up inpatient consult on a new patient? No. Follow-up means that you have seen this patient before.

14. Your physician is called for a confirmatory consultation for a new patient. This will be a comprehensive history and exam and require medical decision making of a moderate complexity. What code would you use? 99274

15. Can you have a confirmatory consultation on an established patient? Yes. Confirmation does not have to be a first visit.

16. A teenage boy is brought into the emergency room. This is a new patient for you. He requires a comprehensive history and exam and medical decision making of a high complexity. What code would you use? 99285

CPT

CPT1

Please look up the following codes in the CPT books:

Code	Type	Pt Type	Problem level
99212	OV	est pt	focused
99201	OV	new pt	focused
99211	OV	est pt	minimal
99218 (observation)	HV	new or est	comprehensive
99221	HV	new or est	comprehensive
99232 (subsequent care)	HV	est pt	focused
99238	HV	est pt	focused
99244	OV	new or est	comprehensive
99254	HV	new or est	comprehensive
99252	HV	new or est	focused

CPT 2

Description	CPT Code
Miller Procedure	28737
Miscarriage, second trimester	59821
Excision, *Metacarpal*	26230
Paternity testing, *blood type*	86910–86911
Face Lift	15824–15828
In Vitro *Fertilization*	89250–89252
Incision and Drainage, Skin with Fluid Collection	10140
Injection, Cyst, Kidney	50390
Intubation, Endotracheal tube	31500
Administration, *Ipecac*	99175
Excision, *Intervertebral* disc Decompression	63075–63078
Intermediate Care Facility Visits	99301–99303
	99311–99313

CPT3

Description	CPT Code
Sensitivity Study-Fungus	87192
Separation, Craniofacial, closed	21431
Excision, *Stomach*, total	43620–43622
Gastric bypass, *Stomach*	43846
Tetanus Immunization	90711
TB (Tuberculosis) Skin test	86580–86585
Tachycardia, heart, recording	93609
Hysterosonography	76831
Heroin Screen	82101
Hernia Repair-Epigastric	49570
Drainage, Abscess, Liver	47010–47011
Diverticulum, Meckel's, Excision	44800

CPT- 4 CODING

Please code the following:

	Description	Code
1.	Office Visit-new patient-comprehensive	99205
2.	Hosp Visit observation-new or est pt, initial	99218
3.	Hosp visit-hosp care, initial, comprehensive of moderate complexity	99222
4.	Hosp visit-subsequent visit-focused of low complexity	99231
5.	Breast reconstruction with tissue expander subsequent expansion	19357
6.	Laparoscopy, surgical transection of vagus nerves, truncal	43651
7.	Diagnostic ultrasound, chest, echography chest B-scan with realtime image documentation	76604
8.	Blood Tests (Chemistry/ Path and Lab)	
	Creatine	82540
	Copper	82525
	Chromium	82495
	Fluoride	82735
	Dihydrocodeinone	82646
9.	Echocardiography, transthoracic for congenital heart anomalies, complete	93303
10.	Cardiac Catheterization	
	Right Heart Cath	93501
	Left Heart Cath	93510
11.	Physical Therapy Evaluation	97001
12.	Prescription and fitting of contact lenses	92310
13.	Cochlear device implantation (hearing aid)	69930
14.	Thyroid Lobectomy	60225
15.	Incision, Gastrotomy	43500

CPT-5 CODING

Please code the following:

1.	Incision, soft tissue, superficial	20000
2.	Incision, deep or complicated	20005
3.	Repair, flexor tendon, primary, each tendon,	26350
	each subsequent tendon	26350–51
4.	Incision and Drainage, Knee joint, hematoma	27301
5.	Fasciotomy, iliotibial open (tenotomy) knee joint or femur, thigh region	27305
6.	Cholangiopancreatography	43260
7.	Vasotomy, Incision vas deferens	55200
8.	Vasectomy, excision vas deferens	55250
9.	Cervical biopsy	57500
10.	Excision endometrial sample (biopsy)	58100
11.	Subdural tap, skull thru fontalenne or suture, infant	61000
12.	X-ray teeth, diagnostic exam	70300
13.	Venography, extremity, bilateral, radiological supervision and interpretation	75822
14.	Diagnostic ultrasound, spinal canal echography	76800
15.	Arthritis panel	80072
16.	(Path and Lab) Blood test for Human Growth Hormone	83003

ICD-9, EXERCISE 1

Please look up the following codes from the ICD-9 books:

717.43	derangement of lateral meniscus-posterior horn
540.0	acute appendicitis with generalized peritonitis
E852	accidental poisoning by other sedatives and hypnotics
V65.1	other person seeking consult without complaint or sickness on behalf of another person
722	Intervertebral disc disorders (needs fourth- or fifth-digit coding)
443.0	Raynaud's syndrome
251.2	Hypoglycemia, unspecified
253.3	Pituitary dwarfism
090	congenital syphilis (needs fourth- or fifth-digit coding)
E880.1	fall from sidewalk or curb

ICD-9 EXERCISE 2

Please look up the following codes from the ICD-9 books:

E970	injury due to legal intervention by fire arms
V455.3	attention to artificial openings-colostomy
780.7	malaise and fatigue
196	malignant neoplasm/lymph nodes (needs fourth- or fifth-digit coding)
056.9	Rubella without complications
102.0	yaws-initial lesions
360.1	disorders of the globe (eye) other endophthalmitis
998.01	postoperative shock
E828	accident involving animal being ridden (needs fourth- or fifth-digit coding)
628.0	infertility, female-anovulation

ICD-9 EXERCISE 3

(Remember to look up in index, then cross reference to tabular to check color coding.)

Description	CPT Code
Fear of Open Spaces with panic attacks	300.21
Hysterical *Parorexia*	300.11
Twisted Bowel (Colon)	560.2
Elephantiasis, Eyelid	374.83
Human Growth Hormone *Deficiency*	253.3
Blood *Clot*, Bladder	596.7
Clumsiness	781.3
Cold	460
Osteoarthritis	715.9
Traumatic Rotator Cuff *Tear*	840.4
Jackson's *Veil*	751.4
Open Ankle *Wound*	891.0

ICD-9 EXERCISE 4

(Remember to look up code in index then cross reference to tabular and check color coding.)

Description	CPT Code
Whooping Cough	033.9
Widening Aorta	441.9
Onychitis	681.9
Malignant *Neoplasm*, Connective Tissue NEC Abdomen, Primary	171.5
Benign *Neoplasm*, Connective Tissue NEC Hand, Secondary	215.2
Neoplasm, Brain NEC Uncertain Behavior	237.5
Eyeball, Superficial	918.9
Abdominal Wall *Fissure*	756.79
Diseased Heart (Organic)	429.9
Cirrhosis, Liver, Chronic	571.5
Osler's Disease polycythemia vera	238.4
Hanging	E913.8

ICD-9 EXERCISE 5

Please answer the following questions using your ICD-9 book as a guide:

1. Does the code 518 require a fourth digit? **Yes** A fifth digit? **No**
2. What is the difference between 512.0 and 512.1? **spontaneous vs. Iatrogenic pneumothorax**
3. What is the code 232.0 for? **CA skin of lip**
4. What does the code 233.0 exclude? **Paget's Disease and CA of skin of breast**
5. What is the first tabular code in the book? **001 Cholera**
6. What is the last tabular code in the book? (Excluding V codes and E codes) **999.9 other unspecified complications of medical care NEC**
7. Does V02 require a fifth digit? **Yes** Where are they? **Listed only three (no gray box, just under main heading)**
8. Does V17 require a fifth digit? **No**

9. What is the code V25 for? **Encounter for contraceptive management (not for men)**
10. What kind of stock doe the code E805 refer to? **Who knows?**
11. Are there any E codes with fifth digits? **No**
12. What is Appendix A? **Morphology of Neoplasms**
13. What is Appendix B? **Glossary of Mental Disorders**
14. What is Appendix C? **Classifications of Drugs by AHIS list**
15. What is Appendix D? **Industrial Accidents According to Agency**
16. What is Appendix E? **Three-Digit Categories**
17. Where are the definitions and illustrations? **In the back of the book, behind the appendices**
18. Where is the general glossary? **Very back of book, last thing**
19. Where is the E code alphabetical list? **After Disease Index (main index)**
20. Where is the V code alphabetical list? (*trick question) **With the main tabular list of diseases**
21. Where is the Table of Drugs and Chemicals? **After Disease Index**
22. Where is the summary of Additions/Deletions/Revisions from the tabular list? **Very beginning, first thing**
23. What does NEC stand for? **Not Elsewhere Classified**
24. What does NOS stand for? **Not Otherwise Specified**
25. Can you get around in this book now? **(The correct answer would be *yes*!)**

ICD-9 Exercise 6

Please code the following:

1.	Manson's Disease (schistosomiasis)	120.1
2.	Semicoma	780.09
3.	Fracture Fibula, Closed	823.81
4.	Hippus	379.49
5.	Seizure	780.39
6.	Self-mutilation	300.9
7.	Glider Crash	E842
8.	Dog Bite	E906.0
9.	Tongue Tie	750.0
10.	False Labor	644.1
11.	Krukenberg's Spindle	371.13
12.	Neck Injury	959.09
13.	Heel Deformity (acquired)	736.76
14.	Mental Health Evaluation	V70.2
15.	Allergy Examination	V72.7

ICD-9 Exercise 7

Please code the following:

1.	Osteomalacia	268.2
2.	chronic deformans hypertrophica	731.0
3.	Psoriasis	696.1
4.	Slowing heart	427.89
5.	Thumb Sucking (child problem)	307.9
6.	Cancer of stomach, primary	151.9
7.	Headache	784.0
8.	Hemorrhage, Intestine	578.9

9.	Herpes, genital	054.10
10.	Iron deficient anemia	280.9
11.	Jackson's membrane	751.4
12.	Ixodiasis	134.8
13.	Abdominal mass	789.3
14.	Herrick's anemia	282.61
15.	Foods intolerance NEC	579.8
16.	Manic depressive psychosis	296.80

ICD-9 AND CPT CODING TOGETHER

ICD-9 and CPT Exercise 1

1. You have a new patient who was admitted to the hospital on 7/3 and discharged on 7/8 for a total of six days. The initial hospital visit was comprehensive, with subsequent days being focused. The discharge on 7/8 took less than thirty minutes. Code this visit.

   Initial exam: **99221**
   Subsequent days: **99231** How many? **4**
   Discharge exam: **99238**
   This patient was admitted for:
       Headache: **784.0**
       and Diabetes: **250.0**

2. You have an established patient who is seen in the office for a focused exam.

   What is the code? **99212**
   This patient was seen for:
       Diarrhea due to bacteria NEC: **008.5**
       and gastric flu: **008.8**

3. You have a patient admitted to the hospital for observation. This is an established patient with a focused exam of low complexity. Patient was admitted on 7/3 and discharged on 7/5.

   Please code 7/3 (admit day): **99218**
   7/4 (subsequent day): **99231**
   and 7/5 (discharge day): **99217**
   This patient also had the following hospital testing:
       Hemoglobin concentration (blood): **85046**
       Blood Cell Enzyme Activity: **82657**
       and Bleeding Time: **85002**
   This patient was admitted for:
       Duchenne's Disease (muscular dystrophy): **094.0**
       and Autonomic Imbalance: **337.9**

4. You have a new patient who is seen as an outpatient in your office for a comprehensive visit.
   Please code the visit: **99204**
   This patient also had the following tests:
       X-ray of Right Ankle: **73600–73610**
       X-ray of Right Lower Leg: **73592**

This patient's diagnosis is:
>   Broken Right Ankle Bone: 825.21 (Fracture)
>   Sprain Right Lower Leg: 844.9

5. You have a patient in the hospital. You are called for a consult. Patient is admitted on 7/3 and discharged on 7/8 for a total of five days. The initial hospital consult is a detailed history of low complexity. The discharge consult took less than thirty minutes. Please code this hospital stay:

    7/3 (admit day): 99253
    Subsequent days: 99231   How many? 4
    7/8 (discharge day): 99238
    This patient's diagnosis is:
    >   Infectious bronchitis with obstruction to airway, chronic: 491.20
    >   and Endocrine Dysfunction NEC: 259.9

6. You are called to examine a new patient in a skilled nursing facility (SNF). This will be a new patient comprehensive visit for evaluation and management. This visit is of high complexity decision making. Please code the:
    Initial visit: 99303
    and, any subsequent visits: 99312
    This patient's diagnosis is:
    >   Emphysema with bronchitis, acute and chronic: 491.21
    >   and Congestive Heart Failure: 428.0

7. You are called to the emergency room to see a patient. This patient is not admitted. This visit is outpatient, treat and release. This is a new patient, comprehensive visit of high complexity. Please code:

    ER Visit: 99285
    This patient's diagnosis is:
    >   Auto Accident, involving another motor vehicle: E812
    >   Concussion with moderate loss of consciousness: 850.2

8. One of your patients delivers a child prematurely. The newborn infant is now your patient. This infant is admitted to the NeoNatal Intensive Care Unit. Please code:

    Initial visit (date of birth): 99295
    Subsequent care days for a stable infant: 99297
    This patient's diagnosis is:
    >   premature birth NEC: 765.1
    >   underdeveloped lungs: 748.5

9. You have a patient that you see either in their own home or a board and care facility, which they sometimes enter for limited periods of time. This is a new patient.

    For a home visit with a detailed history, of moderate complexity, what is the initial visit code? 99343

    For a Domiciliary, or Board and Care Initial visit with an expanded history of moderate complexity, use which code? 99322

This patient's diagnosis is:
Undiagnosed disease: **799.9**
And Failure to Thrive: **783.4**

ICD-9 AND CPT CODING TOGETHER

ICD-9 and CPT Exercise 2

Please code the following diagnostic testing and their corresponding diagnoses:

Procedure	Diagnosis		
Cesarean Section (delivery only)	59620	Pregnancy	V22.2
CAT Scan	70450–70470	Headache	784.0
Brain death (determination)	95824	Murder	E968.9
Chest X-ray Malignant, primary	71010–71035	Lung cancer	162.9
Well Baby Care Single birth, born in hospital	99391–99432	Newborn Infant	V30.00
Throat Biopsy Malignant, secondary	42800–42806	Throat cancer	198.89
Sleep Study With Insomnia	95806–95807	Sleep Apnea, Adult	780.51
Sperm Washing	58323	Male Infertility	606.9
Including Special Handling	99000–99001		
Psychological Testing	96100	Schizophrenia	295.9
Cardiac Massage	32160	Cardiac Arrest	427.5

HCPCS Exercise 1

Please look up the following HCPCS codes: (remember to cross reference them in the index section of the book)

1.	Dental bleaching, external, per tooth	D9973
2.	Aztreonam	S0073
3.	Brachytherapy, prostate	G0261
4.	Body sock	L0984
5.	Benbadryl	J1200
6.	Gravlee jet washer	A4470
7.	Nebulizer, aerosol mask	A7015
8.	Mini-bus, non-ER transportation	A0120
9.	Sodium chloride Injection	J2912
10.	Hypertonic saline	J7130
11.	Irrigation solution	A4323
12.	Dental sealant	D1351
13.	Johnson's thumb immobilizer	L3800
14.	Albumarc	P9041
15.	Carbon filter	A4680
16.	Jenamicin	J1580
17.	IUD (Intra Uterine Device)	J7300
18.	Wig	S8095
19.	Oral Zithromax	Q0144
20.	Wound cleanser	A6260
21.	Shoe Wedges (range)	L3340–L3420
22.	Zantac	J2780

HCPCS Exercise 2

1.	A0428	Ambulance service, basic life support, non-ER
2.	C1122	supply of radiopharmaceutical diagnostic imaging agent Technetium TC 99 m arcitumomab, per vial
3.	E02751	bed pan, standard, metal or plastic
4.	G9016	smoking cessation counseling
5.	J1815	injection, insulin, per 5 units
6.	L1500	THKAO mobility frame
7.	K0105	IV hanger, each
8.	S9435	Medical foods for inborn errors of metabolism
9.	V5364	dysphagia screening
10.	V5299	hearing service, misc.
11.	S0034	injection, ofloxacin, 400 mg.
12.	Q3031	collagen skin test
13.	P9060	fresh frozen plasma, donor retested
14.	L8610	ocular implant
15.	K0098	drive belt for power wheelchair

HCPCS Review

Let's try some exercises. Using the glossary or your HCPCS manual, answer the following questions. In what section of the HCPCS manual would you find the following section headings?

1. Medical/Surgical Supplies?   A
2. Dental Procedures?   D
3. Table of Drugs?   Appendix 3
4. Vision Services?   V
5. Prosthetic Procedures?   L
6. Temporary National Codes?   S
7. Temporary Codes?   K
8. Drugs/other than oral?   J
9. Durable Medical Equipment (DME)?   E
10. Temporary Outpatient PPS?   C
11. Modifiers?   Appendix 1
12. Pathology and Lab?   P

BILLING EXERCISE 1

Assuming all insurance companies mentioned are contracted payers, making these all assigned claims, answer the following questions:

1. A patient has Medicare as their primary insurance and Blue Shield as their second.
   Billed: $150.00
   Allowed: $75.00
   Medicare paid: $53.00
   Patient liability: $22.00
   How much would you bill Blue Shield for? $22.00
   What is your write-off amount? $75.00

2. A patient has Blue Cross insurance
   Billed: $300.00
   Allowed: $250.00
   Blue Cross paid: $250.00
   What is your write-off amount? $50.00
   How much would you bill the patient for? $0.00

3. A Healthnet managed care capitated patient was seen in your office for a routine office visit. This patient has a $10.00 co-pay.
   Total charges: $538.00
   How much would you bill the insurance company for? $0.00 unless stipulated
   How much would you bill the patient for? $10.00
   How much is your write-off amount? $528.00 (remember you have already been paid a monthly stipend for this patient)

4. You have a Medi-Medi patient. (What does Medi-Medi stand for?) Medicare/Medi-Caid
   Billed amount: $378.00
   Allowed amount: $278.00
   Medicare paid: $210.00
   Patient liability: $68.00
   What is your write-off amount? $100.00
   How much would you bill the patient for? $0.00
   Whom would you bill as second? Medi-Caid

5. You have a UFCW patient.
    Billed amount: $62.00
    Allowed: $50.00
    Write-off Amount: $12.00
    UFCW paid: $50.00
    How much would you bill the patient for? $0.00; they paid the whole allowed amount.

6. You have a Medicare patient.
    Billed amount: $458.00
    Allowed amount: $458.00
    Medicare paid: $432.00
    How much would you bill the patient for? $26.00
    What is your write-off amount? $0.00
    Whom would you bill as secondary? Don't know, call the patient.

7. You have a Blue Cross patient
    Billed amount: $325.00
    Allowed amount: $275.00
    Blue Cross paid: $260.00
    What is your write-off amount? $50.00
    What is your patient liability? $15.00

8. For a *non-contracted* insurance company without accepting assignment.
    Billed amount: $5,000.00
    Insurance paid: $3,500.00
    Patient deductible: $500.00
    How much is your write-off portion? $0.00 (non-contracted)
    How much can you bill the patient for? Everything that the insurance did not pay: $1,500.00

BILLING EXERCISE 2

Assuming that these are all contracting payers accepting assignment on these claims, answer the following questions.

1. You have a Blue Cross patient.
    Billed charges: $887.00
    Allowed: $230.00
    B/C paid: $185.00
    What is your write-off amount? $657.00
    How much would you bill the patient for? $45.00

2. You have a patient with Medicare prime and Blue Cross second.
    Billed charges: $545.00
    Allowed: $540.00
    Medicare paid: $350.00
    How much would you bill the patient for? $0.00
    What is your write-off amount? $5.00
    Who is responsible for $190.00? B/C

3. You have a managed care Mercy capitated patient with a $10.00 co-pay.
   Billed charges: $625.00
   What would you bill the insurance company for? $615.00, if stipulated
   How much would you bill the patient for? $10.00
   What is your write-off amount? $615.00 (You have already been paid a monthly stipend for this patient.)

4. You have a Healthnet patient.
   Billed charges: $3,686.00
   Allowed: $25.00
   Healthnet paid: $0.00
   What is your write-off amount? Unsure
   How much will you bill the patient for? Why paid $0? Unclear right now.
   What action would you take on this claim? Call—why denied? Non-covered?

5. You have a Pacificare managed care patient who opted for an out of network physician.
   Total charges: $5,000.00
   Pacificare allowed: $0.00
   Pacificare paid: $0.00
   How much would you write off and why? $0.00, this is an out of network physician
   How much would you bill the patient for? $5,000.00 (When the patient opted to go out of network, their services were non-covered, and therefore patient liability.)

6. You have a Western Health Advantage patient.
   Billed charges: $368.00
   Allowed: $350.00
   WHA paid: $325.00
   What is your write-off amount? $18.00
   How much would you bill the patient for? $25.00

7. You have a Medi-Caid patient.
   Total charges: $5,268.00
   Allowed: $150.00
   Medi-Caid paid: $150.00
   What is your write-off amount? $5,118.00
   How much would you bill the patient for? $0.00

8. You have a Blue Shield patient.
   Total charges: $350.00
   Non-covered: $25.00
   Allowed: $300.00
   B/S paid: $225.00
   What is your write-off amount? $50.00
   What would you bill the patient for? $100.00 (if told of non-covered prior, $75.00 otherwise)

9. You have a UFCW patient.
   Total charges: $1,500.00
   Allowed: $1,500.00
   UFCW paid: $1,000.00
   Patient deductible: $500.00

What is your write-off amount? $0.00
How much would you bill the patient for? $500.00

10. You have a UFCW patient.
    Total charges: $3,000.00
    Allowed: $2,500.00
    UFCW paid: $1,000.00
    Patient deductible: $500.00
    What is your write-off amount? $500.00
    How much would you bill the patient for? $1,500.00

11. You have a patient in an automobile accident. He has no health insurance; you are not contracted with his automobile insurance.
    Total charges: $150.00
    Allowed: $75.00
    Insurance paid: $75.00
    What is your write-off amount? $0.00 (you are non-contracted)
    How much would you bill the patient for? $75.00 (everything not paid by insurance)

12. You have a patient in an automobile accident and are not contracted with the auto insurance company. This patient is also covered by Healthnet.
    Total billed: $575.00
    Allowed: $500.00
    Insurance paid: $450.00
    Who is prime? Auto insurance
    Who is second? Healthnet
    What is your write-off amount? None, non-contracted with auto
    How much would you bill the patient for? $0.00, only if Healthnet denies
    Whom would you bill as second? Healthnet

REVIEW

Let's take a brief review of which forms would be appropriate to use under what circumstances.

1. You work for a single physician's office. A patient comes in for an office visit and you are billing for professional services.

    Will you use a UB-04 or HCFA-1500?   **HCFA-1500**

2. You work for an independent lab. A sample is sent to you from an independent physician's office for processing. You are billing for the physician on staff at the lab to diagnose from the test results as a consult. You are billing for professional services.

    Will you use a UB-04 or HCFA-1500?   **HCFA-1500**

3. You work for a Skilled Nursing Facility. You are billing for long term room and board care for the residents. There are no professional fees involved. You are billing for facility charges involved in running the home.

    Will you use a UB-04 or HCFA-1500?   **UB-04**

4. You work for an outpatient clinic owned and operated by a major hospital. You are billing for clinic fees for the use of the facility. There are no professional fees involved.

   Will you use a UB-04 or HCFA-1500?   **UB-04**

5. You work for a multi-physician group. You work in a private office and bill for physicians' professional services within the office.

   Will you use a UB-04 or HCFA-1500?   **HCFA-1500**

6. You work for a radiology group. You bill for professional fees for the radiologist on staff to read the results of the x-rays and report back to the primary care physician.

   Will you use a UB-04 or HCFA-1500?   **HCFA-1500**

APPENDICES

APPENDICES

PLACE OF SERVICE CODES/CPT
FOR USE WITH HCFA-1500 BILLING FORMS

Code	Description
01–02	Unassigned
03	School
04	Homeless Shelter
05	Indian Health Service Free-standing Clinic
06	Indian Health Service Provider-based Facility
07	Tribal 638 Free-standing Facility
08	Tribal 638 Provider-based Facility
09–10	Unassigned
11	Office
12	Home
13–14	Unassigned
15	Mobile Unit
16–19	Unassigned
20	Urgent Care Facility
21	Inpatient Hospital
22	Outpatient Hospital
23	Emergency Room—Hospital
24	Ambulatory Surgical Center
25	Birthing Center
26	Military Treatment Facility
27–30	Unassigned
31	Skilled Nursing Facility
32	Nursing Facility
33	Custodial Care Facility
34	Hospice
35–40	Unassigned
41	Ambulance—Land
42	Ambulance—Air or Water
43–49	Unassigned
50	Federally Qualified Health Center
51	Inpatient Psychiatric Facility
52	Psychiatric Facility—Partial Hospitalization
53	Community Mental Health Center

54	Intermediate Care Facility/Mentally Retarded
55	Residential Substance Abuse Treatment Facility
56	Psychiatric Residential Treatment Center
57–59	Unassigned
60	Mass Immunization Center
61	Comprehensive Inpatient Rehabilitation Facility
62	Comprehensive Outpatient Rehabilitation Facility
63–64	Unassigned
65	End Stage Renal Disease Treatment Facility
66–70	Unassigned
71	State of Local Public Health Clinic
72	Rural Health Clinic
73–80	Unassigned
81	Independent Laboratory
82–98	Unassigned
99	Other Place of Service

APPROVED CPT MODIFIERS

Modifier	Description
21	Prolonged Evaluation and Management Services
22	Unusual Procedural Services
23	Under Anesthesia
24	Unrelated Evaluation and Management Service by the Same Physician During a Postoperative Period
25	Significant, Separately Identifiable Evaluation and Management Service by the Same Physician on the Same Day of the Procedure or Other Service
26	Professional Component
32	Mandated Service
47	Anesthesia by Surgeon
50	Bilateral Procedure
51	Multiple Procedures
52	Reduced Services
53	Discontinued Procedure
54	Surgical Care Only
55	Postoperative Management Only
56	Preoperative Management Only
57	Decision for Surgery
58	Staged or Related Procedure or Service by the Same Physician During the Postoperative Period

THE POSTOPERATIVE PERIOD

59	Distinct Procedural Service
62	Two Surgeons
63	Procedure Performed on Infants
66	Surgical Team
76	Repeat Procedure by Same Physician
77	Repeat Procedure by Another Physician
78	Return to the Operating Room for a Related Procedure During the Postoperative Period

POSTOPERATIVE PERIOD

79	Unrelated Procedure or Service by the Same Physician During the Postoperative Period
80	Assistant Surgeon
81	Minimum Assistant Surgeon
82	Assistant Surgeon (when qualified resident surgeon not available)
90	Reference (Outside) Laboratory
91	Repeat Clinical Diagnostic Laboratory Test
99	Multiple Modifiers

PHYSICAL STATUS MODIFIERS

MODIFIER	DESCRIPTION
P1	A normal, healthy patient
P2	A patient with mild systemic disease
P3	A patient with severe systemic disease
P4	A patient with severe systemic disease that is a constant threat to life
P5	A moribund patient who is not expected to survive without the operation
P6	A declared brain-dead patient whose organs are being removed for donor purposes

APPROVED HOSPITAL OUTPATIENT MODIFIERS, LEVEL I, CPT

Modifier	Description
25	Significant, Separately Identifiable Evaluation and Management Services by the Same Physician on the Same Day of the Procedure or Other Service
27	Multiple Outpatient Hospital Evaluation and Management Encounters on the Same Day
50	Bilateral Procedure
52	Reduced Services
58	Staged or Related Procedure or Service by the Same Physician During the Post-operative Period
59	Distinct Procedural Service
73	Discontinued Outpatient Procedure Prior to Anesthesia Administration
74	Discontinued Outpatient Procedure After the Anesthesia Administration
76	Repeat Procedure by Same Physician
77	Repeat Procedure by Another Physician
78	Return to the Operating Room for a Related Procedure During the Postoperative Period
79	Unrelated Procedure or Service by the Same Physician During the Postoperative Period
91	Repeat Clinical Diagnostic Laboratory Test

APPROVED HOSPITAL OUTPATIENT MODIFIERS, LEVEL II, HCPCS/NATIONAL

A1	Dressing for one wound
A2	Dressing for two wounds
A3	Dressing for three wounds
A4	Dressing for four wounds

A5	Dressing for five wounds
A6	Dressing for six wounds
A7	Dressing for seven wounds
A8	Dressing for eight wounds
A9	Dressing for nine or more wounds
AA	Anesthesia services performed personally by anesthesiologist
AD	Medical supervision by a physician: More than four concurrent anesthesia procedures
AH	Clinical psychologist
AJ	Clinical social worker
AM	Physician, team member service
AP	Determination of refractive state was not performed in the course of diagnostic ophthalmological examination
AS	Physician assistant, nurse practitioner, or clinical nurse specialist services for assistant at surgery
AT	Acute treatment (This modifier should be used when reporting service 98940, 98941, 98942.)
AU	Item furnished in conjunction with urological, ostomy, or tracheostomy supply
AV	Item furnished in conjunction with a prosthetic device, prosthetic, or orthotic
AW	Item furnished in conjunction with a surgical dressing
AX	Item furnished in conjunction with dialysis services
BA	Item furnished in conjunction with parenteral enteral nutrition (PEN) services
BO	Orally administered nutrition, not by feeding tube
BP	The beneficiary has been informed of the purchase and rental options and has elected to purchase the item
BR	The beneficiary has been informed of the purchase and rental options and has elected to rent the item
BU	The beneficiary has been informed of the purchase and rental options and after thirty days has not informed the supplier of his/her decision
CA	Procedure payable only in the inpatient setting when performed emergently on an outpatient who expires prior to admission
CB	Service ordered by renal dialysis facility (RDF) physician as part of the esrd beneficiary's dialysis benefit, is not part of the composite rate, and is separately reimbursable
CC	Procedure code change (use "CC" when the procedure code submitted was changed either for administrative reasons or because an incorrect code was filed)
E1	Upper left, eyelid
E2	Lower left, eyelid
E3	Upper right, eyelid
E4	Lower right, eyelid
EJ	Subsequent claims for a defined course of therapy, e.g., EPO, Sodium Hyaluronate, Infliximab
EM	Emergency reserve supply (for ESRD benefit only)
EP	Service provided as part of Medicaid early periodic screening diagnosis and treatment (EPSDT) program
ET	Emergency services
EY	No physician or other licensed healthcare provider order for this item or service

FA	Left hand, thumb
F1	Left hand, second digit
F2	Left hand, third digit
F3	Left hand, fourth digit
F4	Left hand, fifth digit
F5	Right hand, thumb
F6	Right hand, second digit
F7	Right hand, third digit
F8	Right hand, fourth digit
F9	Right hand, fifth digit
FP	Service provided as part of Medicaid Family Planning Program
G1	Most recent URR reading of less than 60
G2	Most recent URR reading of 60–64.9
G3	Most recent URR reading of 65–69.0
G4	Most recent URR reading of 70–74.9
G5	Most recent URR reading of 75 or greater
G6	ESRD patient for whom less than six dialysis sessions have been provided in a month
G7	Pregnancy resulted from rape or incest or pregnancy certified by physician as life threatening
G8	Monitored anesthesia care (MAC) for complex, complicated, or markedly invasive surgical procedure
G9	Monitored anesthesia care for patient who has history of severe cardio-pulmonary condition
GA	Waiver of liability statement on file
GB	Claim being resubmitted for payment because it is no longer covered under a global payment demonstration
GC	This service has been performed in part by a resident under the direction of a teaching physician
GE	This service has been performed by a resident without the presence of a teaching physician under the primary care exception
GF	Non-physician (e.g. nurse practitioner [NP], certified registered nurse anesthetist [CRNA], certified registered nurse [CRN], clinical nurse specialist [CNS], physician assistant [PA]) services in a critical access hospital
GG	Performance and payment of a screening mammogram and diagnostic mammogram on the same patient, same day
GH	Diagnostic mammogram converted from screening mammogram on same day
GJ	"Opt out" physician or practitioner emergency or urgent service
GK	Actual item/service ordered by physician, item associated with GA or GZ modifier
GL	Medically unnecessary upgrade provided instead of standard item, no charge, no advance beneficiary notice (ABN)
GM	Multiple patients on one ambulance trip
GN	Services delivered under an outpatient speech language pathology plan of care
GO	Services delivered under an outpatient occupational therapy plan of care
GP	Services delivered under an outpatient physical therapy plan of care
GQ	Via asynchronous telecommunications system
GT	Via interactive audio and video telecommunication systems
GV	Attending physician not employed or paid under arrangement by the patient's hospice provider

GW	Service not related to the hospice patient's terminal condition
GY	Item or service statutorily excluded or does not meet the definition of any Medicare benefit
GZ	Item or service expected to be denied as not reasonable and necessary
H9	Court ordered
HA	Child/adolescent program
HB	Adult program, non geriatric
HC	Adult program, geriatric
HD	Pregnant/parenting women's program
HE	Mental health program
HF	Substance abuse program
HG	Opioid addiction treatment program
HH	Integrated mental health/substance abuse program
HI	Integrated mental health and mental retardation/development disabilities program
HJ	Employee assistance program
HK	Specialized mental health programs for high risk populations
HL	Intern
HM	Less than bachelor degree level
HN	Bachelor degree level
HO	Masters degree level
HP	Doctorate level
HQ	Group setting
HR	Family/couple with client present
HS	Family/couple without client present
HT	Multi-disciplinary team
HU	Funded by child welfare agency
HV	Funded by state addictions agency
HW	Funded by state mental health agency
HX	Funded by county/local agency
HY	Funded by juvenile justice agency
HZ	Funded by criminal justice agency
JW	Drug amount discarded/not administered to any patient
KO	Lower extremity prosthesis functional level 0—does not have the ability or potential to ambulate or transfer safely with or without assistance and a prosthesis does not enhance their quality of life or mobility.
K1	Lower extremity prosthesis functional level 1—has the ability or potential to use a prosthesis for transfers or ambulation on level surfaces at fixed cadence. Typical of the limited and unlimited household ambulator.
K2	Lower extremity prosthesis functional level 2—has the ability or potential for ambulation with the ability to traverse low level environmental barriers such as curbs, stairs, or uneven surfaces. Typical of the limited community ambulator.
K3	Lower extremity prosthesis functional level 3—has the ability or potential for ambulation with variable cadence. Typical of the community ambulator who has the ability to traverse most environmental barriers and may have vocational, therapeutic, or exercise activity that demands prosthetic utilization beyond simple locomotion.
K4	Lower extremity prosthesis functional level 4—has the ability or potential for prosthetic ambulation that exceeds the basic ambulation skills, exhibiting high

	impact, stress, or energy levels, typical of the prosthetic demands of the child, active adult, or athlete.
KA	Add on option/accessory for wheelchair
KB	Beneficiary requested upgrade for ABN, more than 4 modifiers identified on claim
KH	DMEPOS item, initial claim, purchase or first month rental
KI	DMEPOS item, second or third month rental
KJ	DMEPOS item, parenteral enteral nutrition (PEN) pump or capped rental, months four to fifteen
KM	Replacement of facial prosthesis including new impression/moulage
KN	Replacement of facial prosthesis using previous master model
KO	Single drug unit dose formulation
KP	First drug of a multiple drug unit dose formulation
KQ	Second or subsequent drug of a multiple drug unit dose formulation
KR	Rental item, billing for partial month
KS	Glucose monitor supply for diabetic beneficiary not treated with insulin
KX	Specific required documentation on file
KZ	New coverage not implemented by managed care
LC	Left circumflex, coronary artery
LD	Left anterior descending coronary artery
LL	Lease/rental (use the "II" modifier when DME equipment rental is to be applied against the purchase price)
LR	Laboratory round trip
LS	FDA-monitored intraocular lens implant.
LT	Left side
MS	Six-month maintenance and servicing fee for reasonable and necessary parts and labor which are not covered under any manufacturer or supplier warranty
NR	New when rented (use the "NR" modifier when DME, which was new at the time of rental is subsequently purchased)
NU	New equipment
PL	Progressive addition lenses
Q2	HCFA/ORD demonstration project procedure/service
Q3	Live kidney donor surgery and related services
Q4	Services for ordering/referring physician qualifies as a service exemption
Q5	Services furnished by a substitute physician under a reciprocal billing arrangement
Q6	Service furnished by a locum tenens physician
Q7	One class A finding
Q8	Two class B findings
Q9	One class B and two class C findings
QA	FDA investigational device exemption
QB	Physician providing service in a rural HPSA
QC	Single channel monitoring
QD	Recording and storage in a solid state memory by a digital recorder.
QE	Prescribed amount of oxygen is less than 1 liter per minute (LPM)
QF	Prescribed amount of oxygen exceeds 4 liters per minute (LPM) and portable oxygen is prescribed
QG	Prescribed amount of oxygen is greater than 4 liters per minute (LPM)
QH	Oxygen conserving device is being used with an oxygen delivery system

QJ	Services/items provided to a prisoner or patient in state or local custody, however the state or local government, as applicable, meets the requirements in 42 CFR 411.4(b)
QK	Medical direction of two, three, or four concurrent anesthesia procedures involving qualified individuals
QL	Patient pronounced dead after ambulance called
QM	Ambulance service provided under arrangement by a provider of service
QN	Ambulance service furnished directly by a provider of service
QP	Documentation is on file showing that the laboratory test(s) was ordered individually or ordered as a CPT-recognized panel of other than automated profile codes 80002-80019, G0058, G0059, and G0060.
QQ	Claim submitted with a written statement of intent
QS	Monitored anesthesia care service
QT	Recording and storage on tape by an analog tape recorder
QU	Physician providing service in an urban HPSA
QV	Item or service provided as routine care in a Medicare qualifying clinical trial
QW	CLIA waived test
QX	CRNA service: with medical direction by a physician
QY	Medical direction of one certified registered nurse anesthetist (CRNA) by an anesthesiologist
QZ	CRNA service: without medical direction by a physician
RC	Right coronary artery
RP	Replacement and repair—RP may be used to indicate replacement of DME, orthotic, and prosthetic devices that have been in use for some time. The claim shows the code for the part, followed by the "RP" modifier and the charge for the part.
RR	Rental (use the "RR" modifier when DME is to be rented)
RT	Right side
SA	Nurse practitioner rendering service in collaboration with a physician
SB	Nurse midwife
SC	Medically necessary service or supply
SD	Services provided by registered nurse with specialist, highly technical home infusion training
SE	State and/or federally-funded programs/services
SF	Second opinion ordered by a professional review organization (PRO) per section 9401, p. l. 99–272 (100% reimbursement, no Medicare deductible or coinsurance)
SG	Ambulatory surgical center (ASC) facility service
SH	Second concurrently administered infusion therapy
SJ	Third or more concurrently administered infusion therapy
SK	Member of high-risk population (use only with codes for immunization)
SL	State supplied vaccine
SM	Second surgical opinion
SN	Third surgical opinion
SQ	Item ordered by home health
ST	Related to trauma or injury
SU	Procedure performed in physician's office (to denote use of facility and equipment)
SV	Pharmaceuticals delivered to patient's home but not utilized
TA	Left foot, great toe

T1	Left foot, second digit
T2	Left foot, third digit
T3	Left foot, fourth digit
T4	Left foot, fifth digit
T5	Right foot, great toe
T6	Right foot, second digit
T7	Right foot, third digit
T8	Right foot, fourth digit
T9	Right foot, fifth digit

REVENUE CODES
FOR USE WITH UB-04 BILLING FORMS

Rev Code:	Description:	Abbreviation:
0001	Total Charges	TOTAL CHARGE
001X	Reserved for Internal Payor Use	
0020	Reserved	
0021	Reserved	
0022	Skilled Nursing Facility-Prospective Payment System	SNF PPS (RUG)
0023	Home Health -Prospective Payment System	HH PPS (HRG)
0024	Inpatient Rehab Facility -Prospective Payment System	REHAB PPS (CMG)
0025	Reserved	
0026	Reserved	
0027	Reserved	
0028	Reserved	
0029	Reserved	
002X	Health Insurance -Prospective Payment System	HIPPS
0100	All-inclusive room and board plus ancillary	ALL INCL RandB/ANC
0101	All-inclusive room and board	ALL INCL RandB
010X	All-inclusive rate	
0110	General Classification	RandB/PVT
0111	Medical/Surgical/Gyn	MED-SUR-GY/PVT
0112	OB	OB/PVT
0113	Pediatric	PEDS/PVT
0114	Psychiatric	PSYCH/PVT
0115	Hospice	HOSPICE/PVT
0116	Detoxification	DETOX/PVT
0117	Oncology	ONCOLOGY/PVT
0118	Rehabilitation	REHAB/PVT

0119	Other	OTHER/PVT
011X	Room and Board-Private (Medical/General)	
0120	General Classification	RandB/SEMI
0121	Medical/Surgical/Gyn	MED-SUR-GY/2BED
0122	OB	OB/2BED
0123	Pediatric	PEDS/2BED
0124	Psychiatric	PSTAY/2BED
0125	Hospice	HOSPICE/2BED
0126	Detoxification	DETOX/2BED
0127	Oncology	ONCOLOGY/2BED
0128	Rehabilitation	REHAB/2BED
0129	Other	OTHER/SEMI
012X	Room and Board-Semiprivate Two-bed	
0130	General Classification	RandB/3and4BED
0131	Medical/Surgical/Gyn	MED-SUR-GY/3and4BED
0132	OB	OB/3and4BED
0133	Pediatric	PEDS/3and4BED
0134	Psychiatric	PSYCH/3and4BED
0135	Hospice	HOSPICE/3and4BED
0136	Detoxification	DETOX/3and4BED
0137	Oncology	ONCOLOGY/3and4BED
0138	Rehabilitation	REHAB/3and4BED
0139	Other	OTHER/3and4BED
013X	Room and Board-Three and Four Beds	
0140	General Classification	RandB/PVT/DLX
0141	Medical/Surgical/Gyn	MED-SUR-GY/DLX
0142	OB	OB/DLX
0143	Pediatric	PEDS/DLX
0144	Psychiatric	PSYCH/DLX
0145	Hospice	HOSPICE/DLX
0146	Detoxification	DETOX/DLX
0147	Oncology	ONCOLOGY/DLX
0148	Rehabilitation	REHAB/DLX
0149	Other	OTHER/DLX
014X	Room and Board-Private Deluxe	
0150	General Classification	RandB/WARD
0151	Medical/Surgical/Gyn	MED-DUR-BY/WARD

0152	OB	OB/WARD
0153	Pediatric	PEDS/WARD
0154	Psychiatric	PSYCH/WARD
0155	Hospice	HOSPICE/WARD
0156	Detoxification	DETOX/WARD
0157	Oncology	ONCOLOGY/WARD
0158	Rehabilitation	REHAB/WARD
0159	Other	OTHER/WARD
015X	Room and Board-Ward (Medical/General)	
0160	General Classification	RandB
0164	Sterile Environment	RandB/STERILE
0167	Self Care	RandB/SELF
0169	Other	RandB/OTHER
016X	Room and Board Other	
0170	General Classification	NURSERY
0171	Newborn-Level I	NURSERY/LEVEL I
0172	Premature-Level II	NURSERY/LEVEL II
0173	Intermediate-Level III	NURSERY/LEVEL III
0174	Neonatal ICU Level IV	NURSERY/LEVEL IV
0179	Other Nursery	NURSERY/OTHER
017X	Room and Board Nursery	
0180	General Classification	LOA
0181	Reserved	
0182	Patient Convenience	LOA/PT CONV
0183	Therapeutic Leave	LOA/THERAPEUTIC
0184	Reserved	LOA/ICF/MR
0185	Hospitalization	LOA/HOSPITALIZATION
0189	Other Leave of Absence	LOA/OTHER
018X	Leave of Absence	
0190	General Classification	SUBACUTE
0191	Subacute Care-Level I	SUBACUTE/LEVEL I
0192	Subacute Care-Level II	SUBACUTE/LEVEL II
0193	Subacute Care-Level III	SUBACUTE/LEVEL III
0194	Subacute Care-Level IV	SUBACUTE/LEVEL IV
0199	Other Subacute Care	SUBACUTE/OTHER
019X	Subacute Care	
0200	General Classification	ICU

0201	Surgical	ICU/SURGICAL
0202	Medical	ICU/MEDICAL
0203	Pediatric	ICU/PEDS
0204	Psychiatric	ICU/PSTAY
0206	Intermediate ICU	ICU/INTERMEDIATE
0207	Burn Care	ICU/BURN CARE
0208	Trauma	ICU/TRAUMA
0209	Other	ICU/OTHER
020X	Intensive Care	
0210	General Classification	CCU
0211	Myocardial Infarction	CCU/MCY INFARC
0212	Pulmonary Care	CCU/PULMONARY
0213	Heart Transplant	CCU/TRANSPLANT
0214	Intermediate CCU	CCU/INTERMEDIATE
0219	Other Coronary	CCU/OTHER
021X	Coronary Care	
0220	General Classification	SPECIAL CHARGES
0221	Admission Charge	ADMIT CHARGE
0222	Technical Support Charge	TECH SUPPORT CHG
0223	UR Service Charge	UR CHARGE
0224	Late Discharge, Medically Necessary	LATE DISCH/MED NEC
0229	Other Special Charges	OTHER SPEC CHG
022X	Special Charges	
0230	General Classification	NURSING INCREM
0231	Nursery	NUR INCR/NURSERY
0232	OB	NUR INCR/OB
0233	ICU	NUR INCR/ICU
0234	CCU	NUR INCR/CCU
0235	Hospice	NUR/INCR/HOSPICE
0239	Other	NIR/INCR/OTHER
023X	Incremental Nursing Charge Rate	
0240	General Classification	ALL INCL ANCIL
0241	Basic	ALL INCL BASIC
0242	Comprehensive	ALL INCL COMP
0243	Specialty	ALL INCL SPECIAL
0249	Other Inclusive Ancillary	ALL INCL ANCIL/OTHER
024X	All-Inclusive Ancillary	

0250	General Classification	PHARMACY
0251	Generic Drugs	DRUGS/GENERIC
0252	Non-generic Drugs	DRUGS/NONGENERIC
0253	Take Home Drugs	DRUGS/TAKEHOME
0254	Drug Incident to Other Diagnostic Services	DRUGS/INCIDENT ODX
0255	Drug Incident to Radiology	DRUGS/INCIDENT RAD
0256	Experimental Drugs	DRUGS/EXPERIMT
0257	Non-Prescription	DRUGS/NONPSCRPT
0258	IV Solutions	IV SOLUTIONS
0259	Other Pharmacy	DRUGS/OTHER
025X	Pharmacy (Also see 063X, an extension of 025X)	
0260	General Classification	IV THERAPY
0261	Infusion Pump	IV THER/INFSN PUMP
0262	IV Therapy-Pharmacy Services	IV THER/PHARM/SVC
0263	IV Therapy-Drugs/Supply Delivery	IV THER/DRUG/SUPPLY/DELV
0264	IV Therapy-Supplies	IV THER/SUPPLIES
0269	Other IV Therapy	IV THERAPY/OTHER
026X	IV Therapy	
0270	General Classification	MED-SUR SUPPLIES
0271	Non-Sterile Supply	NON-STERILE SUPPLY
0272	Sterile Supply	STERILE SUPPLY
0273	Take Home Supplies	TAKEHOME SUPPLY
0274	Prosthetic-Orthotic Devices	PROSTH/ORTHO DEV
0275	Pacemaker	PACEMAKER
0276	Intraocular Lens	INTRA OC LENS
0277	Oxygen-Take Home	02/TAKEHOME
0278	Other Implants	SUPPLY/IMPLANTS
0279	Other Supplies or Devices	SUPPLY/OTHER
027X	Medical/Surgical Supplies and Devices (Also see 062X, an extension of 027X)	
0280	General Classification	ONCOLOGY
0289	Other Oncology	ONCOLOGY/OTHER
028X	Oncology	
0290	General Classification	MED EQUIP/DURAB
0291	Rental	MED EQUIP/RENT
0292	Purchase of New DME	MED EQUIP/NEW
0293	Purchase of Used DME	MED EQUIP/USED

0294	Supplies-Drugs for DME Effectiveness	MED EQUIP/SUPPLIES/DRUGS
0299	Other Equipment	MED EQUIP/OTHER
029X	Durable Medical Equipment (Other than rental)	
0300	General Classification	LAB or LABORATORY
0301	Chemistry	LAB/CHEMISTRY
0302	Immunology	LAB/IMMUNOLOGY
0303	Renal Patient (Home)	LAB/RENAL HOME
0305	Hematology	LAB/HEMATOLOGY
0306	Bacteriology and Microbiology	LAB/BACT-MICRO
0307	Urology	LAB/UROLOGY
0309	Other Laboratory	LAB/OTHER
030X	Laboratory	
0310	General Classification	PATH LAB or PATHOLOGY LAB
0311	Cytology	PATHOL/CYTOLOGY
0312	Histology	PATHOL/HYSTOL
0314	Biopsy	PATHOL/BIOPSY
0319	Other	PATHOL/OTHER
031X	Laboratory Pathology	
0320	General Classification	DX X-RAY
0321	Angiocardiography	DX X-RAY/ANGIO
0322	Arthrography	DX X-RAY/ARTH
0323	Arteriography	DX X-RAY/ARTER
0324	Chest X-ray	DX X-RAY/CHEST
0329	Other	DX X-RAY/OTHER
032X	Radiology-Diagnostic	
0330	General Classification	RX X-RAY
0331	Chemotherapy Administration-Injected	CHEMOTHER/INJ
0332	Chemotherapy Administration-Oral	CHEMOTHER/ORAL
0333	Radiation Therapy	RADIATION RX
0335	Chemotherapy Administration-IV	CHEMOTHERP-IV
0339	Other Radiology-Therapeutic	RX X-RAY/OTHER
033X	Radiology-Therapeutic and/or Chemotherapy Administration	
0340	General Classification	NUCLEAR MED or NUC MED
0341	Diagnostic Procedures	NUC MED/DX
0342	Therapeutic Procedures	NUC MED/RX
0343	Diagnostic Radiopharmaceuticals	NUC MED/DX RADIOPHARM

0344	Therapeutic Radiopharmaceutials	NUC MED/RX RADIOPHARM
0349	Other	NUC MED/OTHER
034X	Nuclear Medicine	
0350	General Classification	CT SCAN
0351	Head Scan	CT SCAN/HEAD
0352	Body Scan	CT SCACN/BODY
0359	Other CT scans	CT SCAN/OTHER
035X	CT Scan	
0360	General Classification	OR SERVICES
0361	Minor Surgery	OR/MINOR
0362	Organ Transplant-Other than Kidney	OR/ORGAN TRANS
0367	Kidney Transplant	OR/KIDNEY
0369	Other Operating Room Services	OR/OTHER
036X	Operating Room Services	
0370	General Classification	ANESTHESIA
0371	Anesthesia Incident to Radiology	ANESTHE/INCIDENT RAD
0372	Anesthesia Incident to Other Diagnostic Service	ANESTHE/INCDNT OTHER DX
0374	Acupuncture	ANESTH/ACUPUNC
0379	Other Anesthesia	ANESTHE/OTHER
037X	Anesthesia	
0380	General Classification	BLOOD
0381	Packed Red Cells	BLOOD/PKD RED
0382	Whole Blood	BLOOD/WHOLE
0383	Plasma	BLOOD/PLASMA
0384	Platelets	BLOOD/PLATELETS
0385	Leucocytes	BLOOD/LEUCOCYTES
0386	Other Components	BLOOD/COMPONENTS
0387	Other Derivatives (cryopricipitates)	BLOOD/DERIVATIVES
0389	Other Blood	BLOOD/OTHER
038X	Blood	
0390	General Classification	BLOOD/STOR-PROC
0391	Blood Administration	BLOOD/ADMIN
0399	Other Blood Storage and Processing	BLOOD/OTHER STOR
039X	Blood and Blood Component Administration, Processing and Storage	
0400	General Classification	IMAGING SERVICE
0401	Diagnostic Mammography	DIAG MAMMOGRAPHY

0402	Ultrasound	ULTRASOUND
0403	Screening Mammography	SCRN MAMMOGRAPHY
0404	Positron Emission Tomography	PET SCAN
0409	Other Imaging Services	OTHER IMAGING SVC
040X	Other Imaging Services	
0410	General Classification	RESPIRATORY SVC
0412	Inhalation Services	INHALATION SVC
0413	Hyperbaric Oxygen Therapy	HYPERBARIC 02
0419	Other Respiratory Services	OTHER RESPIR SVC
041X	Respiratory Services	
0420	General Classification	PHYSICAL THERAP
0421	Visit Charge	PHYS THERAP/VISIT
0422	Hourly Charge	PHYS THERAP/HOUR
0423	Group Rate	PHYS THERAP/GROUP
0424	Evaluation or Re-evaluation	PHYS THERAP/EVAL
0429	Other Physical Therapy	OTHER PHYS THERAP
042X	Physical Therapy	
0430	General Classification	OCCUPATION THERAP
0431	Visit Charge	OCCUP THERAP/VISIT
0432	Hourly Charge	OCCUP THERAP/HOUR
0433	Group Rate	OCCUP THERAP/GROUP
0434	Evaluation or Re-Evaluation	OCCUP THERAP/EVAL
0439	Other Occupational Therapy	OTHER OCCUP THER
043X	Occupational Therapy	
0440	General Classification	SPEECH PATHOL
0441	Visit Charge	SPEECH PATH/VISIT
0442	Hourly Charge	SPEECH PATH/HOUR
0443	Group Rate	SPEECH PATH/GROUP
0444	Evaluation or Re-Evaluation	SPEECH PATH/EVAL
0449	Other Speech-Language Pathology	OTHER SPEECH PATH
044X	Speech-Language Pathology	
0450	General Classification	EMERGENCY ROOM
0451	EMTALA Emergency Medical Screening Serv.	ER/EMTALA
0452	ER Beyond EMTALA Screening	ER/BEYOND EMTALA
0456	Urgent Care	URGENT CARE
0459	Other	OTHER EMER ROOM
045X	Emergency Room	

0460	General Classification	PULMONARY FUNC
0469	Other Pulmonary Function	OTHER PULMON FUNC
046X	Pulmonary Function	
0470	General Classification	AUDIOLOGY
0471	Diagnostic	AUDIOLOGY/DX
0472	Treatment	AUDIOLOGY/RX
0479	Other Audiology	OTHER/AUDIOL
047X	Audiology	
0480	General Classification	CARDIOLOGY
0481	Cardiac Cath Lab	CARDIAC CATH LAB
0482	Stress Test	STRESS TEST
0483	Echocardiology	ECHOCARDIOLOGY
0489	Other Cardiology	OTHER CARDIOLOGY
048X	Cardiology	
0490	General Classification	AMBULATORY SURG
0499	Other Ambulatory Surgical Services	OTHER AMBL SURG
049X	Ambulatory Surgical Care	
0500	General Classification	OUTPATIENT SVC
0509	Other Outpatient Services	OUTPATIENT/OTHER
050X	Outpatient Services	
0510	General Classification	CLINIC
0511	Chronic Pain Center	CHRONIC PAIN CL
0512	Dental Clinic	DENTAL CLINIC
0513	Psychiatric Clinic	PSYCH CLINIC
0514	OB-GYN Clinic	OB-GYN CLINIC
0515	Pediatric Clinic	PEDS CLINIC
0516	Urgent Care Clinic	URGENT CLINIC
0517	Family Practice Clinic	FAMILY CLINIC
0519	Other Clinic	OTHER CLINIC
051X	Clinic	
0520	General Classification	FREESTAND CLINIC
0521	Rural Health-Clinic	RURAL/CLINIC
0522	Rural Health-Home	RURAL/HOME
0523	Family Practice Clinic	FR/STD FAMILY PRAC
0526	Urgent Care Clinic	FR/STD URGENT CLINIC
0529	Other Free Standing Clinic	OTHER FR/STD CLINIC
052X	Free Standing Clinic	

0530	General Classification	OSTEOPATH SVC
0531	Osteopathic Services	OSTEOPATH RX
0539	Other Osteopathic Services	OTHER OSTEOPATH
053X	Osteopathic Services	
0540	General Classification	AMBULANCE
0541	Supplies	AMBUL/SUPPLY
0542	Medical Transport	AMBUL/MED TRANS
0543	Heart Mobile	AMBUL/HEARTMOBL
0544	Oxygen	AMBUL/OXY
0545	Air Ambulance	AIR AMBULANCE
0546	Neonatal Ambulance Services	AMBUL/NEONAT
0547	Pharmacy	AMBUL/PHARMACY
0548	Telephone Transmission EKG	AMBUL/TELEPHONIC EKG
0549	Other Ambulance	OTHER AMBULANCE
054X	Ambulance	
0550	General Classification	SKILLED NURSING
0551	Visit Charge	SKILLED NURS/VISIT
0552	Hourly Charge	SKILLED NURS/HOUR
0559	Other Skilled Nursing	SKILLED NURS/OTHER
055X	Skilled Nursing	
0560	General Classification	MED SOCIAL SVC
0561	Visit Charge	MED SOC SERVS/VISIT
0562	Hourly Charge	MED SOC SERVS/HOUR
0569	Other Medical Social Services	MED SOC SERVS/OTHER
056X	Medical Social Services	
0570	General Classification	AID/HOME HEALTH
0571	Visit Charge	AIDE/HOME HLTH/VISIT
0572	Hourly Charge	AIDE/HOME HLTH/HOUR
0579	Other Home Health Aide	AIDE/HOME HLTH/OTHER
057X	Home Health Aide (Home Health)	
0580	General Classification	VISIT/HOME HEALTH
0581	Visit Charge	VISIT/HOME HLTH/VISIT
0582	Hourly Charge	VISIT/HOME HLTH/HOUR
0589	Other Home Health Aide	VISIT/HOME HLTH/OTHER
058X	Other Visits (Home Health)	
0590	General Classification	UNIT/HOME HEALTH
0599	Home Health Other Units	UNIT/HOME HLTH/OTHER

059X	Units of Service (Home Health)	
0600	General Classification	02/HOME HEALTH
0601	Oxygen-State/Equipment/Supply/ or Cont.	02/STAT EQUIP/SUPPL/CONT
0602	Oxygen-State/Equip/Suppl/Under 1 LPM	02/STAT EQUIP/UNDER 1 LPM
0603	Oxygen-State/Equip/ Over 4 LPM	02/STAT EQUIP/OVER 4 LPM
0604	Oxygen-Portable Add-on	02/PORTABLE ADD-ON
0609	Other Oxygen	02-OTHER
060X	Oxygen Home Health	
0610	General Classification	MRT
0611	Brain (including brain stem)	MRI-BRAIN
0612	Spinal Cord (including spine)	MRI-SPINE
0613	Reserved	
0614	MRI-Other	MRI-OTHER
0615	MRI-Head and Neck	MRI-HEAD AND NECK
0616	MRI-Lower Extremities	MRI-LOWER EXT
0617	Reserved	
0618	MRI-Other	MRI-OTHER
0619	Other-MRT	MRT-OTHER
061X	MRT (Magnetic Resonance Technology)	
0621	Supplies Incident to Radiology	MED-SUR SUPP/INCDT RAD
0622	Supplies Incident to Other Diagnostic Services	MED-SUR SUPP/INCDT ODX
0623	Surgical Dressing	SURG DRESSING
0624	FDA Investigational Devices	FDA INVEST DEVICE
062X	Medical Surgical Supplies (See also 027X)	
0630	Reserved (Eff. 01/01/98)	
0631	Single Source Drug	DRUG/SINGLE
0632	Multiple Source Drug	DRUG/MULT
0633	Restrictive Prescription	DRUG/RSTR
0634	Erythropoietin (EPO) less than 10,000 units	DRUG/EPO<10,000 UNITS
0635	Erythropoietin (EPO) more than 10,000 units	DRUG/EPO>10,000 UNITS
0636	Drugs requiring detailed coding (a)	DRUGS/DETAIL CODE
0637	Self-administerable drugs (b)	DRUGS/SELF ADMN
063X	Drugs requiring specific identification (See also 025X)	
0640	General Classification	IV THERAPY SVC
0641	Non-routine Nursing, Central Line	NON RT NURSING/CENTRAL
0642	IV Site Care, Central Line (HCPCS related)	IV SITE CARE/CENTRAL

0643	IV Started/Changed, Peripheral Line	IV STRT/CHNG/PERIPHRL
0644	Non-routine Nursing, Peripheral Line	NON RT NURSING/PERIPHRL
0645	Training patient/Caregiver, Central Line	TRNG PT/CAREGVR/CENTRAL
0646	Training Disabled Patient, Central Line	TRNG DSBLPT/CENTRAL
0647	Training Patient/Caregiver, Peripheral Line	TRNG PT/CAREGVR/PERIPHRL
0648	Training Disabled Patient, Peripheral Line	TRNG DSBLPAT/PERIPHRL
0649	Other IV Therapy Services	OTHER IV THERAPY SVC
064X	Home IV Therapy Services	
0650	General Classification	HOSPICE
0651	Routine Home Care	HOSPICE/RTN HOME
0652	Continuous Home Care	HOSPICE/CTNS HOME
0653	Reserved	
0654	Reserved	
0655	Inpatient Respite Care	HOSPICE/IP RESPITE
0656	General Inpatient Care	HOSPICE/IP NONRESPITE
0657	Physician Services	HOSPICE/PHYSICIAN
0658	Hospice RandB Nursing Facility	HOSPICE/RandB/NURS FAC
0659	Other Hospice	HOSPICE/OTHER
065X	Hospice Services	
0660	General Classification	RESPITE CARE
0661	Hourly Charge/Nursing	RESPITE/NURSE
0662	Hourly Charge/Aide/Homemaker/Companion	RESPITE/AIDE/HMEMKR/COMP
0663	Daily Respite Charge	RESPITE DAILY
0669	Other Respite Care	RESPITE OTHER
066X	Respite Care	
0670	General Classification	OP SPEC RES
0671	Hospital Based	OP SPEC RES/HOSP BASED
0672	Contracted	OP SPEC RES/CONTRACTED
0679	Other Special Residence Charges	OP SPEC RES/OTHER
067X	Outpatient Special Residence Charges	
0680	Not Used	
0681	Level I	TRAUMA LEVEL I
0682	Level II	TRAUMA LEVEL II
0683	Level III	TRAUMA LEVEL III
0684	Level IV	TRAUMA LEVEL IV
0689	Other Trauma Response	TRAUMA OTHER
068X	Trauma Response	

069X	Not Assigned	
0700	General Classification	CAST ROOM
0709	Other Cast Room	OTHER CAST ROOM
070X	Cast Care	
0710	General Classification	RECOVERY RM
0719	Other Recovery Room	OTHER RECOV RM
071X	Recovery Room	
0720	General Classification	DELIVERYROOM/LABOR
0721	Labor	LABOR
0722	Delivery	DELIVERY ROOM
0723	Circumcision	CIRCUMCISION
0724	Birthing Center	BIRTHING CENTER
0729	Other Labor/Delivery Room	OTHER/DELIV-LABOR
072X	Labor/Delivery Room	
0730	General Classification	EKG/ECG
0731	Holter Monitor	HOLTER MONITOR
0732	Telemetry	TELEMETRY
0739	Other EKG/ECG	OTHER EKG-ECG
073X	EKG/ECG (Electrocardiogram)	
0740	General Classification	EEG
0749	Other EEG	OTHER EEG
074X	EEG (Electroencephalogram)	
0750	General Classification	GASRT-INTS SVC
0759	Other Gastrointestinal	OTHER GASTRO-INTS
075X	Gastrointestinal Services	
0760	General Classification	TREATMT/OBSERVATION RM
0761	Treatment Room	TREATMENT RM
0762	Observation Room	OBSERVATION RM
0769	Other Treatment/Observation Room	OTHER TREAT/OBSERV RM
076X	Treatment or Observation Room	
0770	General Classification	PREVENT CARE SVC
0771	Vaccine Administration	VACCINE ADMIN
0779	Other Preventive Care Services	OTHER PREVENT
077X	Preventive Care Services	
0780	General Classification	TELEMEDICINE
0789	Other Telemedicine	TELEMEDICINE/OTHER
078X	Telemedicine	

0790	General Classification	ESWT
0799	Other ESWT	ESWT/OTHER
079X	Extra-Corporeal Shock Wave Therapy (ESWT), formerly lithotripsy	
0800	General Classification	RENAL DIALYSIS
0801	Inpatient Hemodialysis	DAILY/INPT
0802	Inpatient Peritoneal (Non-CAPD)	DAILY/INPT/PER
0803	Inpatient Continuous Ambulatory Peritoneal Dialysis	DAILY/INPT/CAPD
0804	Inpatient Continuous Cycling Peritoneal Dialysis	DAILY/INPT/CCPD
0809	Other Inpatient Dialysis	DAILY/INPT/OTHER
080X	Inpatient Renal Dialysis	
0810	General Classification	ORGAN ACQUISIT
0811	Living Donor	LIVING DONOR
0812	Cadaver Donor	CADAVER DONOR
0813	Unknown Donor	UNKNOWN DONOR
0814	Unsuccessful Organ Search-Donor Bank Charges	UNSUCCESSFUL SEARCH
0819	Other Donor	OTHER DONOR
081X	Organ Acquisition	
0820	General Classification	HEMO/OP or HOME
0821	Hemodialysis/Composite or Other Rate	HEMO/COMPOSITE
0822	Home Supplies	HEMO/HOME/SUPPL
0823	Home Equipment	HEMO/HOME/EQUIP
0824	Maintenance 100%	HEMO/HOME/100%
0825	Support Services	HEMO/HOME/SUPSERV
0829	Other Outpatient Hemodialysis	HEMO/HOME/OTHER
082X	Hemodialysis-Outpatient or Home	
0830	General Classification	PERITONEAL/OP or HOME
0831	Peritoneal/Composite or Other Rate	PERTNL/COMPOSITE
0832	Home Supplies	PERTNL/HOME/SUPPL
0833	Home Equipment	PERTNL/HOME EQUIP
0834	Maintenance 100%	PERTNL/HOME 100%
0835	Support Services	PERTNL/HOME SUPSERV
0839	Other Outpatient Peritoneal	PERTNL/HOME/OTHER
083X	Peritoneal Dialysis-Outpatient or Home	
0840	General Classification	CAPD/OP or CAPD/HOME
0841	CAPD/Composite or other Rate	CAPD/COMPOSITE

0842	Home Supplies	CAPD/HOME/SUPPL
0843	Home Equipment	CAPD/HOME/EQUIP
0844	Maintenance 100%	CAPD/HOME/100%
0845	Support Services	CAPD/HOME/SUPSERV
0849	Other Outpatient CAPD	CAPD/HOME/OTHER
084X	Continuous Ambulatory Peritoneal Dialysis (CAPD) Outpatient or Home	
0850	General Classification	CCPD/OP or CCPD/HOME
0851	CCPD/Composite or Other Rate	CCPD/COMPOSITE
0852	Home Supplies	CCPD/HOME/SUPPL
0853	Home Equipment	CCPD/HOME/EQUIP
0854	Maintenance 100%	CCPD/HOME/100%
0855	Support Services	CCPD/HOME/SUPSERV
0859	Other Outpatient CCPD	CCPD/HOME/OTHER
085X	Continuous Cycling Peritoneal Dialysis (CCPD) Outpatient or Home	
086X	Reserved for Dialysis (National Assignment)	
087X	Reserved for Dialysis (National Assignment)	
0880	General Classification	DAILY MISC
0881	Ultrafiltration	DAILY/ULTRAFILT
0882	Home Dialysis Aid Visit	HOME DIALYSIS AID VISIT
0889	Misc. Dialysis Other	MISC. DIALYSIS OTHER
088X	Misc. Dialysis	MISC. DIALYSIS
089X	Reserved for National Assignment	
0900	General Classification	BH
0901	Electroshock Treatment	BH/ELECTRO SHOCK
0902	Milieu Therapy	BH/MILIEU THERAPY
0903	Play Therapy	BH/PLAY THERAPY
0904	Activity Therapy	BH/ACTIVITY THERAPY
0905	Intensive Outpatient Services-Psychiatric	BH/INTENS OP/PSYCH
0906	Intensive Outpatient Services Chemical Dependency	BH/INTENS OP/CHEM DEP
0907	Community Behavioral Health Program Day Treatment	BH/COMMUNITY
0908	Reserved	
0909	Reserved	
090X	Behavioral Health Treatments/Services (See also 091X)	
0910	Reserved	

0911	Rehabilitation	BH/REHAB
0912	Partial Hospitalization-Less Intensive	BH/PARTIAL HOSP
0913	Partial Hospitalization-Intensive	BH/PARTIAL INTENSIVE
0914	Individual Therapy	BH/INDIV RX
0915	Group Therapy	BH/GROUP RX
0916	Family Therapy	BH/FAMILY RX
0917	Biofeedback	BH/BIOFEED
0918	Testing	BH/TESTING
0919	Other Behavioral Health Treatment Services	BH/OTHER
091X	Behavioral Health Treatments/Services (See also 090X)	
0920	General Classification	OTHER DX SVC
0921	Peripheral Vascular Lab	PERI VASCUL LAB
0922	Electromyogram	EMG
0923	Pap Smear	PAP SMEAR
0924	Allergy Test	ALLERGY TEST
0925	Pregnancy Test	PREG TEST
0929	Other Diagnostic Services	ADDITIONAL DX SVC
092X	Other Diagnostic Services	
0931	Half Day	HALF DAY
0932	Full Day	FULL DAY
093X	Medical Rehabilitation Day Program	
0940	General Classification	OTHER RX SVC
0941	Recreational Therapy	RECREATION RX
0942	Educational/Training	EDUC/TRAINING
0943	Cardiac Rehabilitation	CARDIAC REHAB
0944	Drug Rehabilitation	DRUG REHAB
0945	Alcohol Rehabilitation	ALCOHOL REHAB
0946	Complex Medical Equipment-Routine	CMPLX MED EQUIP-ROUT
0947	Complex Medical Equipment-Ancillary	CMPLX MED EQUIP-ANC
0949	Other Therapeutic Services	ADDITIONAL RX SVC
094X	Other Therapeutic Services (See also 095X)	
0950	General Classification	PRO FEE
0951	Athletic Training	ATHLETIC TRAINING
0951	Psychiatry	PRO FEE/PSYCH
0952	Ophthalmology	PRO FEE/EYE
0952	Kinesiotherapy	KINESIOTHERAPY

0953	Anesthesiology MD	PRO FEE/ANES MD
0954	Anesthetist (CRNA)	PRO FEE/ANES CRNA
0959	Other Professional Fees	OTHER PRO FEE
095X	Other Therapeutic Services (See also 094X)	
0960	General Classification	PRO FEE
0961	Psychiatric	PRO FEE/PSYCH
0962	Ophthalmology	PRO FEE/EYE
0963	Anesthesiologist MD	PRO FEE/ANES MD
0964	Anesthetist (CRNA)	PRO FEE/ANES CRNA
0969	Other Professional Fees	OTHER PRO FEE
096X	Professional Fees (See also 097X and 098X)	
0971	Laboratory	PRO FEE/LAB
0972	Radiology-Diagnostic	PRO FEE/RAD DX
0973	Radiology-Therapeutic	PRO FEE/RAD RX
0974	Radiology-Nuclear Medicine	PRO FEE/NUC MED
0975	Operating Room	PRO FEE/OR
0976	Respiratory Therapy	PRO FEE/RESPIR THPY
0977	Physical Therapy	PRO FEE/PHYSICAL THPY
0978	Occupational Therapy	PRO FEE/OCUPA THPY
0979	Speech Pathology	PRO FEE/SPEECH PATH
097X	Professional Fees (See also 096X)	
0981	Emergency Room	PRO FEE/ER
0982	Outpatient Services	PRO FEE/OUTPT
0983	Clinic	PRO FEE/CLINIC
0984	Medical Social Services	PRO FEE/SOC SVC
0985	EKG	PRO FEE/EKG
0986	EEG	PRO FEE/EEG
0987	Hospital Visit	PRO FEE/HOSP VISIT
0988	Consultation	PRO FEE/CONSULT
0989	Private Duty Nurse	PRO FEE/PVT NURSE
098X	Professional Fees (See also 096X and 097X)	
0990	General Classification	PT CONVENIENCE
0991	Cafeteria/Guest Tray	CAFETERIA or GUEST TRAY
0992	Private Linen Service	LINEN
0993	Telephone/Telegraph	TELEPHONE
0994	TV/Radio	TV/RADIO
0995	Non-patient Room Rentals	NONPT ROOM RENT

0996	Late Discharge Charge	LATE DISCHARGE
0997	Admission Kit	ADMIT KITS
0998	Beauty Shop/Barber	BARBER/BEAUTY
099X	Patient Convenience Items	
1000	General Classification	BH Rand B
1001	Residential Treatment-Psychiatric	BH Rand B RES/PSYCH
100X	Behavioral Health Accommodations	PT CONVENCE/OTH
2100	General Classification	ALTTHERAPY
2101	Acupuncture	ACUPUNCTURE
2102	Acupressure	ACUPRESSURE
2103	Massage	MASSAGE
2104	Reflexology	REFLEXOLOGY
2105	Biofeedback	BIOFEEDBACK
2106	Hypnosis	HYPNOSIS
2109	Other Alternative Therapy Services	OTHER ALTTHERAPY
210X	Alternative Therapy Services	
3100	Not Used	
3101	Adult Day Care-Medical and Social-Hourly	ADULT MED/SOC HR
3102	Adult Day Care-Social-Hourly	ADULT SOC HR
3103	Adult Day Care-Medical and Social-Daily	ADULT MED/SOC DAY
3104	Adult Day Care-Social-Daily	ADULT SOC DAY
3105	Adult Foster Care-Daily	ADULT FOSTER DAY
3109	Other Adult Care	OTHER ADULT
310X	Adult Care	

EXTRA FORMS

[1500]

HEALTH INSURANCE CLAIM FORM

APPROVED BY NATIONAL UNIFORM CLAIM COMMITTEE 08/05

| | PICA | | | | | | | | | | PICA | | |

1. MEDICARE	MEDICAID	TRICARE CHAMPUS	CHAMPVA	GROUP HEALTH PLAN	FECA BLK LUNG	OTHER	1a. INSURED'S I.D. NUMBER	(For Program in Item 1)
(Medicare #)	(Medicaid #)	(Sponsor's SSN)	(Member ID#)	(SSN or ID)	(SSN)	(ID)		

2. PATIENT'S NAME (Last Name, First Name, Middle Initial)

3. PATIENT'S BIRTH DATE MM DD YY   SEX   M   F

4. INSURED'S NAME (Last Name, First Name, Middle Initial)

5. PATIENT'S ADDRESS (No., Street)

6. PATIENT RELATIONSHIP TO INSURED   Self   Spouse   Child   Other

7. INSURED'S ADDRESS (No., Street)

CITY   STATE

8. PATIENT STATUS   Single   Married   Other

CITY   STATE

ZIP CODE   TELEPHONE (Include Area Code) ( )

Employed   Full-Time Student   Part-Time Student

ZIP CODE   TELEPHONE (Include Area Code) ( )

9. OTHER INSURED'S NAME (Last Name, First Name, Middle Initial)

10. IS PATIENT'S CONDITION RELATED TO:

11. INSURED'S POLICY GROUP OR FECA NUMBER

a. OTHER INSURED'S POLICY OR GROUP NUMBER

a. EMPLOYMENT? (Current or Previous)   YES   NO

a. INSURED'S DATE OF BIRTH MM DD YY   SEX   M   F

b. OTHER INSURED'S DATE OF BIRTH MM DD YY   SEX   M   F

b. AUTO ACCIDENT?   PLACE (State)   YES   NO

b. EMPLOYER'S NAME OR SCHOOL NAME

c. EMPLOYER'S NAME OR SCHOOL NAME

c. OTHER ACCIDENT?   YES   NO

c. INSURANCE PLAN NAME OR PROGRAM NAME

d. INSURANCE PLAN NAME OR PROGRAM NAME

10d. RESERVED FOR LOCAL USE

d. IS THERE ANOTHER HEALTH BENEFIT PLAN?   YES   NO   *If yes*, return to and complete item 9 a-d.

READ BACK OF FORM BEFORE COMPLETING & SIGNING THIS FORM.
12. PATIENT'S OR AUTHORIZED PERSON'S SIGNATURE I authorize the release of any medical or other information necessary to process this claim. I also request payment of government benefits either to myself or to the party who accepts assignment below.

SIGNED _____ DATE _____

13. INSURED'S OR AUTHORIZED PERSON'S SIGNATURE I authorize payment of medical benefits to the undersigned physician or supplier for services described below.

SIGNED _____

14. DATE OF CURRENT: MM DD YY   ILLNESS (First symptom) OR INJURY (Accident) OR PREGNANCY(LMP)

15. IF PATIENT HAS HAD SAME OR SIMILAR ILLNESS. GIVE FIRST DATE MM DD YY

16. DATES PATIENT UNABLE TO WORK IN CURRENT OCCUPATION MM DD YY   FROM   TO MM DD YY

17. NAME OF REFERRING PROVIDER OR OTHER SOURCE

17a.

17b. NPI

18. HOSPITALIZATION DATES RELATED TO CURRENT SERVICES MM DD YY   FROM   TO MM DD YY

19. RESERVED FOR LOCAL USE

20. OUTSIDE LAB?   YES   NO $ CHARGES

21. DIAGNOSIS OR NATURE OF ILLNESS OR INJURY (Relate Items 1, 2, 3 or 4 to Item 24E by Line)

1. _____ . _____   3. _____ . _____

2. _____ . _____   4. _____ . _____

22. MEDICAID RESUBMISSION CODE   ORIGINAL REF. NO.

23. PRIOR AUTHORIZATION NUMBER

24. A. DATE(S) OF SERVICE						B. PLACE OF SERVICE	C. EMG	D. PROCEDURES, SERVICES, OR SUPPLIES (Explain Unusual Circumstances) CPT/HCPCS	MODIFIER	E. DIAGNOSIS POINTER	F. $ CHARGES	G. DAYS OR UNITS	H. EPSDT Family Plan	I. ID. QUAL	J. RENDERING PROVIDER ID. #
From MM	DD	YY	To MM	DD	YY										
1															NPI
2															NPI
3															NPI
4															NPI
5															NPI
6															NPI

25. FEDERAL TAX I.D. NUMBER   SSN EIN

26. PATIENT'S ACCOUNT NO.

27. ACCEPT ASSIGNMENT? (For govt. claims, see back)   YES   NO

28. TOTAL CHARGE $

29. AMOUNT PAID $

30. BALANCE DUE $

31. SIGNATURE OF PHYSICIAN OR SUPPLIER INCLUDING DEGREES OR CREDENTIALS (I certify that the statements on the reverse apply to this bill and are made a part thereof.)

SIGNED _____ DATE _____

32. SERVICE FACILITY LOCATION INFORMATION

a.   b.

33. BILLING PROVIDER INFO & PH # ( )

a.   b.

1500

HEALTH INSURANCE CLAIM FORM

APPROVED BY NATIONAL UNIFORM CLAIM COMMITTEE 08/05

PICA   PICA

| 1. MEDICARE (Medicare #) | MEDICAID (Medicaid #) | TRICARE CHAMPUS (Sponsor's SSN) | CHAMPVA (Member ID#) | GROUP HEALTH PLAN (SSN or ID) | FECA BLK LUNG (SSN) | OTHER (ID) | 1a. INSURED'S I.D. NUMBER (For Program in Item 1) |

| 2. PATIENT'S NAME (Last Name, First Name, Middle Initial) | 3. PATIENT'S BIRTH DATE MM DD YY | SEX M F | 4. INSURED'S NAME (Last Name, First Name, Middle Initial) |

| 5. PATIENT'S ADDRESS (No., Street) | 6. PATIENT RELATIONSHIP TO INSURED Self Spouse Child Other | 7. INSURED'S ADDRESS (No., Street) |

| CITY | STATE | 8. PATIENT STATUS Single Married Other | CITY | STATE |

| ZIP CODE | TELEPHONE (Include Area Code) ( ) | Employed Full-Time Student Part-Time Student | ZIP CODE | TELEPHONE (Include Area Code) ( ) |

| 9. OTHER INSURED'S NAME (Last Name, First Name, Middle Initial) | 10. IS PATIENT'S CONDITION RELATED TO: | 11. INSURED'S POLICY GROUP OR FECA NUMBER |

| a. OTHER INSURED'S POLICY OR GROUP NUMBER | a. EMPLOYMENT? (Current or Previous) YES NO | a. INSURED'S DATE OF BIRTH MM DD YY SEX M F |

| b. OTHER INSURED'S DATE OF BIRTH MM DD YY SEX M F | b. AUTO ACCIDENT? PLACE (State) YES NO | b. EMPLOYER'S NAME OR SCHOOL NAME |

| c. EMPLOYER'S NAME OR SCHOOL NAME | c. OTHER ACCIDENT? YES NO | c. INSURANCE PLAN NAME OR PROGRAM NAME |

| d. INSURANCE PLAN NAME OR PROGRAM NAME | 10d. RESERVED FOR LOCAL USE | d. IS THERE ANOTHER HEALTH BENEFIT PLAN? YES NO *If yes*, return to and complete item 9 a-d. |

READ BACK OF FORM BEFORE COMPLETING & SIGNING THIS FORM.

12. PATIENT'S OR AUTHORIZED PERSON'S SIGNATURE I authorize the release of any medical or other information necessary to process this claim. I also request payment of government benefits either to myself or to the party who accepts assignment below.

SIGNED _____ DATE _____

13. INSURED'S OR AUTHORIZED PERSON'S SIGNATURE I authorize payment of medical benefits to the undersigned physician or supplier for services described below.

SIGNED _____

| 14. DATE OF CURRENT: MM DD YY ◀ ILLNESS (First symptom) OR INJURY (Accident) OR PREGNANCY(LMP) | 15. IF PATIENT HAS HAD SAME OR SIMILAR ILLNESS. GIVE FIRST DATE MM DD YY | 16. DATES PATIENT UNABLE TO WORK IN CURRENT OCCUPATION MM DD YY FROM TO MM DD YY |

| 17. NAME OF REFERRING PROVIDER OR OTHER SOURCE | 17a. 17b. NPI | 18. HOSPITALIZATION DATES RELATED TO CURRENT SERVICES MM DD YY FROM TO MM DD YY |

| 19. RESERVED FOR LOCAL USE | 20. OUTSIDE LAB? YES NO $ CHARGES |

21. DIAGNOSIS OR NATURE OF ILLNESS OR INJURY (Relate Items 1, 2, 3 or 4 to Item 24E by Line)

1. |____ . ____| 3. |____ . ____|

2. |____ . ____| 4. |____ . ____|

22. MEDICAID RESUBMISSION CODE   ORIGINAL REF. NO.

23. PRIOR AUTHORIZATION NUMBER

24. A. DATE(S) OF SERVICE		B. PLACE OF SERVICE	C. EMG	D. PROCEDURES, SERVICES, OR SUPPLIES (Explain Unusual Circumstances)		E. DIAGNOSIS POINTER	F. $ CHARGES	G. DAYS OR UNITS	H. EPSDT Family Plan	I. ID. QUAL.	J. RENDERING PROVIDER ID. #
From MM DD YY	To MM DD YY			CPT/HCPCS	MODIFIER						
1										NPI	
2										NPI	
3										NPI	
4										NPI	
5										NPI	
6										NPI	

| 25. FEDERAL TAX I.D. NUMBER SSN EIN | 26. PATIENT'S ACCOUNT NO. | 27. ACCEPT ASSIGNMENT? (For govt. claims, see back) YES NO | 28. TOTAL CHARGE $ | 29. AMOUNT PAID $ | 30. BALANCE DUE $ |

| 31. SIGNATURE OF PHYSICIAN OR SUPPLIER INCLUDING DEGREES OR CREDENTIALS (I certify that the statements on the reverse apply to this bill and are made a part thereof.) SIGNED _____ DATE _____ | 32. SERVICE FACILITY LOCATION INFORMATION a. NPI b. | 33. BILLING PROVIDER INFO & PH # ( ) a. NPI b. |

NUCC Instruction Manual available at: www.nucc.org

APPROVED OMB-0938-0999 FORM CMS-1500 (08-05)

CARRIER

PATIENT AND INSURED INFORMATION

PHYSICIAN OR SUPPLIER INFORMATION

1500

HEALTH INSURANCE CLAIM FORM

APPROVED BY NATIONAL UNIFORM CLAIM COMMITTEE 08/05

☐☐☐ PICA   PICA ☐☐☐

CARRIER →

1. MEDICARE   MEDICAID   TRICARE CHAMPUS   CHAMPVA   GROUP HEALTH PLAN   FECA BLK LUNG   OTHER   1a. INSURED'S I.D. NUMBER   (For Program in Item 1)

☐ (Medicare #)   ☐ (Medicaid #)   ☐ (Sponsor's SSN)   ☐ (Member ID#)   ☐ (SSN or ID)   ☐ (SSN)   ☐ (ID)

2. PATIENT'S NAME (Last Name, First Name, Middle Initial)   3. PATIENT'S BIRTH DATE   MM ┊ DD ┊ YY   SEX   M ☐   F ☐   4. INSURED'S NAME (Last Name, First Name, Middle Initial)

5. PATIENT'S ADDRESS (No., Street)   6. PATIENT RELATIONSHIP TO INSURED   Self ☐   Spouse ☐   Child ☐   Other ☐   7. INSURED'S ADDRESS (No., Street)

CITY   STATE   8. PATIENT STATUS   Single ☐   Married ☐   Other ☐   CITY   STATE

ZIP CODE   TELEPHONE (Include Area Code)   ( )   Employed ☐   Full-Time Student ☐   Part-Time Student ☐   ZIP CODE   TELEPHONE (Include Area Code)   ( )

9. OTHER INSURED'S NAME (Last Name, First Name, Middle Initial)   10. IS PATIENT'S CONDITION RELATED TO: 11. INSURED'S POLICY GROUP OR FECA NUMBER

a. OTHER INSURED'S POLICY OR GROUP NUMBER   a. EMPLOYMENT? (Current or Previous)   ☐ YES   ☐ NO   a. INSURED'S DATE OF BIRTH   MM ┊ DD ┊ YY   SEX   M ☐   F ☐

b. OTHER INSURED'S DATE OF BIRTH   MM ┊ DD ┊ YY   SEX   M ☐   F ☐   b. AUTO ACCIDENT?   ☐ YES   ☐ NO   PLACE (State) ___   b. EMPLOYER'S NAME OR SCHOOL NAME

c. EMPLOYER'S NAME OR SCHOOL NAME   c. OTHER ACCIDENT?   ☐ YES   ☐ NO   c. INSURANCE PLAN NAME OR PROGRAM NAME

d. INSURANCE PLAN NAME OR PROGRAM NAME   10d. RESERVED FOR LOCAL USE   d. IS THERE ANOTHER HEALTH BENEFIT PLAN?   ☐ YES   ☐ NO   *If yes*, return to and complete item 9 a-d.

READ BACK OF FORM BEFORE COMPLETING & SIGNING THIS FORM.

12. PATIENT'S OR AUTHORIZED PERSON'S SIGNATURE I authorize the release of any medical or other information necessary to process this claim. I also request payment of government benefits either to myself or to the party who accepts assignment below.

SIGNED _____ DATE _____

13. INSURED'S OR AUTHORIZED PERSON'S SIGNATURE I authorize payment of medical benefits to the undersigned physician or supplier for services described below.

SIGNED _____

PATIENT AND INSURED INFORMATION →

14. DATE OF CURRENT: ◀ ILLNESS (First symptom) OR INJURY (Accident) OR PREGNANCY(LMP)   MM ┊ DD ┊ YY   15. IF PATIENT HAS HAD SAME OR SIMILAR ILLNESS. GIVE FIRST DATE   MM ┊ DD ┊ YY   16. DATES PATIENT UNABLE TO WORK IN CURRENT OCCUPATION   FROM MM ┊ DD ┊ YY   TO MM ┊ DD ┊ YY

17. NAME OF REFERRING PROVIDER OR OTHER SOURCE   17a. _____   17b. NPI _____   18. HOSPITALIZATION DATES RELATED TO CURRENT SERVICES   FROM MM ┊ DD ┊ YY   TO MM ┊ DD ┊ YY

19. RESERVED FOR LOCAL USE   20. OUTSIDE LAB?   ☐ YES   ☐ NO $ CHARGES

21. DIAGNOSIS OR NATURE OF ILLNESS OR INJURY (Relate Items 1, 2, 3 or 4 to Item 24E by Line)

1. |___ . ___   3. |___ . ___

2. |___ . ___   4. |___ . ___

22. MEDICAID RESUBMISSION CODE _____ ORIGINAL REF. NO. _____

23. PRIOR AUTHORIZATION NUMBER

24. A. DATE(S) OF SERVICE						B. PLACE OF SERVICE	C. EMG	D. PROCEDURES, SERVICES, OR SUPPLIES (Explain Unusual Circumstances)		E. DIAGNOSIS POINTER	F. $ CHARGES	G. DAYS OR UNITS	H. EPSDT Family Plan	I. ID. QUAL	J. RENDERING PROVIDER ID. #
From			To					CPT/HCPCS	MODIFIER						
MM	DD	YY	MM	DD	YY										
1														NPI	
2														NPI	
3														NPI	
4														NPI	
5														NPI	
6														NPI	

25. FEDERAL TAX I.D. NUMBER   ☐ SSN ☐ EIN   26. PATIENT'S ACCOUNT NO.   27. ACCEPT ASSIGNMENT? (For govt. claims, see back)   ☐ YES   ☐ NO   28. TOTAL CHARGE $ 29. AMOUNT PAID $ 30. BALANCE DUE $

31. SIGNATURE OF PHYSICIAN OR SUPPLIER INCLUDING DEGREES OR CREDENTIALS (I certify that the statements on the reverse apply to this bill and are made a part thereof.)

SIGNED _____ DATE _____

32. SERVICE FACILITY LOCATION INFORMATION   a. NPI   b.

33. BILLING PROVIDER INFO & PH # ( )   a. NPI   b.

PHYSICIAN OR SUPPLIER INFORMATION →

NUCC Instruction Manual available at: www.nucc.org   APPROVED OMB-0938-0999 FORM CMS-1500 (08-05)

1500

HEALTH INSURANCE CLAIM FORM

APPROVED BY NATIONAL UNIFORM CLAIM COMMITTEE 08/05

CARRIER

| | PICA | | | | | | PICA | |

1. MEDICARE (Medicare #) MEDICAID (Medicaid #) TRICARE CHAMPUS (Sponsor's SSN) CHAMPVA (Member ID#) GROUP HEALTH PLAN (SSN or ID) FECA BLK LUNG (SSN) OTHER (ID) 1a. INSURED'S I.D. NUMBER (For Program in Item 1)

2. PATIENT'S NAME (Last Name, First Name, Middle Initial) 3. PATIENT'S BIRTH DATE MM DD YY SEX M F 4. INSURED'S NAME (Last Name, First Name, Middle Initial)

5. PATIENT'S ADDRESS (No., Street) 6. PATIENT RELATIONSHIP TO INSURED Self Spouse Child Other 7. INSURED'S ADDRESS (No., Street)

CITY STATE 8. PATIENT STATUS Single Married Other Employed Full-Time Student Part-Time Student CITY STATE

ZIP CODE TELEPHONE (Include Area Code) ( ) ZIP CODE TELEPHONE (Include Area Code) ( )

9. OTHER INSURED'S NAME (Last Name, First Name, Middle Initial) 10. IS PATIENT'S CONDITION RELATED TO: 11. INSURED'S POLICY GROUP OR FECA NUMBER

a. OTHER INSURED'S POLICY OR GROUP NUMBER a. EMPLOYMENT? (Current or Previous) YES NO a. INSURED'S DATE OF BIRTH MM DD YY SEX M F

b. OTHER INSURED'S DATE OF BIRTH MM DD YY SEX M F b. AUTO ACCIDENT? YES NO PLACE (State) b. EMPLOYER'S NAME OR SCHOOL NAME

c. EMPLOYER'S NAME OR SCHOOL NAME c. OTHER ACCIDENT? YES NO c. INSURANCE PLAN NAME OR PROGRAM NAME

d. INSURANCE PLAN NAME OR PROGRAM NAME 10d. RESERVED FOR LOCAL USE d. IS THERE ANOTHER HEALTH BENEFIT PLAN? YES NO *If yes*, return to and complete item 9 a-d.

READ BACK OF FORM BEFORE COMPLETING & SIGNING THIS FORM.
12. PATIENT'S OR AUTHORIZED PERSON'S SIGNATURE I authorize the release of any medical or other information necessary to process this claim. I also request payment of government benefits either to myself or to the party who accepts assignment below. SIGNED _____ DATE _____
13. INSURED'S OR AUTHORIZED PERSON'S SIGNATURE I authorize payment of medical benefits to the undersigned physician or supplier for services described below. SIGNED _____

PATIENT AND INSURED INFORMATION

14. DATE OF CURRENT: ILLNESS (First symptom) OR INJURY (Accident) OR PREGNANCY(LMP) MM DD YY 15. IF PATIENT HAS HAD SAME OR SIMILAR ILLNESS. GIVE FIRST DATE MM DD YY 16. DATES PATIENT UNABLE TO WORK IN CURRENT OCCUPATION FROM MM DD YY TO MM DD YY

17. NAME OF REFERRING PROVIDER OR OTHER SOURCE 17a. 17b. NPI 18. HOSPITALIZATION DATES RELATED TO CURRENT SERVICES FROM MM DD YY TO MM DD YY

19. RESERVED FOR LOCAL USE 20. OUTSIDE LAB? YES NO $ CHARGES

21. DIAGNOSIS OR NATURE OF ILLNESS OR INJURY (Relate Items 1, 2, 3 or 4 to Item 24E by Line) 1. ___ . ___ 3. ___ . ___ 2. ___ . ___ 4. ___ . ___ 22. MEDICAID RESUBMISSION CODE ORIGINAL REF. NO. 23. PRIOR AUTHORIZATION NUMBER

24. A. DATE(S) OF SERVICE From MM DD YY To MM DD YY	B. PLACE OF SERVICE	C. EMG	D. PROCEDURES, SERVICES, OR SUPPLIES (Explain Unusual Circumstances) CPT/HCPCS MODIFIER	E. DIAGNOSIS POINTER	F. $ CHARGES	G. DAYS OR UNITS	H. EPSDT Family Plan	I. ID QUAL.	J. RENDERING PROVIDER ID. #
1								NPI	
2								NPI	
3								NPI	
4								NPI	
5								NPI	
6								NPI	

25. FEDERAL TAX I.D. NUMBER SSN EIN 26. PATIENT'S ACCOUNT NO. 27. ACCEPT ASSIGNMENT? (For govt. claims, see back) YES NO 28. TOTAL CHARGE $ 29. AMOUNT PAID $ 30. BALANCE DUE $

31. SIGNATURE OF PHYSICIAN OR SUPPLIER INCLUDING DEGREES OR CREDENTIALS (I certify that the statements on the reverse apply to this bill and are made a part thereof.) SIGNED _____ DATE _____ 32. SERVICE FACILITY LOCATION INFORMATION a. NPI b. 33. BILLING PROVIDER INFO & PH # ( ) a. NPI b.

PHYSICIAN OR SUPPLIER INFORMATION

1500

HEALTH INSURANCE CLAIM FORM

APPROVED BY NATIONAL UNIFORM CLAIM COMMITTEE 08/05

| | PICA | | | | | | | | | PICA | |

1. MEDICARE	MEDICAID	TRICARE CHAMPUS	CHAMPVA	GROUP HEALTH PLAN	FECA BLK LUNG	OTHER	1a. INSURED'S I.D. NUMBER	(For Program in Item 1)
(Medicare #)	(Medicaid #)	(Sponsor's SSN)	(Member ID#)	(SSN or ID)	(SSN)	(ID)		

2. PATIENT'S NAME (Last Name, First Name, Middle Initial)

3. PATIENT'S BIRTH DATE MM | DD | YY   SEX   M☐ F☐

4. INSURED'S NAME (Last Name, First Name, Middle Initial)

5. PATIENT'S ADDRESS (No., Street)

6. PATIENT RELATIONSHIP TO INSURED   Self☐ Spouse☐ Child☐ Other☐

7. INSURED'S ADDRESS (No., Street)

CITY   STATE

8. PATIENT STATUS   Single☐ Married☐ Other☐

CITY   STATE

ZIP CODE   TELEPHONE (Include Area Code) (   )

Employed☐ Full-Time Student☐ Part-Time Student☐

ZIP CODE   TELEPHONE (Include Area Code) (   )

9. OTHER INSURED'S NAME (Last Name, First Name, Middle Initial)

10. IS PATIENT'S CONDITION RELATED TO:

11. INSURED'S POLICY GROUP OR FECA NUMBER

a. OTHER INSURED'S POLICY OR GROUP NUMBER

a. EMPLOYMENT? (Current or Previous)   ☐YES ☐NO

a. INSURED'S DATE OF BIRTH MM | DD | YY   SEX M☐ F☐

b. OTHER INSURED'S DATE OF BIRTH MM | DD | YY   SEX   M☐ F☐

b. AUTO ACCIDENT?   PLACE (State)   ☐YES ☐NO

b. EMPLOYER'S NAME OR SCHOOL NAME

c. EMPLOYER'S NAME OR SCHOOL NAME

c. OTHER ACCIDENT?   ☐YES ☐NO

c. INSURANCE PLAN NAME OR PROGRAM NAME

d. INSURANCE PLAN NAME OR PROGRAM NAME

10d. RESERVED FOR LOCAL USE

d. IS THERE ANOTHER HEALTH BENEFIT PLAN? ☐YES ☐NO *If yes,* return to and complete item 9 a-d.

READ BACK OF FORM BEFORE COMPLETING & SIGNING THIS FORM.

12. PATIENT'S OR AUTHORIZED PERSON'S SIGNATURE I authorize the release of any medical or other information necessary to process this claim. I also request payment of government benefits either to myself or to the party who accepts assignment below.

SIGNED _____ DATE _____

13. INSURED'S OR AUTHORIZED PERSON'S SIGNATURE I authorize payment of medical benefits to the undersigned physician or supplier for services described below.

SIGNED _____

14. DATE OF CURRENT: ILLNESS (First symptom) OR INJURY (Accident) OR PREGNANCY(LMP) MM | DD | YY

15. IF PATIENT HAS HAD SAME OR SIMILAR ILLNESS. GIVE FIRST DATE MM | DD | YY

16. DATES PATIENT UNABLE TO WORK IN CURRENT OCCUPATION MM | DD | YY FROM   TO MM | DD | YY

17. NAME OF REFERRING PROVIDER OR OTHER SOURCE

17a. | 17b. NPI

18. HOSPITALIZATION DATES RELATED TO CURRENT SERVICES MM | DD | YY FROM   TO MM | DD | YY

19. RESERVED FOR LOCAL USE

20. OUTSIDE LAB?   ☐YES ☐NO $ CHARGES

21. DIAGNOSIS OR NATURE OF ILLNESS OR INJURY (Relate Items 1, 2, 3 or 4 to Item 24E by Line)

1. |___.___   3. |___.___

2. |___.___   4. |___.___

22. MEDICAID RESUBMISSION CODE   ORIGINAL REF. NO.

23. PRIOR AUTHORIZATION NUMBER

24. A. DATE(S) OF SERVICE From MM DD YY To MM DD YY	B. PLACE OF SERVICE	C. EMG	D. PROCEDURES, SERVICES, OR SUPPLIES (Explain Unusual Circumstances) CPT/HCPCS	MODIFIER	E. DIAGNOSIS POINTER	F. $ CHARGES	G. DAYS OR UNITS	H. EPSDT Family Plan	I. ID QUAL	J. RENDERING PROVIDER ID. #
1									NPI	
2									NPI	
3									NPI	
4									NPI	
5									NPI	
6									NPI	

25. FEDERAL TAX I.D. NUMBER   ☐SSN ☐EIN

26. PATIENT'S ACCOUNT NO.

27. ACCEPT ASSIGNMENT? (For govt. claims, see back) ☐YES ☐NO

28. TOTAL CHARGE $

29. AMOUNT PAID $

30. BALANCE DUE $

31. SIGNATURE OF PHYSICIAN OR SUPPLIER INCLUDING DEGREES OR CREDENTIALS (I certify that the statements on the reverse apply to this bill and are made a part thereof.)

SIGNED _____ DATE _____

32. SERVICE FACILITY LOCATION INFORMATION

a. ___ NPI   b.

33. BILLING PROVIDER INFO & PH # (   )

a. ___ NPI   b.

APPROVED OMB-0938-0999 FORM CMS-1500 (08-05)

CARRIER

PATIENT AND INSURED INFORMATION

PHYSICIAN OR SUPPLIER INFORMATION

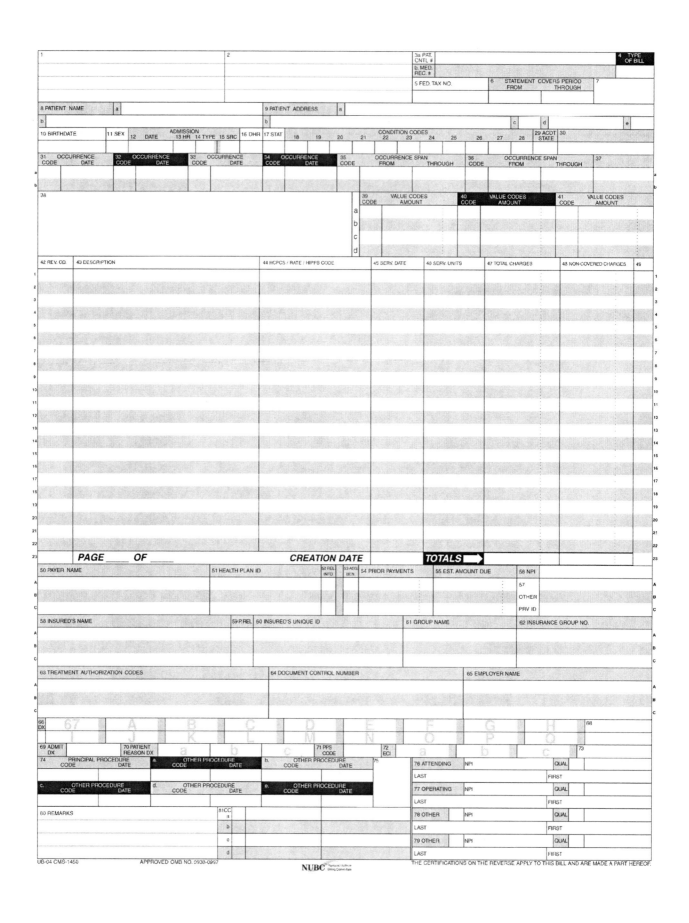

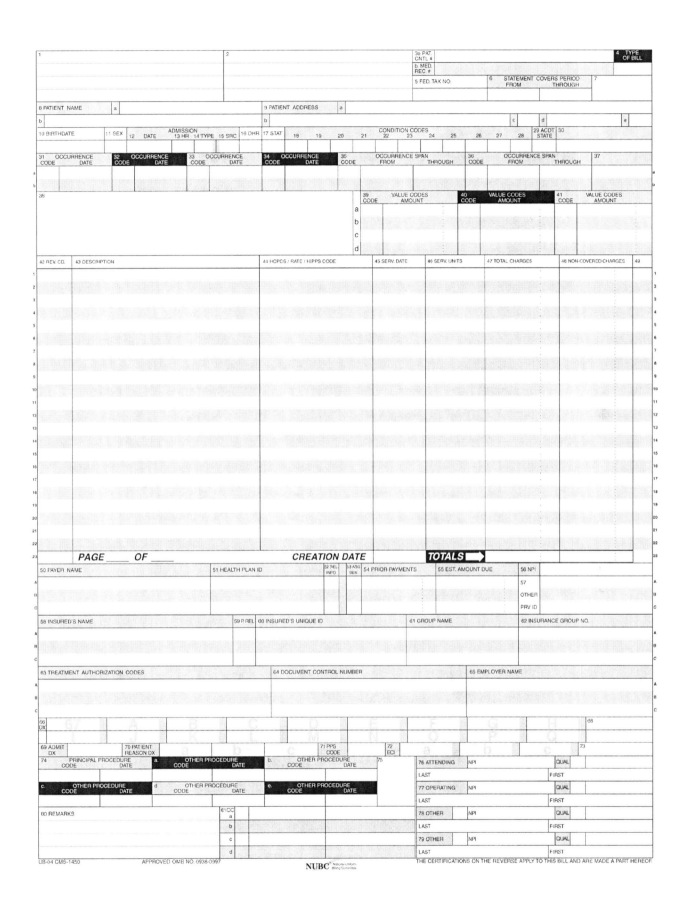

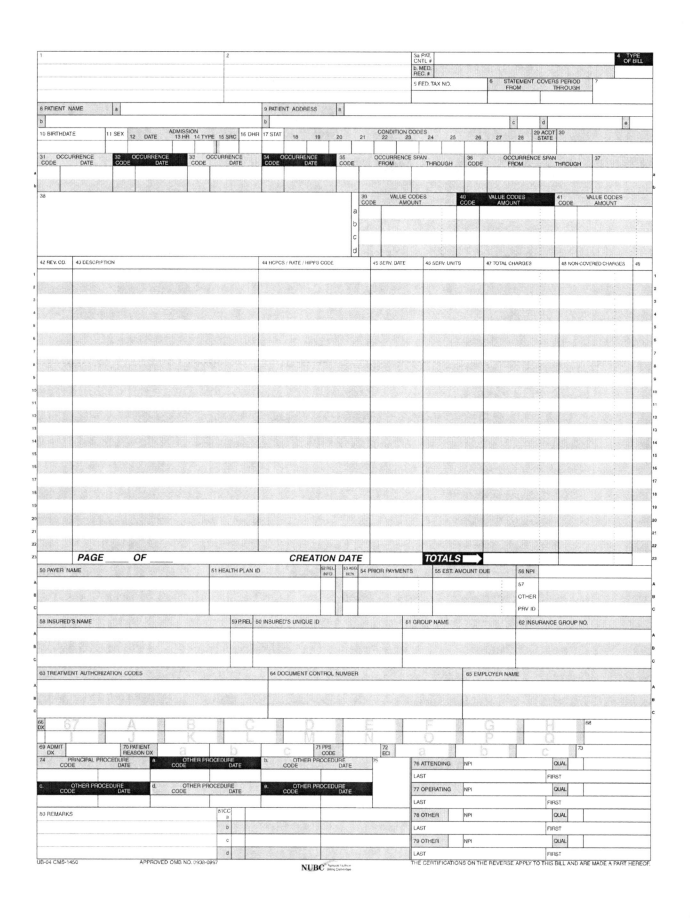

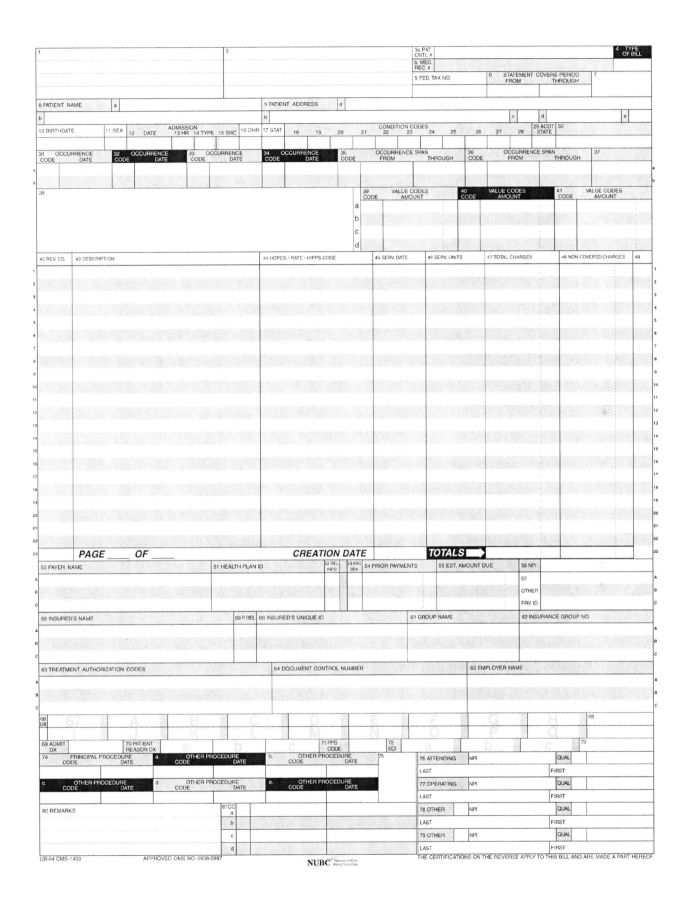

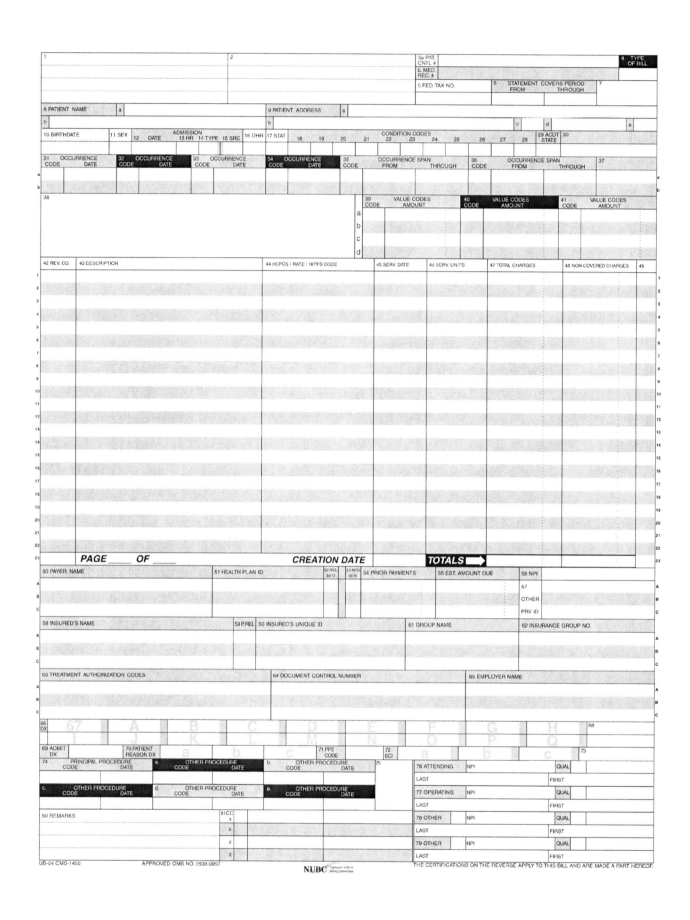

BIBLIOGRAPHY

Current Procedural Terminology, (CPT)
Copyright 1995-2006: American Medical Association™
All Rights Reserved
Cited Under United States Copyright Law
Chapter 1, Section 107, Fair Use Limitations on Exclusive Rights

International Classification of Diseases, 9th Edition (ICD-9)
Copyright 1995-2006: U.S. Dept. of Health & Human Services
All Rights Reserved
Cited Under United States Copyright Law
Chapter 1, Section 107, Fair Use Limitations on Exclusive Rights

Healthcare Common Procedure Coding System (HCPCS)
Copyright 1995-2006: U.S. Dept. of Health & Human Services
All Rights Reserved
Cited Under United States Copyright Law
Chapter 1, Section 107, Fair Use Limitations on Exclusive Rights